IN transition:
A Paris Anthology

IN

IN Paris

transition An

Anthology

transition: A
Paris Anthology

WRITING AND ART FROM *transition* MAGAZINE 1927-30

With an Introduction by Noel Riley Fitch

Contributions by
**Samuel BECKETT, Paul BOWLES, Kay BOYLE,
Georges BRAQUE, Alexander CALDER,
Hart CRANE, Giorgio DE CHIRICO, André GIDE,
Robert GRAVES, Ernest HEMINGWAY,
James JOYCE, C. G. JUNG, Franz KAFKA,
Paul KLEE, Archibald MacLEISH, MAN RAY,
Joan MIRÓ, Pablo PICASSO,
Katherine Anne PORTER, Rainer Maria RILKE,
Diego RIVERA, Gertrude STEIN, Tristan TZARA,
William Carlos WILLIAMS**
and others

ANCHOR BOOKS
DOUBLEDAY
NEW YORK   LONDON   TORONTO   SYDNEY   AUCKLAND

AN ANCHOR BOOK

PUBLISHED BY DOUBLEDAY
a division of Bantam Doubleday Dell Publishing Group, Inc.
666 Fifth Avenue, New York, N.Y. 10103

This book was created by

4 Doughty Street
London WC1N 2PH
England

Library of Congress Cataloging-in-Publication Data
In Transition: a Paris anthology / with
an introduction by Noel Riley Fitch.—1st ed.
    p.   cm.
    1. Literature. Modern—20th century.
I. Transition (1927)
PN6012.I46   1990   89-77184
820.8'00912—dc20   CIP

ISBN: 0-385-41161-8

Typesetting by SX Composing Ltd, Rayleigh, Essex, England
Halftone origination by Fotographics Ltd, London/Hong Kong
PRINTED IN THE UNITED STATES OF AMERICA
October, 1990
FIRST ANCHOR BOOKS EDITION

TABLE OF CONTENTS

[F] Fiction; [P] Poetry; [NF] Nonfiction

Read about us and marvel!
You did not live in our time — be sorry!
— *Ilya Ehrenburg*

...with fixed barone *Lord of ladders, what for lungitube!* *N. I am hather of of the missed. Areed.*

falling hair and for would be joybells to ring sadly ringless hands. The dame dowager to stay kneeled how she is as first mutherer with cord in coil. The two princes of the tower royal, daulphin and devlin, to lie how they are without to see. The dame dowager's duffgerent to present wappon and about wheel without to be seen of them. The infants Isabella from her coign to do obeisence toward the duffgerent as first futherer with drawn brand. Then the court to come in to full morning. Herein see ye fail not —
— Vidu Porkegg Ili vi rigardas Returnu, Porkego Maldelikato *O Sire!*

Hummels! That crag! Those hullocks! What have you therefore? I fear lest we have lost ours respecting these wildy parts. How shagsome all and beastful! What do you show on? I show because I must see before my misfortune so a stark pointing pole. Can you read the verst legend hereon? To the dunleary obelisk via the rock what myles knots furlongs; to the general's post office howsands of patience; to the Wellington memorial half a league wrongwards; to sara's bridge good hunter and nine to meet her; to the point, one yeoman's yard. He, he, he! At that do you leer? I leer because I must see a buntingcap of so a pinky on the point. It is for a true glover's greetings and many burgesses by us uses to pink it in this way. Do you not have heard that the queen lying abroad her king shall come tomorrow, michaelmas? He shall come by jubilarian with — who can doubt it? — His golden beagles and his white elkox terriers for a hunting on our littlego illcome faxes, meynhir mayour, our boorgomaister, in best bib and tucker, surrounded on his full cooperation and all our pueblos, shall receive dom king at broadstone barrow with a keys of goodmorrow onto his pompey cushion. It will give piketurns on the tummlipplads and crosshurdles and dollmanovers and vicuvious gyrolyphics at darkfall for cur fancy ladies. You do not have heard? I have heard anyone tell it yesterday how one should come on morrow here but it is never here today. Well but remind that it is always tomorrow in another place. Amen. True! True! Is rich Mr. Pornter always in his such strong health? I thank you for the best, he is exceedingly herculeneous. One sees how he is lot stoutlier than of formerly. One would say him to hold whole a litteringture of kidlings under his aproham. Has handsome Mr. Pournter always been so long married? O yes Mr. Pournter familys has been marryingman ever since so long time

of lateenth dignisties

It stays in book of that which is.

meet

all assured

Grace's Mamnesty and

INTRODUCTION

by Noel Riley Fitch

P ARIS, IN THE YEARS FOLLOWING THE FIRST WORLD WAR AND THE RUSSIAN Revolution, was an irresistible magnet for creative artists of all kinds. Americans particularly were drawn to the City of Light by low prices, freedom of expression and behavior, and the free-flowing alcohol forbidden in the United States. They helped to make Paris the center of the Western world's artistic life, and created, in the words of Archibald MacLeish, "the greatest period of literary and artistic innovation since the Renaissance."

Far from the provincialism, censorship and Prohibition of America, this expatriate avant-garde flourished. Shunned by large traditional publishers, the adventurous writers, artists, editors and wealthy hangers-on of fashionable Bohemia created a number of peripheral publishing houses and "little magazines." These small publications – many printed in editions of a hundred or less – are the documents of record for the exhilarating creative adventure of the Twenties and Thirties. Their now-yellowing pages contain treasures, and none more so than the magazine called *transition*.

Transition, founded in 1927 by Eugene Jolas, was different in many ways from other small journals of literature and art between the wars. It lasted longer – from 1927 to 1938, although it moved to The Hague and changed in character in 1932; it was larger, sometimes containing as many as four hundred pages; it had a truly international position – no English-language journal carried more European literature; and its editorials and manifestos reflected European intellectual movements.

Most importantly, *transition* earned a place in literary history for publishing eighteen segments of James Joyce's *Finnegans Wake* (called at the time simply *Work in Progress*). Because this serial publication, along with explanations and defenses of it, accounted for more pages than any other subject, the magazine later became known as *la maison de Joyce*, or, as the *Saturday Evening Post* dubbed it, "The James Joyce Adulation and Interpretation Union, Local 69."

Leading this distinguished international group was a small team of editors, mostly professional journalists, mostly Americans. Eugene Jolas had been the literary critic and city editor of the Paris edition of the *Chicago Tribune*. He was born in New Jersey in 1894, but his French father and German mother moved the family back to their native Lorraine when he was two years old, giving him a linguistic facility which opened many doors for *transition*; significantly, he called his unpublished autobiography *Man from Babel*. He was a handsome, robust man, known for his appreciation of alcohol and intelligent conversation. An avid reader and idealist, Jolas was caught up in Dada and Surrealist activities, in psychology and in the philosophy of the German romantics. Fifty of his own pieces appeared in the magazine between 1927 and 1938, in addition to numerous translations. Some of the more fanciful were signed with his pseudonym Theo Rutra. It was Eugene Jolas, also, who wrote most of *transition*'s controversial manifestos.

Elliot Paul (a colleague from the *Tribune*, who later became famous for his nostalgic wartime book *The Last Time I Saw Paris*) served as co-editor from the start until the spring of 1928, when his chaotic love life demanded more of his attention. Robert Sage (also of the *Tribune*) took over Paul's responsibilities, and Maeve Paul, his wife, became secretary. Later assistant and contributing editors included Stuart Gilbert, an Englishman who had moved to Paris in 1927, becoming a member of the small Joyce circle and assisting with the French translation of *Ulysses*. Another peripheral member of the "staff" was Harry Crosby, whose inherited wealth gave him the means to pay entirely for Issue No. 14. Harry Crosby, the sun-mystic as Paul called him, was also a gifted writer and founder of the Black Sun Press in Paris (whose authors included Archibald MacLeish, Kay Boyle and Hart Crane). His suicide with his mistress in New York in 1929 was a traumatic event in the history of this group, inspiring a large memorial special section in the magazine and perhaps, with hindsight, symbolizing the end of the carefree era of the Twenties. Kay Boyle, who had come to France with her French husband (originally living with him in Le Havre before escaping to Paris), while never officially part of the staff, was a frequent contributor and visitor to the offices. Extremely important, but not always enough acknowledged, was Jolas's wife Maria, an American from Kentucky, whom he had met when she was a music student. She was office manager, consulting editor and frequent translator.

The magazine's offices in a fourth-floor hotel room at 40, rue Fabert may have had a grand view of the esplanade des Invalides, but the quarters were cramped, and the plumbing fixtures so characteristic of French hotel rooms supported boards which were piled high with stacks of manuscripts. "The walls of Room 16 should be saturated with arguments, jokes, discussions, worries, mockeries and those pleasant meandering conversations which at college we called pea-talks," reminisced Robert Sage when the magazine suspended publication in 1930.

Introduction

Transition made its first appearance in April 1927 as a monthly magazine. After twelve issues it was cut back to four times a year, styled as "An International Quarterly for Creative Experiment." Typical early issues contained about ten short prose pieces, a dozen poems and some paintings, along with reviews and essays by the editors. Issues grew in size but became sporadic in 1929 and 1930, when publication was suspended altogether as the financial losses became too great for the Jolases to bear and the illness of James Joyce halted his installments of the *Work in Progress.*

Two years later, *transition* was revived by the Servire Press of The Hague, appearing annually or bi-annually through 1938. In this second incarnation it was subtitled "International Workshop for Orphic Creation," signalling a change which prompted its frequent critic Waverley Root of the *Chicago Tribune* Paris edition to claim that the editors had gone "completely haywire." Eugene Jolas, who was again at the helm, filled more and more of its pages with dreams, hypnosis and automatic writing. This present collection limits itself (with one or two exceptions) to *transition*'s first phase, Issues 1 through 20, which appeared from April 1927 through June 1930.

To provoke the critics, Eugene Jolas and Elliot Paul chose to render the title of the magazine without capitalization. The name derives from Edwin Muir's 1926 collection of critical essays called *Transition* (published by Leonard and Virginia Woolf's Hogarth Press) which expressed sympathy for the artist in revolt against the past.

Transition was an immediate and controversial success. As the magazine's biographer Dougald McMillan has said, "For Americans at home (and for a smaller number of English intellectuals) it came to stand for all that was new in contemporary writing. . . . Most people never saw a copy but nodded in agreement as book review pages of newspapers pronounced it unintelligible or laughed as *Life* magazine satirized it in a cartoon as the quintessence of expatriate extremism."

Transition saw it as its task to declare war on traditional literature and herald the source of creation in the irrational, unconscious world of dreams, calling for a new language to express that creation. These sentiments were in harmony with the Dadaists and Surrealists whose work appeared in its pages. A twelve-point Proclamation of 1929, signed by Jolas, Elliot Paul, Hart Crane and Kay Boyle among others, declared that "The revolution in the English language is an accomplished fact." Harry Crosby titled one of his short *transition* pieces "The New Word," which he defined as "the clean piercing of a Sword through the rotten carcass of the Dictionary."

Eugene Jolas kept a door open to all experimental writing – "We are not troubled by manuscripts we do not understand," he wrote – paying thirty francs per printed page. Remarkable today is the number of the great and the near-great whose work appeared in its pages. In addition to James Joyce, issues from 1927 to 1930 included

Introduction

works by Samuel Beckett, Paul Bowles, Kay Boyle, Erskine Caldwell, Hart Crane, Robert Graves, the poet H.D., Ernest Hemingway, Archibald MacLeish, Katherine Anne Porter, Laura Riding, Gertrude Stein and William Carlos Williams. In The Hague, Henry Miller, Anaïs Nin, William Saroyan and Dylan Thomas were among others who joined the impressive roster.

Eugene Jolas' knowledge of languages brought important writers from across Europe to *transition.* From France, he published André Gide (who appeared in the first issue), Tristan Tzara, and the Surrealists, whose fascination with dreams and automatic writing coincided with his own. These included Paul Eluard and Robert Desnos, whose haunting silent film scenario is reproduced in this volume. From the German came poems by Rainer Maria Rilke, a short story by Franz Kafka and an essay by Carl Gustav Jung; and from further afield, poetry by the Hungarian Lorincz Szabó, the Russian Serge Essenin and the Mexican Alfonso Reyes, and fiction by the Yiddish writer I. M. Veissenberg.

The leading artists of the period also made appearances in these pages. *Transition* showed the latest works by Man Ray, Picasso, Max Ernst, Alexander Calder, Paul Klee, Berenice Abbott, Giorgio de Chirico, Yves Tanguy and Diego Rivera (so little known at the time that he was mistakenly listed as Piedro Rivera) among others, often with appreciative essays. Photographs of pre-Columbian sculptures and rock-crystal skulls in the British Museum rounded out the unpredictable visual mix. The originals of many of these works of art by later-famous artists have now been lost, making their record in *transition* all the more precious.

The main star of *transition* was of course James Joyce, who, though forty-five years old in 1927, was the quintessential modern revolutionary artist on the Paris scene. It was Sylvia Beach, the owner of the famous bookshop and lending library Shakespeare and Company near the *Odéon*, and publisher of Joyce's *Ulysses*, who arranged a meeting in which Joyce read from his *Work in Progress* to an enthusiastic small audience, including Eugene Jolas; Sylvia Beach was *transition*'s official distributor in Europe, while Frances Steloff at the Gotham Book Mart in New York was her counterpart in the United States.

All who have heard James Joyce read aloud from his work have remarked on the almost magical effect of his voice. Jolas sincerely believed that Joyce was inventing the "universal language," and recognized that the presence of the leader of the avant-garde would ensure the magazine's fame.

Joyce also needed *transition* as an outlet for the "novel" which took him eighteen years to write. He preferred serial publication for this new work, which Ford Maddox Ford's *transatlantic review*, Marianne Moore's *The Dial*, Ezra Pound's *The Exile* and Wyndham Lewis's

Introduction

The Enemy had already rejected as unintelligible or obscene. Publication in Europe was also a way of avoiding American and British censorship.

Transition agreed to reprint pieces which had appeared earlier and then continue with further installments. Jolas not only helped Joyce with rewriting, revising and editing his "night world" before publication, he also provided a steady flow of essays explaining and defending the work. In 1932, with Joyce's blessing, the new *transition* took the bold step of translating the last four pages of the "Anna Livia Plurabelle" section into plain English. The Jolases eventually became the major supporters and friends of the Joyce family. James Joyce reciprocated by making *transition* famous and by including in this *Work in Progress* numerous hidden references to the magazine.

The second major presence among the contributors was Gertrude Stein, chiefly thanks to the enthusiasm of Elliot Paul, who had fallen under her spell at the rue Fleurus. Although her work was quite dissimilar to Joyce's, she certainly satisfied Jolas's love of creation by instinctive and automatic processes. The egos of both Joyce and Stein prevented them from understanding why *transition* published the work of the other. Gertrude Stein's work appeared regularly until March 1932. After the publication of her *Autobiography of Alice B. Toklas* the next year, in which she claimed that Elliot Paul had really founded *transition* and that she had been its most important contributor, she was denounced in a special supplement to *transition* Issue 23, titled "Testimony Against Gertrude Stein." Matisse, Tristan Tzara and Georges Braque joined the Jolases in refuting her assertions.

The presence of radical though widely diverse writers like Gertrude Stein, James Joyce, Tristan Tzara and the Surrealists led to charges that the magazine was a mindless, even dangerous, conspiracy of artists with a sinister purpose. Provocative manifestos – containing inflammatory pronouncements such as "The writer expresses. He does not communicate. The plain reader be damned" – inspired *transition*'s reputation as far out and eccentric. One of the most celebrated of these manifestos was *Hands Off Love*, which came to the defense of Charlie Chaplin, on trial in the United States for requiring his wife to perform "unnatural sexual acts." Wyndham Lewis insisted that the magazine was part of a Communist-Surrealist plot headed by Joyce and Stein (who had never met each other). Any protest of innocence in the face of these charges was greeted by the accusers as further proof of a conspiracy.

Far removed from these debates, it is astonishing today to witness these grand old men and women of literature and art in their youth, for most were in their twenties when they wrote these pieces. The unevenness of some of their contributions is as fascinating as their

Introduction

flashes of genius. Truly, we can see before our eyes many members of this brilliant generation finding their voice.

The writing and art in *transition* have survived the decades with enormous freshness and power. The French writer and publisher Philippe Soupault wrote at the end of the magazine's first phase, in 1930, that it was in France the "only living force, the only review which did not despair of poetry." Critics in the United States, meanwhile, referred to it as "that irritating mixture of brilliance and nonsense." But perhaps the epitaph which the *transition* group would have wished was formulated by Robert Sage himself in a letter to Eugene Jolas. *Transition* he wrote, "fired the first shots in the Revolution of the Word."

A PARIS ANTHOLOGY

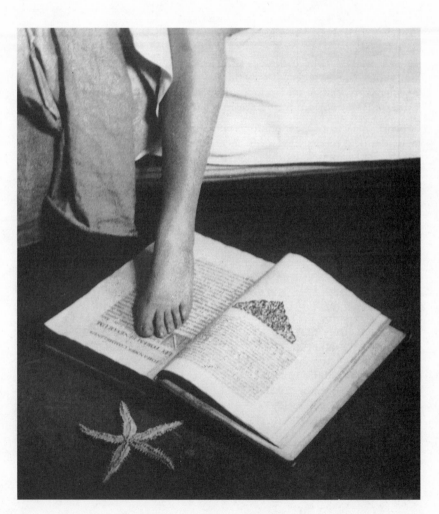

MAN RAY

Film [DETAIL]

[SUMMER 1928]

NOTES
ON THE TEXT

All material in this anthology appears exactly as it was published in *transition*. Where Eugene Jolas and his associate editors allowed erratic (or erroneous) spellings and punctuation to escape them, these have been preserved; only obvious printers' errors have been rectified.

Artwork, likewise, appears in its original form. Whenever possible, however, new identical prints have been located, to obtain the best reproduction quality. The captions are the original ones, and the full titles of most of the works are listed in the Acknowledgments section.

Issues of *transition* are customarily referred to by number. In the interest of clarity, however, the pieces in this book have been identified by issue date.

Selections in this anthology have been taken from the following issues:

Issue 1 : April 1927	Issue 11 : February 1928
2 : May 1927	12 : March 1928
3 : June 1927	13 : Summer 1928
4 : July 1927	14 : Fall 1928
5 : August 1927	15 : February 1929
6 : September 1927	16-17 : June 1929
7 : October 1927	18 : November 1929
8 : November 1927	19-20 : June 1930
9 : December 1927	21 : March 1932
10 : January 1928	24 : June 1936

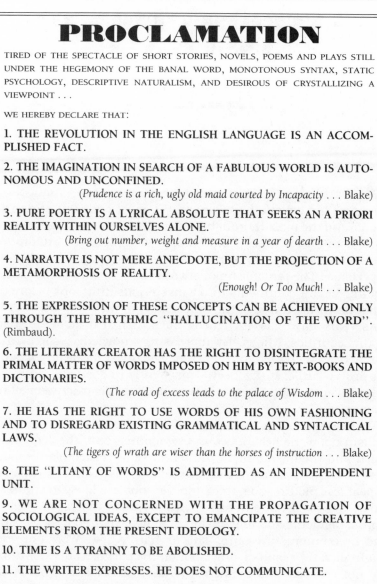

PROCLAMATION

TIRED OF THE SPECTACLE OF SHORT STORIES, NOVELS, POEMS AND PLAYS STILL UNDER THE HEGEMONY OF THE BANAL WORD, MONOTONOUS SYNTAX, STATIC PSYCHOLOGY, DESCRIPTIVE NATURALISM, AND DESIROUS OF CRYSTALLIZING A VIEWPOINT . . .

WE HEREBY DECLARE THAT:

1. THE REVOLUTION IN THE ENGLISH LANGUAGE IS AN ACCOMPLISHED FACT.

2. THE IMAGINATION IN SEARCH OF A FABULOUS WORLD IS AUTONOMOUS AND UNCONFINED.
> *(Prudence is a rich, ugly old maid courted by Incapacity . . . Blake)*

3. PURE POETRY IS A LYRICAL ABSOLUTE THAT SEEKS AN A PRIORI REALITY WITHIN OURSELVES ALONE.
> *(Bring out number, weight and measure in a year of dearth . . . Blake)*

4. NARRATIVE IS NOT MERE ANECDOTE, BUT THE PROJECTION OF A METAMORPHOSIS OF REALITY.
> *(Enough! Or Too Much! . . . Blake)*

5. THE EXPRESSION OF THESE CONCEPTS CAN BE ACHIEVED ONLY THROUGH THE RHYTHMIC "HALLUCINATION OF THE WORD". (Rimbaud).

6. THE LITERARY CREATOR HAS THE RIGHT TO DISINTEGRATE THE PRIMAL MATTER OF WORDS IMPOSED ON HIM BY TEXT-BOOKS AND DICTIONARIES.
> *(The road of excess leads to the palace of Wisdom . . . Blake)*

7. HE HAS THE RIGHT TO USE WORDS OF HIS OWN FASHIONING AND TO DISREGARD EXISTING GRAMMATICAL AND SYNTACTICAL LAWS.
> *(The tigers of wrath are wiser than the horses of instruction . . . Blake)*

8. THE "LITANY OF WORDS" IS ADMITTED AS AN INDEPENDENT UNIT.

9. WE ARE NOT CONCERNED WITH THE PROPAGATION OF SOCIOLOGICAL IDEAS, EXCEPT TO EMANCIPATE THE CREATIVE ELEMENTS FROM THE PRESENT IDEOLOGY.

10. TIME IS A TYRANNY TO BE ABOLISHED.

11. THE WRITER EXPRESSES. HE DOES NOT COMMUNICATE.

12. THE PLAIN READER BE DAMNED.
> *(Damn braces! Bless relaxes! . . . Blake)*

— *Signed*: KAY BOYLE, WHIT BURNETT, HART CRANE, CARESSE CROSBY, HARRY CROSBY, MARTHA FOLEY, STUART GILBERT, A. L. GILLESPIE, LEIGH HOFFMAN, EUGENE JOLAS, ELLIOT PAUL, DOUGLAS RIGBY, THEO RUTRA, ROBERT SAGE, HAROLD J. SALEMSON, LAURENCE VAIL.

INTRODUCTION TO ISSUE N° 1

O<small>F ALL THE VALUES CONCEIVED BY THE MIND OF MAN THROUGHOUT</small> the ages, the artistic have proven the most enduring. Primitive people and the most thoroughly civilized have always had, in common, a thirst for beauty and an appreciation of the attempts of the other to recreate the wonders suggested by nature and human experience. The tangible link between the centuries is that of art. It joins distant continents into a mysterious unit, long before the inhabitants are aware of the universality of their impulses.

As years have passed, truths have turned to folly and back again, countless times. By increasing knowledge, sorrow has surely been increased, but joy also. The quest for beauty has not yet proven futile. It has been consistently in good standing as a means of enriching life. It has been the least destructive of all the major urges.

We hear much talk, nowadays, of the encroachment of commercialism upon the field of art, of the dominance of the acquisitive spirit and the dwindling of the reflective or contemplative faculties. The threat does not seem grave, to us. Our age does not appear less picturesque, than another, nor less likely to stimulate a desire to perpetuate it, along with its predecessors, in terms of words, pigments and tones. The artist is harrassed by laws, a bit, and by economic pressure. This is hardly new. Works of great originality, the result of long labor on the part of a superior mind, are not grasped in a moment by hasty, lesser folk. This is not ground for despair.

Art has never confused itself with commerce. The same gulf exists today. It has always surmounted chauvinism, greed and vulgarity.

Perhaps, because America is young, from the white man's standpoint, and has been constantly adapting itself to changing conditions, without a single tranquil decade, it has been less affected by literature, music or painting than any other land.

The EDITORS

Surely it is the only country, in recent centuries, which has accepted ready-made cultures from other peoples before having developed one characteristically its own. The early settlers, if their architecture is indicative, were not insensitive to beauty, but they destroyed or ignored the wealth of art which the Indians offered them and let the amazing monuments and relics of the Mound Builders be broken with plowshares.

Lately, Americans have shown unmistakeable signs of artistic awakening. Poets and novelists have come forward with work of unquestionable genuineness and originality. More important, still, a small group of intelligent readers has developed. As yet there is only a beginning but it gives glorious promise.

It is quite natural that the new interest in American literature should stimulate a curiousity about the literature of other lands. Languages are badly taught, in the United States, and geographic isolation makes it still more difficult to follow contemporaneous European literature. Translators have often selected the easiest or the least expensive works. Coincidently, the government has placed such obstacles in the way of frank expression that the work of almost every capable American novelist has been suppressed, in whole or in part. Publishers have become frankly merchants and the magazines, with one or two brilliant exceptions, have discarded all literary pretensions. In spite of these difficulties, men have continued to write and to interest themselves in books and poems. The modern American writers, composers and painters are gradually gaining recognition abroad.

TRANSITION wishes to offer American writers an opportunity to express themselves freely, to experiment, if they are so minded, and to avail themselves of a ready, alert and critical audience. To the writers of all other countries, TRANSITION extends an invitation to appear, side by side, in a language Americans can read and understand. The result should be mutually helpful and inspiring. Contributions will be welcomed from all sources and the fact that an author's name is unknown will assure his manuscript a more favorable examination.

We do not hold with the dogma that contemporary works of art cannot be evaluated. It is easier to judge a contemporary work because it arises from sources more readily and directly understandable. No rigid artistic formulae will be applied in selecting the contents of TRANSITION. If the inspiration is genuine, the conception clear and the result artistically organized, in the judgement of the editors, a contribution will be accepted. Originality will be its best recommendation. Neither violence nor subtlety will repel us.

We believe, that although art and literature are, in many quarters, growing more definitely racial and national in coloring and texture, their appeal is becoming distinctly international. The reader is coming into his own. Whatever tendencies appear, we want them to be reflected in TRANSITION if they have real artistic value. The bulk of the space will be devoted to stories, plays, sketches or poems. Critical articles will be subjected to the same tests as other kinds of creative work. If writers employ longer forms that can be included *in toto*, extracts will be given.

At the outset, the editors have found the foremost writers of all countries ready to cooperate in a most courteous and generous fashion, and we wish to acknowledge this with thanks. We should like to think of the readers as a homogeneous group of friends, united by a common appreciation of the beautiful, – idealists of a sort, – and to share with them what has seemed significant to us.

The Editors.

SUGGESTIONS FOR A NEW MAGIC

transition WILL ATTEMPT TO PRESENT THE QUINTESSENCE OF the modern spirit in evolution. It may be interesting, therefore, to re-define some of the concepts that symbolize this spirit which both on the American and European continents is surrounded by a certain confusion.

We believe in the ideology of revolt against all diluted and synthetic poetry, against all artistic efforts that fail to subvert the existing concepts of beauty. Once and for all let it be stated that if there is any real choice to be made, we prefer to skyscraper spirituality, the immense lyricism and madness of illogic.

Realism in America has reached its point of saturation. We are no longer interested in the photography of events, in the mere silhouetting of facts, in the presentation of misery, in the anecdotic boredom of verse.

We are not interested in dillettantism as a means of literary expression. We denounce the *farceurs* whose sole claim to contemporary consideration is a facile sense of lilting rhythms. The epigones of Whitman and his followers have become hopelessly entangled in sentimentality, eclecticism, "delicate perceptions".

We are not interested in literature that wilfully attempts to be of the age. Unless there be a perception of eternal values, there can be no new magic. The point of departure is unimportant. The poet may use the rythm of his age, if he be so inclined, and thus tell us, with accelerated intensity, the Arabian Nights' adventures of his brain. But let him not forget that only the dream is essential.

The rushing of new springs can be heard only in silence. To be sure, few of us can have Paul Valery's ecstatic and fertile silence. That is more of the spirit of poetry than the roar of machines. Out of it may come finally a vertical urge.

We believe that there is no hope for poetry unless there be disintegration first. We need new words, new abstractions, new hieroglyphics, new symbols, new myths. These values to be organically evolved and hostile to a mere metaphorical conception must seek freer association. Thus there may be produced that sublimation of the spirit which grows imminently out of the modern consciousness. By re-establishing the simplicity of the word, we may find again its old magnificence. Gertrude Stein, James Joyce, Hart Crane, Louis Aragon, Andre Breton, Leon-Paul Fargue, August Stramm and others are showing us the way.

We who live in this chaotic age, are we not aware that living itself is an inferno? And having experienced it, can we not express it by seeking new outlets and new regions of probability? Are not the working of the instincts and the mysteries of the shadows more beautiful than the sterile world of beauty we have known? It is Arthur Rimbaud who captured this idea first. In him broke forth savagely intensified the feeling of the subconscious, pure emergence of the instinct, child-like and brutal.

Perhaps we are seeking God. Perhaps not. It matters little one way or the other. What really matters is that we are on the quest. Piety or savagery have both the same bases. Without unrest we have stagnation and impotence.

The Editors.

[JUNE 1927]

POEM

by Berenice Abbott

DON'T DISCUSS LIFE, PEOPLE, PROBLEMS. DON'T VOICE POVERTY.

[JUNE 1927]

SOME OPINIONS [1929]

— A casual look at the last number of *Transition*, that brilliant publication edited by my friend Eugene Jolas, was the starting point for some reflections on the state of contemporary poetry. So far as they are clearly formulated, I cannot understand the critical theories of that paper, nor can any man to whom words are supposed to fulfill their ancient function of corresponding in an arbitrary way to arbitrary sounds which in turn finally correspond to definite concepts. That this sort of thing is still waiting for its great critic is in a way unimportant; what matters is to read what these young people are doing and to determine if they have something to say and are saying it . . .

— Alex Small in the *Chicago Tribune*, Paris edition.

Berenice Abbott

James Joyce

[SUMMER 1928]

STAIRWAY OF PAIN

by Richard Aldington

unyielding
there is no way out
mosaic mask threatens and laughs
that blood was wasted
so were his hers mine
I always knew that brought the gravest pang
there is no way out
who said so? he said so
no I said so
up those winding stairs
so long and tedious to mount alone
always the mosaic mask
that nothing says and says too much
there is no way out
except the inevitable final plunge
and that's not soon
and yet too soon
round and up they wind
and up and round
blind feeling with finger tips
up and round
there is no way out
but why have entered?
yes why have entered?
entered? well the mask said enter
so beautiful a mask
I forgot the blood
so beautifully so like a god
said enter I forgot the blood
ran stumbling upwards too eagerly
then the mask changed
and yes there is no way out.

[FALL 1928]

THE LIGHT-SHUNNING PARADISE (Fragment)

by Hans Arp

we fire the oracle gun with the left hand
we rustle with our cenacle leaves
we feed the mature sea-wonders with wampun bones
one has to laugh
one has to laugh haha
we wipe the addresses from our lips
we beat our wood into chains
our daily wood to sustain our flesh
we skim off the precocious stones
one has to laugh
one has to laugh hehe
we wear bagatelle shoes
we wrap the a the e the i the o in water
   turned on a lathe
and only the u we leave unwrapped
we know the feminine a b c by heart
anna bertha clara e t c
we know that seven is the opposite of lean
and so we light a fire under the last tail
then every third one wants to join in three times
nor do the other two say no
no no and no again
one has to laugh
one has to laugh hihi
because we live we resemble watchmen
we have noses to smell at the flag-poled easels of love
we have ears to have ears ready to listen
we have eyes for a moment
one has to laugh
one has to laugh hoho
we have countermanded our souls
we curtesy still like flesh three days after our death
o you heaven crying u
o you all crushing u
one has to weep
one has to weep huhu

Translated from the German by EUGENE JOLAS.

[OCTOBER 1927]

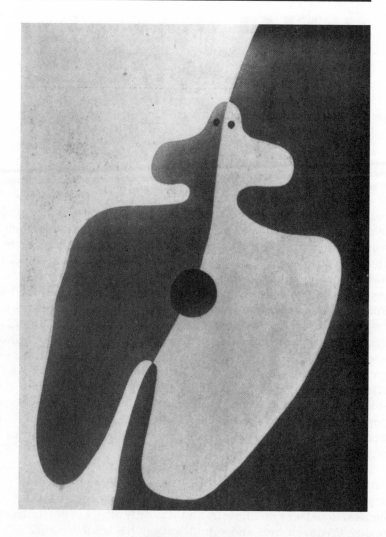

Hans Arp

Arping

Hans Arp lives in Strasbourg, where he is
constantly occupied in the curious experiments
specimens of which have been published in
transition.   [OCTOBER 1927]

[SEPTEMBER 1927]

EUGENE ATGET
(with an Essay by B.J. Kospoth)

PARISIANS PASSING IN THE STREETS WERE PUZZLED AND ALARMED A FEW years ago by the strange behaviour of an old man, staggering under the weight of a cumbrous camera and tripod, who stopped before sordid house-fronts and in obscure corners to focus his lens on a shabby dress-suit hanging in front of a second-hand dealer's window or a heap of tin cans and rubbish in a dirty courtyard. Near seventy, always wearing an overcoat many sizes too big for him, from the long sleeves of which protruded hands bitten and burned by poisonous acids, he seemed like a character in Balzac, intent on the satisfaction of some extraordinary dominating passion. Shop-keepers and other bourgeois regarded him with suspicion, and even the beggars and outcasts with whom he fraternized were stirred with feelings of condescending pity for what they considered his mental aberration. But, utterly unmoved by popular miscomprehension, the old man, with infinite trouble and care, went on taking his queer pictures and walking the streets until he died.

Such was Eugene Atget, who has done for the Paris of our days what the old engravers did for the Paris of the French kings and the first revolution in fixing on their plates all its aspects in streets and homes, in palaces and hovels, and it is only after his death that we realize the magnitude and significance of his achievement.

For Eugene Atget was not a painter, nor an etcher; he was "only" a photographer. It seems singularly fitting that he should have been nothing else, for none but a photographer can hope today to fix for posterity the image of the modern city. Atget realised that it was his mission as a photographer to replace the old engravers in recording the Paris of his time, for the delectation of future generations, and he gave his life to his self-imposed task careless of material success, with the result that he left behind him, assembled in a vast array of albums, the thousand plates fixing every conceivable angle of the aspect and life of the Paris he had known.

Eugene Atget's photographs, which I saw for the first time the

Eugene Atget

Shopfront

other day in Berenice Abbott's studio are an artistic revelation quite apart from their immense documentary value. Some of Atget's plates stir the imagination like a Daumier etching or a Lautrec lithograph; at first sight one might mistake them for reproductions of one or the other. There is a photograph of street musicians by Atget which is an absolute Daumier in technique and conception, and one of women's hats in a *modiste's* window might have been drawn by Lautrec on the stone. Pieces like this (and there are many others among the thousands composing Atget's life-work) must convince the most sceptical of the possibility of transforming photography into a means of personal, artistic expression. Atget was an artist, and his albums, when they are published, will deserve a place beside the albums of the greatest pictorial recorders of Parisian life and manners.

It was Atget's ambition to make a *complete* pictorial record of the Paris of his day. When he died, a year ago, over seventy years old, he could rest satisfied that he had realized his dream. His vast work comprises the whole city: its architecture, its streets, its old and historic houses, its ancient signs over crumbling doorways and curious shops, the displays in its store windows, its markets and moving crowds, the prosperous bourgeois of its boulevards and the outcasts of its proletarian suburbs, even to the rooms in which they live and eat and sleep. He has a series of bourgeois *interiors* that are as suggestive as a page out of Flaubert or Huysmans, and visions of *brocanteurs* and gypsies camping on the Paris fortifications that Steinlen would have been proud to claim for his own. Indeed, Atget sold many of his photographs to painters in search of "documentation;" one of the first to buy was Luc-Olivier Merson, famous designer of the French hundred franc note. How many modern pictures of Paris, signed by celebrated artists, were more or less directly inspired by this humble photographer's plates, will probably never be known.

Eugene Atget's life and personality make one think of the great Parisian artists and poets of the past. His was the same misery, the same seemingly hopeless struggle against a materialistic world, the same self-denial, invincible faith and alas! posthumous glory. His, too, was the uncommon, existence that seems inseparable from genius. He was born at Bordeaux, and in early youth he shipped as a cabinboy on distant voyages. Afterwards, he was during a great part of his long life an actor, playing secondary roles in suburban theatres. Finding it impossible to make a living, he thought first of learning to paint, for he knew many artists and felt the urge to express himself pictorially; but he took up photography instead, using the camera lens as others would the brush or pencil or etching needle, to fix on paper what struck his vision. It was a thing, so far as I know, that had never been done before; inevitably, few people understood it.

Gazing at the fine, almost tragic portrait which Berenice Abbott made of him in the last years of his life one seems to see him indefatigably walking the city streets, intent on perpetuating scenes on which no man before him had ever thought it worth while to focus a lens. The publication of Atget's albums, which Berenice Abbott is aiming to bring about, will enrich the pictorial immortalization of Paris by a work of unparalleled variety, truth and power.

[FEBRUARY 1929]

SOME OPINIONS [1929]

— Several numbers read in context permit us a comprehensive view as to tendency and fulfillment of *transition* which appears in Paris in English under the direction of Eugene Jolas. The modesty with which, in the subtitle, the experimental and searching qualities of this publication are emphasized, causes hopes for an extraordinary achievement. They are not disappointed ... What amazes us at first sight is the surety of selection ... How long ago is it since the sound of a name like Tristan Tzara, tore for the first time the curtain which hid from us the view into the future? Of names like Lissitzky, Ray, Schwitters, Gertrude Stein? Here, too, the framework is everything. In a bourgeois publication, made by snobs for snobs, these names would be *vieux jeu*; but here they are still prophetic. The philistine during the first months of the war — later on he made it cheaper — demanded many tens of thousands of captured Russians: the same appetite today demands in every morning newspaper, with its coffee and rolls, a newly discovered visionary, producer or conductor. *Transition* is satisfied with the iron ration. It wants to be what it indicates: a passing from one state to another ... Why have we no reviews like this one? Ours are almost without exception ephemeral or dull. Nowhere this grip which gathers what belongs together; nowhere this charming freshness of a good conscience: nowhere this audacity of an exquisite taste ... How much have we read about James Joyce? We accepted him and were secretly ready to acknowledge that we did not understand him. But here Stuart Gilbert finds the redeeming words ... But how could we attempt to render fragmentarily here such plenitude? ... But let the reader be warned. After a few hours of reading *Transition*, we apprehend in a kind of hallucination: that ultimately there is nothing more vital, interesting, amusing than the good and the valuable. This hallucination, of course, is just as ephemeral as the one about perpetual peace, about the future of the film, about the recurrence of the Maecenas. But in three months there will be another number of *Transition*.

— Dora Sophie Keilner in *Die Literarische Welt*, Berlin

RAPE AND REPINING

by Djuna Barnes

Lock windows, bolt doors!
Fie! Whores!

WHAT HO! SPRING AGAIN! RAPE AGAIN! AND THE COCK NOT YET AT HIS crowing! Fie, alack, 'tis Rape, yea Rape it is, and the Hay-shock left a 'leaning! Ah, dilly, dilly, dilly, hath Tittencote brought forth a Girl once again, no longer what she should be, but forever and forever of Tomorrow, and yet another day!

S'bloods death! Is it right, m'Lords? Ravished and the Cream not risen in the Pantry; Ravished and the Weather Fork not turned twice upon its Vane. Ravished and no Star pricked upon its point? Can Hounds track her down to Original Approval; the Law frame her Maidenly again; the not oft-occurring-particular-Popish-dispensation reset her Virginal? Can conclaves and Hosts, Mob and Rabble, Stone her back into that Sweet and Lost condition? Nay, nor one Nun going down before the down going Candle pray her Neat.

A Girl is gone! a Girl is lost! A simple Rustic Maiden but Yesterday swung upon the Pasture Gate, with Knowledge nowhere, yet is now today, no better than her Mother, and her Mother's Mother before her! Soiled! Dispoiled! Handled! Mauled! Rumpled! Rummaged! Ransacked! No purer than the Fish in Sea, no sweeter than Bird on Wing, no cleaner than Beasts of Earth!

Hark! Doth the Eland crying in the Forests of the Night so tweak at your Hearts Blood, good Husbandmen? Hath heard Panther Howl, or Lynx or Deer, or Fox or Owl, of such Deflowering? Doth any crouching, ambushed Flesh, in leash of Fur, turn moaning on Clenched paw, for loss of Filament of Film? Bewailing with Grim Hackled Jowl its Seasons knowledge? Hath any Stag slunk down against the Wind, loosing such a difference? Nay, but read me aright, 'tis another Matter this! A Girl hath come to Mourning, in Spring again. Fare forth then, wind loud the Horn, and call a Spade a Spade! 'Tis Ripe time for it, when Unripe Woman falls to Ripening! Set the Black glove by the White glove, who shall say our Judge wears not the one or the other, come this time Nine Months? Oh for a digression in that exact duration! Come Seven, come Eleven, were she a Wanton still? Damned she is, and set a counting, her Days are numbered, and her Nights are timed, she shall not put her Foot outside of it! A Wife in Bed only, and all in Merrie England, and in the Month of May! Drab of Tittencote! (Thatched Tottencote, the Stocks tidy under the Butter Cross!)

Alas! Alack! Woe is me! Rape has stalked abroad and found one capable of alteration . . . 'twas ever thus! Hath the Leg drawn on the Tight Boot! La, what a Wicked Wakeful Waking for a Lass! Turn backward, oh Time, in thy flight! Doth Rape sit hot among the Wheat; springs it up in the Corn? The unlawful, carnal knowledge of a Woman (before she was teachable), has been gained, the Lad, in the full Legal sense (being but fourteen) incapable, but for all that a Satisfaction, and a Regret.

Girl, hast Fornicated and become Wanton before thy Time? What Presage had you of it? Woke you early the Madman's Bell, and his cry of "Six o-clock, and all Good People to the Brook!" Or was your Back from the Cradle seeking for the Soft Grass, and your Neck for the Warm Arm? Who told you, Hussy, to go ramping at the Bit, and laying about you for Trouble? What thing taken from your Father's table turned you Belly up; what Word in your Mother's Mouth set your Ears outward? Bawd! Slattern! Slut! Who gave you Rope to turn on? Slain you are of Slumber, and your Family Mown down before that Sword of Sorrow! Thy Brother weeps amid his diapers, and thy Father behind his Beard! No longer has thy Mother Pride in the Century old *prop ocreis Reginae*; for the annual rent paid to the Queen, to keep her in Leggings, cannot make Tittencote smack of Tittencote, and you gone sipping down to Hell!

Great things by Little are thus brought to Dust. Fair Rome sees men come buttoning up her Appian Way, and an Ass Brays over Babylon. Strong Nations rise and come to flower under the Hee of one Emperor, and are brought low by the Haw of the next. And here, in the heart of excellent small things, a County over which no Blood has been shed, save once, in a Slip of History, a Girl has brought the very Rafters and Pinnacles of her House about her Ears, her one Nocturnal Tear bringing down many in the morning.

Yet: Is it not a Woman's quickest way of laying herself open to Legend? For now some say, she has Whelped Sad Melancholy, and that she do run about in the Night from Hedge to Hedge, and has a look as if the One who brought her to Great Grief had been Dead a Thousand years, for such Thick Sorrow is given off by her, sitting and standing; her Soul springing from vein to vein, a Hound sensing a thing not common to it, while at the waist a solemn silence hangs!

But of all this, what can be said to better purpose, than that she is Raped, yea, Horrid Raped! Oh Beastly Stale! All the World knows no thing so Mad, so Daft, so Poisonous, so balmy Glut of all ill Luck! Doth not the shudder of it crack the paint of Historic Beds?

Ear to the Ground, my Gossips! Hear you not a sound of it, though you touch Dirt a thousand miles from Home! This way, good Wives, Muzzles to Windward! Is there not a Stench of the matter in every Breeze, blow it East, West, North, or South! Have on, — Milling, Trampling Wrangling multitudes. The Hare is running and you are well behind! She whisks over the common, and you cannot get scent of her! Darted she Left or Right? Whom is the most infallible Pointer among you? Mylady or her

Slattern? 'Tis one and the same, white Meat or dark, would you let the Quarry off? Lift up your Hundred Feet, and let down your Hundred, have you not at your Beck and Call twice your numerical Hate, with which to catch her and make of her an Example? Now! Now! She falls at yonder Ditch, and like a Deer, turns face on, weeping for Clemency. Now, have at her!

"And how was it, my Pretty Love – Box her Ears, the Dirty Wanton! – and was it coming over the Stile, or was it this side of the Fence or the other? How went he about it? Did he Lie to you, Frowsy Smelt! Said he that you had Sweet Chops and a Winter Eye? And you, how fared you at that moment? Were you easily Bedabbled, or came you Reluctant to the Filthing? Backward looking, or leaping at the Bait? Leaping it was, I warrant me, and I'll give my Neighbor here my second best Rolling-Pin, and I am not in the Right of it! Or were you, Little Cabbage, in a state of Coma, wherein a Man may step, the Beggar! And find you all he would, though nowhere at all Yourself. 'Tis a Pox of a Pity that a Womans Wits may be as scattered as Chaff, yet her Chastity well enough in one place to bring her to Damnation! Out then! What will your Mother say to this, and what will you do from now on for a Life? Thou art less than a Farthing, and may be spent at one Ale House. Or have you a Philosophy ready Risen for the Deed, as some Panders, have, but the instant they step upon the stoop of Ill Fame so that there be those in the Market Place who think their Wits are better for the vending of their Wares, thanks to his Vain and Empty Prating, and loose Rein in High Places. These several and such do shake the very Matrix of Truth, and Spawn a thousand Lies, which Flood upon us like a Rain of Stars, but though most Gaudy Showy are no mans Verity. Oh Fie upon you! What have you done, but make some Pimpish Fellow a Braggart and a Nuisance in all the Streets that run a Blind Alley. And shall the child, Girl or Boy, stand in after Years a little at the Pump, and say aught that shall Contradict the Wry proportion of its Begetting? 'Tis such who Poison Wells, and make the Hackle rise on every Pubic Inch, and do split the very Bells by which we tell the time!

Adder in the Grass, Ibex on the Peak, Fish in the Wet, Bird in the Air, know something of it, but do they write Books, or talk at Bedsides, or Whisper in Galleries, or make the Laws? Still, Girl, such shall Judge you, perchance even more Rigorously than we.

To the Oblong Eye of the Deer, is not your Condition Lengthened? By the Owl is there not purchased a Dreadful rotundity? To the Shallow Eye of the Fish you are but a little Staled, but to the Bossy eye of the Ox, you may ride as High, and Damned as Jezebel. And what of the Multitudinous Insects, and the Infinitesimal Conclusions of the Ether? To the Myriad Pupil of the Fly, what can it, but Manifold your Grievance? Consider those yet others, infirm of condition, who have Spots on the Iris, or suffer Jaundice or Bloody Issue, would they not impute their malady to you, saying that Death settles on your Cheek, Decay Rides your Flesh? And what of your own Eyes, and you saw not the Tops of your Boots, but

the Sole? Is it not, therefore, imrative, that while in the World, you consider the World's Eye, and of how many Facets your Crime consists,
according to the thing it walks before?

Were not all Philosophies of Avoidance Penned for you? Do not Mathematics, take them where you will, prove there is always a Deviation that
brings down a Marvelously different Total, and you had wished? Has not
Science proved that no Bodkin takes the Ribband but at will, the Thread
makes no conquest of the Needle, and the Needle has not a leaning to the
Thread? Have not Logicians, from Senica to Plato, settled it that no Prop-
osition may come to a Head, and there be Wit for evading? Shall not a
Council of Women, such as we, make clear to you, in a Sitting, that had
you a Vocabulary of Movement, the case had been a Riddle still, and not a
certainty? Must we send our Girls to School that they may learn how to
say "No" with fitting intonation, both for Dish of Porridge and for Dish of
Love? There is a "No" with a "Yes" wrapped up in it, and there is a "No"
with "No" enough in the Weave, and we have been sorry amiss that our
Girls have not learned of it. Learn now and it is too late, Learn Yesterday,
and To-morrow had been a different dawning. Thus the Bobbin Fats with
knotted Thread, and when it comes to sewing, what Garment shall be
Stitched of it that shall not Rip in open places, and shame the Leg? It is
the unpleasant Nature of Mans mind (being what it is in these days) that
he does not, like the Ancients, need to magnify your deed to make it most
Stinking large and Awful!

Or put it thus:

Have you not taken that which Better Women have refused, and in so
doing, been most unmannerly? Is it well to Grab Sweets that an Hundred
Guests, at the same Gathering, have left untouched, and thus greedily, to
Limn their Savour? You have but one Life, yet in one Night you have
changed the Complexion of all Nights, thus Pilfering from the Community, who have honoured you as true coin, only to discover you Counter-
feit, thereby changing a known sum into a sum in need of recount. Have
you not, therefore, made the whole of Society a Dupe, and shall we not, for
that, have you in the just distaste we evince to the Forger? You Mint with
your false Metal, Metal as false, so that from now on we must watch our
Change that no Lead be in it, or such Alloy as might make us sadly out at
Pocket. You have corrupted the Fabric of our Council by this one brief
act; made of Society an unknown quantity, and this we are not built to
bear, for this a Man will Fury all his Days, and none shall commerce with
you, without first turning you over to see where the Die stamps Treason!

Or put it thus:

You have Stolen Time, such Time as lies Thick about Tittencote; Time
made stout by Good Wives, stitching and Washing, Baking and Praying.
Firm with Household duties well done within the narrow excellence of
Wedlock, paced to Monogamy, fortified with Temperance; made durable
with Patience. You have bent Time with the Tooth of Lust, torn the Hem
of Righteous, and the Wind may enter and the Cyclone follow.

Or thus:

Man is Born to Die, and we, with Fortitude, have made the farthest out-posts of Death a lawful Goal. But you, in this Wanton act, have advanced that mark, and your Child shall, on the Day it first takes Breath, set before the World the farthest point yet gained in this misfortune. And at that Hour when the Child cried its first Cry, will Tittencote reach a point more distant in sorrow than any as yet prepaired for. As if Death were not Terrible enough, this on which all Eyes must direct themselves, is a Divided and a Bastard Death, and like a false Monument, must destroy, rather than Dignify that which it is set to Commemorate.

Think you what this must inevitably do to corrupt a whole Body? It is wretched enough that a Man must continually pace Himself to his End, taking Measure of his First Hour by folding it over until it touch his Last, like a Linen Draper that He may not be too much caught up and des-poiled of his Yard, by creeping, unwarned, upon its salvage; that the list may not run upon him when he is Naked; that his whole Life may not shrivel into naught because of the concussion of this Last Moment.

How much more Miserable then, is that Man who contemplates, with what Fortitude he may, the spectacle of an outpost that flies an uncertain Ensign?

Or so!

Whose Child do you Harvest? Whose First-Born springs forth from your Lap? Is he not your Neighbor's Son had you clung fast to the Laws of your Country? Is he not made Fatherless by too fast Fathering? Is this not turning the just proportion of Generations Backward? Does he not Ride before his Mother, seeking his Mother? What Nation has the Son first and the Mother second? What Tree springs up before the Orchard, saying "Orchard, Orchard, here is the Tree!" What Infant gives Birth to its Parents, what Child crawls out of the Cradle that its Mother may have where to lay her Head?

Who plants the Staff, Crook down? Who Suckles the Wind for a Mother? Who Combs the Wind for a Parent?

Who sets the Child Backward upon the Beast of Time? Who makes of his Son no Kin but the Tomb, no Generation but the Dead? Nay, Bequeaths Him no Living and no Dead, no Future and no Past. He must move forward seeking, and Backward Lamenting. He is whirled about in an Uncertainty, and His People shall Inherit Him for a Birthright, and His Father and His Mother shall say: "We resemble that hereafter which was before, and is not."

Or better:

Thou art Witless Whey, and should be Scourged and Flayed, Whipped and Stocked, Cried against, and Howled over, and spent quickly, that you get from out our Country and over the border and into some Neigh-bouring Land, there to lie, until some Blithering Scabby Potsherd mends a Stewpan with you, or lays you between Hot Iron and Hot Iron, and so melts you down to make a Cap for his Heel. So Shaken Loose, so Cutpursed, that the uncertainty is out of you, and so set you back as Current Coin. So lay about you, so Scratch, Slap, Pinch, Pull, that you turn to Honest Flesh. Thus, to come to the very Pip and Core of Truth, through Good Women's Reasoning – though to that faculty no credence has been given by Philosopher or Scribe adown the very Ageless Ages – to make of a Point no Point on which to Haggle, that indeed no Wits be spent on you, no candle burned to a Wick in Attics and Dens, by Grizzled Beard and Shiny Pate; throw Lots for you between us, to determine to which of us you shall fall, there trust to that Pity which passeth Human Understanding – which God forbid we should have hereabouts! – and so make of you what we will, now, that you have Filched what you Would. And I myself ask no better Portion than that you should fall to me, for then should all Eyes behold the Bone of Truth, the Marrow of Justice! For I'd have all Destruction in you well Destroyed before the Striking of another Midnight Bell!"

Or thus!

It is Spring again, Oh Little One the Waters melt, and the Earth divides, and the Leaves put forth, and the Heart sings dilly, dilly, dilly! It is Girls Weather, and Boys Luck!

[DECEMBER 1927]

SOME OPINIONS [1929]

— Plomer is probably the best novelist in South Africa today. D.H. Lawrence in England, and Sherwood Anderson in America are the very best writers produced by those countries recently; and as to Paris, is it necessary to say that almost all that is good, in formal tendency, or in actual achievement, as either painting or writing, (and there is not much) is to be found here and there between the covers of *Transition*? You may not accept this as true but it is what I believe and it is upon that basis that I am arguing . . .

— Wyndham Lewis in *The Enemy*.

NEW ORLEANS LETTER

by Hamilton Basso

D EAR JOLAS:

I've just come home and it's pretty late. I had intended to come home right after work and write this letter to you but I went to eat breakfast at Gluck's with Delos Smith and we had a long argument about New Orleans. Smith loves New Orleans much more than I do. That's because he's an immigrant from Missouri and is impressed by the French Quarter. I'm a native and not at all impressed by the French Quarter. In the days of its decay, when all the houses were ramshackle and falling down — like the one in which Sherwood Anderson used to live — I used to think it one of the lovliest places in the world but now they've started to preserve it and I see it only as another indication of the American self-consciousness that is coming over us.

It's all the fault of immigrants like Smith. I sometimes think of them as a flaxon flood, coming from the north and the east and the west, from Kansas, from Pennsylvania, from Iowa, Goths and Visigoths waving the American flag. They've changed us.

Before they came we didn't give a damn about anything. Life was very simple and ordinary. We were provincial and proud of it. We lived our own lives and minded our own business. Other people could do as they pleased.

All that is being changed. We have been made to salute the flag. We are in just the same position, I imagine, that Europe is in today. Only here it is a fulfilment rather than a threat. You wouldn't know the place anymore. Skyscrapers have been built, streets have been paved, new lights have been put up and the state militia has raided the gamblers. We've become self-conscious, just as the rest of America is self-conscious.

Matthew Josephson, in transition no. 14, didn't say anything about it but I can't rid myself of the belief that to this state of national mind, more than anything else, can be traced the downfall of Al Smith. I ask you, Mr. Jolas, as one man who is proud of his country to another, could we have a man like that meeting the Prince of Wales? Could we have him advising our children to get their early training in the Fulton Fish Market? Could we have Mrs. Smith's picture in the London Times? The first lady of the United States? Of course not.

Delos Smith doesn't agree with me about New Orleans. He wouldn't. He's too self-conscious himself and besides that he's an immigrant and a sentimentalist. The thing I talk about is not apparent on the surface. It is millions of miles deep. You feel it more than you see it. And if you hadn't lived here all your life you wouldn't even feel it. Anyway, if you ever think of coming back, come back soon. It won't be the same place in ten years. Take my word for it.

John McClure and I talked for a long time last night. We talked about a great many things but mostly about how disgusted we were with literature. There is a good reason for our disgust. Everybody we know talks about literature. Even the waiters in Gluck's talk about literature. I went to see a reporter who works on the paper who was arrested and put in jail for embezzling $176,000 from a Los Angeles bank two years ago and the first thing he did was to talk about literature. With murderers and thieves and dope-peddlers all around him, men waiting in cells to be hung, he started talking about literature. Jesus!

You know, when I think of a whole world going about with the smudge of typewriter ribbon on its fingers, I become so ashamed I want to go off somewhere and hide. I become ashamed of my own smudged fingers. I become ashamed of the book I have written and all the books I want to write. I become ashamed even of the thoughts I think. If I were half-way logical I should never write another line.

Take the crowd in the French Quarter for instance — the ones who sit around the book-shops and swap ideas. They make me feel as though I ought to hurry home and take a bath. Possibly there is some genuine work being done, some sincere emotion being felt, but if so I am sure it is being done and felt in an obscure garret that nobody knows about. Now they've started a magazine and a publishing company. The magazine is called *The Quarter* and the publishing company is the *Provincial Press*. They've had one decent thing in the magazine thus far. A slight poem Louis Gilmore wrote about five years ago.

The *Provincial Press* has just issued its first publication, a book of poems by John Fineran. Fineran, whom I don't know, comes under the classification of a worthy young man. I thought his poems were exceptionally bad, derivative from all the sweet English voices, but he does show a certain measure of unrest and rebellion. Most of his faults, McClure says, may be condoned because of his youth. That might be all right for Fineran but I don't think youth is an excuse for poor poetry. I'm still very young myself, going through the process of feeling youth very keenly, but I think I'd vomit if anybody said I was a promising young writer. If what I do is bad it should be called bad. There is too damned much appreciation anyway.

We've got another poet here too. He is typical of the people who mess up the French Quarter. He's publishing his book of poems himself. The title of his book is "*Just Thoughts.*" Isn't that cute? Isn't that just too god-damned cute?

You think I'm suffering from a sour stomach? Then also think of a guy like that, who ran an "inspirational" column in an Alabama newspaper, leading whatever revolt there is. Think of his army sitting around before a picture of Thornton Wilder. I don't want to be dismal. I'm not snarling in a corner like a dog with fleas. I'd almost give an arm to write of agony and torment, of young men and women spitting at skyscrapers, dancing about a bonfire of Cabell and Mencken and Sinclair Lewis.

There are young men and women like that. They are working in factories and stock-yards, writing obids for newspapers and ads for ladies underwear. We know nothing of them as yet because they haven't found their voice. They are working and suffering in silence, afraid, hesitant, ashamed. But they won't be silent forever. There will be torches in the windows and screams in the streets. This sort of thing can't last forever. But give us time. Just give us time.

Hamilton Basso.

[FEBRUARY 1929]

SOME OPINIONS [1929]

I always read the magazine *transition* faithfully. It is now trying to crystallize its esthetic viewpoint: recently it published a proclamation. "The imagination in search of a fabulous world is autonomous and unconfined", is one of the theses. Yet when I examine the products of their fabulous world, I understand these but too well. A man's dreams and fantasies are as real as his waking life; both are an organic whole. The fantasies of the *transition* writers are not autonomous. They are mainly horror-dreams of world catastrophe, disgust, and destruction. Their "real" world is falling down; but they will confess it only in dreams ... One does not need to create through dreams. Reality is more miraculous, more terrific, more satisfying a material. It is the great exciting truth in which we all live. Time and space were given us to mould; this is the great art Jane Heap dreams about. The world is our workshop; that is what the Social Revolution means: collective arts shaping the world. It is coming fast; it will change empires, cities, workers, artists, gangsters, children, machines, rivers, cows and geniuses; organize everything into new conscious fabulous art. History up to now has been an uncontrolled animal dream ...
— Michael Gold in the *New Masses.*

MALACODA

by Samuel Beckett

thrice he came
the undertaker's man
impassible behind his scutal bowler

to measure
is he not paid to measure
this incorruptible in the vestibule
this malebranca knee-deep in the lilies
Malacoda knee-deep in the lilies
Malacoda for all the expert awe
that felts his perineum mutes his signal
sighing up through the heavy air
must it be it must be it must be
find the weeds engage them in the garden
hear she may see she need not

to coffin
with assistant ungulata
find the weeds engage their attention
hear she must see she need not

to cover
to be sure cover cover all over
your targe allow me hold your sulphur

divine dogday glass set fair
stay Scarmilion stay stay
lay this Huysum on the box
mind the imago it is he
hear she must see she must
all aboard all souls
half-mast aye aye

nay

[JUNE 1936]

ENUEG II

by Samuel Beckett

world world world world
and the face grave
cloud against the evening

de morituris nihil nisi

and the face crumbling shyly
too late to darken the sky
blushing away into the evening
shuddering away like a gaffe

veronica mundi
veronica munda
give us a wipe for the love of Jesus

sweating like Judas
tired of dying
tired of policemen
feet in marmalade
perspiring profusely
heart in marmalade
smoke more fruit
the old heart the old heart
breaking outside congress

doch I assure thee
lying on O'Connell Bridge
goggling at the tulips of the evening
the green tulips
shining round the corner like an anthrax
shining on Guinness's barges

the overtone the face
too late to brighten the sky
doch doch I assure thee

[JUNE 1936]

DORTMUNDER

by Samuel Beckett

IN THE MAGIC THE HOMER DUSK
past the red spire of sanctuary
I null she royal hulk
hasten to the violet lamp to the thin K'in music
   of the bawd.
She stands before me in the bright stall
sustaining the jade splinters
the scarred signaculum of purity quiet
the eyes the eyes black till the plagal east
shall resolve the long night phrase.
Then, as a scroll, folded,
and the glory of her dissolution enlarged
in me, Habbakuk, mard of all sinners.
Schopenhauer is dead, the bawd
puts her lute away.

[JUNE 1936]

ENTITY

by Paul Bowles

THE INTIMACY OF SPIRALS HAS BECOME STONE TO HIM. THIS IS IN REALITY only the last prayer urge. As it is, all the crimson of stamps has resolved into loops. These fold up and seek sounds beyond lime rinds.

Let it not be understood that the frenzied fingers were here wishing us to leave. It was only that he went away and shells returned. An urn of disgust cannot stop up the pores for they are after his creases of intelligence. Or, let us say, if one end were rubbed blue and all edges left green we should have a pleasing effect. But all this is uncertain. One does not feel the imperative qualities soon because behind lapels there are buttons of unrest.

Eradicate, if you can, the adaptability of my nature to joy. It is our heritage, this abandoned cerise; – perhaps the only one we have left. The steel of now cannot be rounded like letters of the system into laughing hordes of misunderstanding. We cannot permit these unflinching bones to perform such elegies. There may be abysms in our fingers. There may be falsehoods about ponds. Last week occurred a strange step. Paradise stalked, and seizing a trombone from the wall, stumbled. In this way all such margins weaken.

Can you not all discover how ennui will creep thus? There is no object in such flight. Masses have power.

At any rate, I shall not have panted entirely beyond borders of limpness. Our sycamores need repose. Is it possible that ever we shall be able to trace our responsibilities to such commands? We cannot ignore successfully the call of feathers. We must heed somewhat bristles. As it is, we are not entirely beyond aluminum fences. This is the reason for his dialogue. The origin of power is everywhere.

If any such enmity is discovered let us discard our yawning.

The susceptibility of emotionalism to unguarded caves may be readily realized by all of us. His smiles fall slowly into jars of porcelain. Even if his pain persists, all these losing forces discover their positions.

A rubber is black. The eternal verities are not. In this effigy we may discern a long boulevard. Leaves of such tendencies shall impale him, and he will be certain to remain poised over lavender pebbles.

The immutability of spheres is constant. All about us are carcasses of planets. Whirling continues a short while. Close her eyes and fold her hands above. We are ready for the treatise on hexagonal tiles.

When all shall have been immersed in brass, it will be easily recognized. Only then shall the grain of the pelt be held by fundamental hands. The only tense is the future and futility is taken for granted.

[SUMMER 1928]

DELICATE SONG

by Paul Bowles

I

IT WAS A LONG TRIP BACK.
White lilies waved by walls.
The sweat from blue grapes
Shone like glass globules.
A wind blown straight from the harbor
Brushed the long grass carelessly.
I suppose we thought of the harbor
And of how it looked with its blue water
And its sailboats moving

II

But even though the wind smelt of the waves
And of the swamp grass nearer
Our thoughts were of the road.

III

Flutes are scarcer these days
And flutists are unskilled.
The white lilies were by walls.

[JUNE 1930]

VACATION-TIME

by Kay Boyle

I WAS WALKING AROUND LIKE A NUT IN THE STREETS AFTER THE TRAIN HAD gone off, and the black was all running down my face from my eyes. I was going like a crazy-woman from one place to another thinking that tonight I must get into something deeper, the eyes full, the mouth full, to be sunk in it, to wallow like a sow. What good would it do to drink if to go home to that place empty of any sound. A good deal of your violence is not I thought. The trouble with you is.

I went into one place where there was a man I knew at the bar drinking and I sat talking for a long time to this man I knew. I was listening to him talking with my eyes rocking in my head and when I had a lot to drink I said I just sent my little girl off to the south I said. He was a Jewish fellow, fat like a mother, and he sat nodding his head. That's too bad he said. Yes, I could believe very much in something I said I could believe in something but what it is I cannot explain. I am seeing that to be a believer you are to be blinded to your own satisfaction. You cannot believe and see clear at the same time. What about your religion I said I've tucked it away he said and taking something to drink in the place of it. I shall persist I said I shall persist in my belief in the spring in spite of the mud the eternal because of the moss gone soft under the soles of my feet I shall believe in the chicken-dirt the cow-flops the sow's battle ground lousy with hoofs. I am convinced of the importance in smelling out the snouting out the moment I am at present as sufficient as anyone without a philosophy.

And am I now gentlemen we ourselves seeking to outwit the interior to ravage the exterior I am not able to sit home in intellectual quiet I am beginning to get tired of what is sensitive unable to acclimatize I am for the gay the biddy a great thing it is to roll home in the furnace of anybody's mouth blasting rust like wine all night and no sleep but the brain too going hot as a black bottom.

but then the morning gentlemen oh the morning with the long sad face the black eyes crooked in the mirror the rouge standing up like an army oh beauty not lovely enough or strong enough someday I'll give you a piece of my mind and it'll be a great gift to you

I prefer the heart winging across the pillow out into the garden. How flat the clouds lie on mornings like these when I remember other mornings other clouds riding the wind of the last breath of do you see the light in the window the dawn has come over Monte Carlo isnt it too lovely lovely and he answered me I can't hear you the cocaine is ringing too loud in my ears were those his last words to you

no there were more

and which my lovely strained-eyed lady pull your gaze out of the mirror for five minutes and answer the district gendarmerie. His last words to me were harsh ones I cannot bring myself to repeat them here before all this these unmelting hearts have melted. He said I cannot hear you the cocaine

Did he amplify that statement

Yes he said that the cocaine was ringing like. She hung her head and said she did not remember. We must have the scene arrange itself cher with dawning yawning over Monte Carlo and the Sister of Mercy drawing her wet thumb along her head-dress pleats and the bags of oxygen deflated in the corner. What were his last words Mrs. Stick-in-the-Mud

He did not draw himself up to his full height as a poet he sagged in the middle there was a bright fan of red velvet fluttering from his mouth and he was saying speak louder for Christ'sake the cocaine is ringing like hell in my head

I looked into the bottom of my glass of and I murmured to the soft blue clouds of gin I too I too should have spat my way to heaven with him

I said I am going home

[FALL 1928]

ON THE RUN

by Kay Boyle

THE LITTLE ALPS WERE BAKED DRY AND THE GRASS ON THEM WAVED IN June like a slow fire along the rails. These little mountains ran in a sharp sea in the windows and the smoke from the engine twisted in in strong white ropes through the car. He opened his mouth to say "St. André-les-Alpes" and when he had opened it the smoke came in and filled it with bitterness. As the train stopped a soft pink tide of pigs rose out of the station-yard and ran in under the wheels of the wagon. The crest of little alps was burning across the roofs of the town, with the dry crumbling finger of the church lifted and the sky gaping white and hot upon decay.

He lay down on the bed in the hotel and when the bonne came to the door he sat up quickly and lit a cigaret. He talked to her,

smiling, moving his hands, with his eyes insisting that she understand him. He wanted pigs' feet grilled in batter and breadcrumbs.
He insisted with his hands moving to convince her of the natural
beauty of his hunger. A sick man would not want pigs' feet grilled
in batter and breadcrumbs. She answered him shaking her head
that they were not this time of the year as if they sprang up like
seeds in the garden. She nodded sternly, seeing that he was dying.
"Later," she said, "later..."

Get her out of here he said I am going to cough Christ is this
where the death will get me take the cigaret and when I cough walk
around the room and sing or something so they won't hear me

The bonne came back to them saying that the washer-woman had
so much work to do that she couldn't take in their laundry this
summer. "Here's your laundry back," said the bonne, "because
the washerwoman has so much work." "What?" said he. "What?"
The alps were closed like dry fists and the grass burned up to the
window. "My God," he said, "we'll clear out of here. Saint André-
les-Alpes what a hole. I'll come back and haunt you. I'll eat your
heart out Saint-André I'll curse and rot you."

If there were a nice fine cold now to tighten up whatever it is
shaking around in me hop around the room now and sing to keep
them from hearing me a tight cold now pulling me together to say
to them

The bonne came back to say that the shoemaker had so much
work to do now that he couldn't touch their shoes for them. The
mountain-trains were screaming like cats at the window. We're
awfully near the railway anyway he said. If I laugh too much at he
said my girl you don't understand the Irish until the sun kills me
I'll be here none of your washwomen or your shoemakers if there
were a fine tight cold to pull me together now he said I'd get out of
here faster than the pigs hitting the dust get her out of the room he
said I'm going to cough

The bonne came back to say that the proprietor the woman luxu-
riously in mourning for her entire family bereaved in the fullness
of middle-age would speak with Madame. Bereaved in the full sal-
low of her cheeks bereaved and the tombstones rising politely
polished with discreet sorrow bereaved and remembered with bubbles of jet frosted on her bosoms and mourned under waves of
hemmed watered crepe. I have mourned people for years and years
this is the way it is done.

She stood in the stairpit with her eyes starting out of her you'll
have your bread and your butter and your coffee Madame when
you've talked to me. "Come in here," she said. "Finish to enter."

The sweet sorrow of the crucifix faced them the rosary hanging

like false-teeth on the bed-stead the sacred smile the Christ bled
with artistry in the well-rounded arms of the Virgin. "Madame,"
she said without any hesitation, "your husband cannot die here,"
she said, "we are not prepared for death."

He sat up on the bed when he heard her coming back down the
hall and he said what do you leave me for you've been gone a
hundred years is she being rude to you? I called her a bitch he said
keep your temper please keep it it worries me when you slam the
door

"Saint-André," he said into the pillow, "I'm a sick man. I'm
afraid. This time I'm afraid to go on."

You you afraid listen here packing the bags again the hairy-
legged brushes pointed ampoules as beautiful as earrings bottles of
ergotine and striped pajamas we're going on somewhere else and
have pigs' feet grilled and champagne and peaches with flames running on them this hole dries the guts in you do you remember
Menton last February and everytime you read Umbra the cabinay
flushed may the Gods speak softly of us in days hereafter

and the very small sausages for breakfast at the Ruhl
Saint-André-les-Alpes you're a perfectly ordinary piss-pot
With a blue eye painted in the bottom of it
Fit only to be put in a cheap room under the bed
With education refinement and all the delicate belly-aches
Here's to bigger and better pigs' feet
Keep on keep on keep on he said maybe I'm going to bleed

[JUNE 1929]

MADE IN BOHEMIA [1927]

"A Montparnasse group headed by Elliot Paul is emitting a review
named *transition* which contains contributions by almost everybody
in the Who's Who of Montparnasse."

Portland (Ore.) *Journal.*

LETTER TO ARCHIBALD CRAIG

by Kay Boyle

I

THERE IS ONE COUNTRY
and no shame to it
For having a heart hot in the bosom
or songs in the mouth humming
That servant-girls sing at their dishes
Wherever the men of it are
Are the laughter and the sorrowing
of their own land
And whenever a stranger speaks
it is a sad word he is saying

The rich coins sing in the hands of them
But whether it is I am deaf now
Or whether it is I am blinded
By the thought of the dead
rank in my eyes even
I am weary
for speech like new cress in the river
I am sick for a sight of him
for when my tears fall

II

I ask more of this season
Than leaves seeking the ground
birds guiding the wind south
or a deerstep swept clean for winter

No lest things
   fingers of stars pointing
   out steps on the wet grass
   the moon ringing the hay-bells
      the frogs crying
   upon what a mouth said or remembered

Or the eyelids of one town lifting
      No answer
From fields struck dumb with frost
But a new season blooming
   a new history of feast-days
For a young man who died one autumn

III

If I thought
   this is the way I'd be
waiting if the door
   let him in
   lock of hair blown on the room's face
I'd be combing it
   back of my ears if I
thought he'd be growing up in the glass
this is the way my legs
      crossed and my hands
         lying
If I thought I could
   see him make sugars fly
up his cuffs after dinner find
      potatoes hot in the dogs' ears
if I thought I could
   hear the thin bark of
his shoes on the gravel this is the way
      my eyes waiting
and my heart crying until
         I be dead with him.

[SUMMER 1928]

THE UNITED STATES
(for William Carlos Williams)

by Kay Boyle

*Not a land, or like other lands, with trees coming out and
the grass growing,
Or of waters shriveling in the wind like the faces of old
women;
But however the body turns there are days when the blood in
the veins even
Flows to the north stars for warmth like the cold blood of a
compass,
And nights with the birch moon drifting cold as Maine water,
And the pleiades running like snipes' feet on the rivers.
But whatever you asked of it, not the seeking or the finding of
your own kind
But the Indian, the silent ways of the old men you were
asking;
Days with the sun worn thin as a 'coon's skin, deep creeks
where salmon took the falls,
Coming to timber towns, the frontier, and to England,
To barns where your grandmother danced with her lovers,
with her young heels shining like white apples in the
dark;
Asking of history one Englishman not watching his own
shadow,
Singing a false note, limping: one Englishman blind, naked,
humming it out of tune,
To give you a taste for horse-shoes and the white eyes of
miners;
Whatever you asked of it, not the mountain-kids of other
countries,*

Kay BOYLE

To jump through the flames of bonfires, or the goats to return
    from the hills,
Running on their black hoofs to snuff the sugar from your
    palms;
Nor questions to tickle and flutter the stiff wings of the goats'
    ears
As they titter together and slide their coarse eyes in their
    faces;
Nor to go back into the hills and to see them, the beasts
    struck dumb in the bush,
Tentative, with their eyes in the darkness like the lights of
    tall houses,
And their tongues tasting the sweet night, and their horned
    teeth crunching the thick leaves of summer,
Nor the owls crying softly in the rain.

But to go back, to go back to another country, to go back
And to say from here I can see it;
Here and here a leaf opening, here the cherry-gum dripping,
Here a stream broken through, here and here and here a
    horse run wild.

[SUMMER 1928]

Constantin Brancusi

Photo of His Studio

[taken by the artist]

[JUNE 1929]

Georges Braque

Nature Morte

[JUNE 1929]

Georges Braque

Nature Morte

[JUNE 1929]

Bob BROWN

THE READIES

by Bob Brown

THE WORD "READIES" SUGGESTS TO ME A MOVING TYPE SPECTACLE, READING at the speed rate of the day with the aid of a machine, a method of enjoying literature in a manner as up-to-date as the lively talkies. In selecting "The Readies" as title for what I have to say about modern reading and writing I hope to catch the reader in a receptive progressive mood, I ask him to forget for the moment the existing medievalism of the BOOK (God bless it, it's staggering on its last leg and about to fall) as a conveyor of reading matter, I request the reader to fix his mental eye for a moment on the ever-present future and contemplate a reading machine which will revitalize this interest in the Optical Art of Writing.

In our aeroplane age radio is rushing in television, tomorrow it will be a commonplace. All the arts are having their faces lifted, painting (the moderns), sculpture (Brancusi), music (Antheil), architecture (zoning law), drama (Strange Interlude), dancing (just look around you tonight) writing (Joyce, Stein, Cummings, Hemingway, *transition*). Only the reading half of Literature lags behind, stays old-fashioned, frumpish, beskirted. Present-day reading methods are as cumbersome as they were in the time of Caxton and Jimmy-the-Ink. Though we have advanced from Gutenberg's movable type through the linotype and monotype to photo-composing we still consult the book in its original form as the only oracular means we know for carrying the word mystically to the eye. Writing has been bottled up in books since the start. It is time to pull out the stopper.

To continue reading at today's speed I must have a machine. A simple reading machine which I can carry or move around and attach to any old electric light plug and read hundred thousand word novels in ten minutes if I want to, and I want to. A machine as handy as a portable phonograph, typewriter or radio, compact, minute, operated by electricity, the printing done microscopically by the new photographic process on a transparent tough tissue roll which carries the contents of a book and is no bigger than a typewriter ribbon, a roll like a miniature serpentine that can be put in a pill box. This reading film unrolls beneath a narrow magnifying glass four or five inches long set in a reading slit, the glass brings up the otherwise unreadable type to comfortable reading size, and the reader is rid at last of the cumbersome book, the inconvenience of holding its bulk, turning its pages, keeping them clean, jiggling his weary eyes back and forth in the awkward pursuit of words from the upper left hand corner to the lower right, all over the vast confusing reading surface of a page.

Extracting the dainty reading roll from its pill box container the reader slips it smoothly into its slot in the machine, sets the speed regulator, turns on the electric current and the whole, 100,000; 200,000; 300,000 or million words, spills out before his eyes and rolls on restfully or restlessly as he wills, in one continuous line of type, its meaning accelerated by the natural celerity of the eye and mind (which today are quicker than the hand); one moving line of type before the eye, not blurred by the presence of lines above and below as they are confusingly placed on a columned page.

My machine is equipped with controls so the reading record can be turned back or shot ahead, a chapter reread or the happy ending anticipated. The magnifying glass is so set that it can be moved nearer to or farther from the type, so the reader may browse in 6 points, 8, 10, 12, 16 or any size that suits him. Many books remain unread today owing to the unsuitable size of type in which they are printed. A number of readers cannot stand the strain of small type and other intellectual prowlers are offended by Great Primer. The reading machine allows free choice in type-point, it is not a fixed arbitrary bound object but an adaptable carrier of flexible, flowing reading matter. Master-compositors have impressed upon apprentices for years that there is no rubber type. Well, now that the reading machine exists with a strong glass to expand to contract the size of letters, compositors can't ding on that anymore.

The machine is equipped with all modern improvements. By pressing a button the roll slows down so an interesting part can be read leisurely, over and over again if need be, or by speeding up, a dozen books can be skimmed through in an afternoon without soiling the fingers or losing a dust wrapper. Taken at high gear ordinary literature may be absorbed at the rate of full length novels in half hours or great pieces of writing may be reread in half lifetimes. The underlying principle of reading remains unaffected, merely its scope is enlarged and its latent possibilities pointed.

To save the labor of changing rolls or records, a clip of a dozen assorted may be put in at one time and automatically fed to the machine as phonograph discs are changed at present. The Book of the Day or Book of the Hour Club could sell its output in clips of a dozen ready to slip into the reading machine. Maybe a book club called the Dozen A Day would result. Reading by machinery will be as simple and painless as shaving with a Schick razor and refills could be had at corner drug stores or telephone booths from dawn to midnight.

With the present speeding up of publishing a machine is needed to handle the bulk and cut down the quantity of paper, ink, binding and manual labor wasted in getting out massive books.

The material advantages of my reading machine are obvious, paper saving by condensation and elimination of waste margin space which alone takes up a fifth or a sixth of the bulk of the present-day book. Ink saving in proportion, a much smaller surface needs to be covered, the magnifying glass multiplies the ink at no additional cost, the ratio is one part ink to ten parts magnifier. Binding will be unnecessary, paper pill boxes are produced at a fraction of the cost of cloth cases. Manual labor will be minimized.

Bob BROWN

Reading will be cheap and independent of advertising which today carries the cost of the cheap reading matter purveyed exclusively in the interests of the advertiser.

All that is needed to modernize reading is a little imagination and a high powered magnifying glass. The Lord's Prayer has been printed in type an inch high with illuminated initials as long as your nose and bound in plush elephantine folios; also it has been etched on the head of a pin. Personally I should have been better pleased if Anthony Trollope had etched his three volume classics on the head of a pin. Maybe no more trilogies will be written when Readies are the vogue. Anyway, if they are, they may be read at one sitting.

By photographic composition, which is rapidly taking the place of antiquated methods, type since 1925 has been turned out which is not readable without the aid of a magnifying glass. The English August-Hunter Camera Composing Machine fired the first gun in this revolution five years ago. Experiments with diamond type, like the old Chiswick Press Shakespeare Complete in one and miniature books of the 64mo Clubs have already shown what a multitude of words can be printed in a minimum of space and yet be readable to the naked eye. Even Cicero mentioned having seen a copy of the Iliad no bigger than a fingernail. Publishers of our day have perfected Oxford Bibles and compressed all of the short stories of De Maupassant into one volume by using thin paper. Dumb, inarticulate efforts have been made for centuries to squeeze more reading matter into less space; but the only hint I have found of Moving Reading is in the title of Stephen Crane's "Black Riders," which suggests the dash of inky words at full gallop across the plains of pure white pages. Roger Babson recently listed the needed invention of a Talking Book in a list of a dozen ways to make a million. But he missed the point. What's needed is a Bookless Book and certainly a silent one, because reading is for the eye and the INNER Ear. Literature is essentially Optical — not Vocal. Primarily, written words stand distinct from spoken ones as a colorful medium of Optical Art.

Reading is intrinsically for the eye, but not necessarily for the naked optic alone. Sight can be comfortably clothed in an enlarging lens and the light on a moving tape-line of words may be adjusted to personal taste in intensity and tint, so the eye may be soothed and civilized, and eventually become ashamed of its former nakedness.

Already we are familiar with news and advertisements reeling off before our eyes in huge illuminated letters from the tops of corner buildings, and smaller propaganda machines tick off tales of commercial prowess before our eyes in shop windows. All that is needed is to bring the electric street signs down to the ground, move the show-window reading device into the library by reducing the size of the letter photographically and refining it to the need of an intimate, handy, rapid reading conveyor.

In New York a retired Admiral by the name of Fiske has patents on a hand reading machine which sells for a dollar; it is used in reading microscopic type through a lens. Admiral Fiske states: "I find that it is entirely feasible, by suitable photographic or other process, to reduce a two and one-half inch column of typewritten or printed matter to a column one-quarter of an inch wide, so that by arranging five of such columns side by side and on both sides of a paper tape, which need not have a width greater than one and one-half inches, it becomes possible to present one hundred thousand words, the length of an average book, on a tape slightly longer than forty inches."

Recently the company that publishes the New York telephone book, because of the alarming increase in the ponderosity of its tomes, considered the idea of using the Fiske machine and printing its product, advertisements and all, in pages three inches tall, in microscopic type. The idea is excellent and eventually will force its way into universal acceptance because the present bulk of phone directories can hardly be expanded unless rooms and booths are enlarged. The inconvenience of searching through the massive volumes of several boroughs has brought New York to the necessity of giving birth to an invention.

But book me no books. In the Fiske Machine we have still with us the preposterous page and the fixity of columns. It is stationary, static, antiquated already before its acceptance.

The accumulating pressure of reading and writing alone will budge type into motion, force it to flow over the column, off the page, out of the book where it has snoozed in apathetic contentment for half a thousand years. The only apparent change the amateur reader may bemoan is that he cannot fall asleep as promptly before a spinning reading roll as he can over a droning book in his lap, but again necessity may come to the rescue with a radio attachment which will shut off the current and automatically stop the type-flow on receipt of the first sensitive vibration of a snore.

Revolutionize reading and the Revolution of the Word is inklessly achieved. There have been rumbling of word battles from Rabelais and Shakespeare through the inarticulate arm-waving time of Whitman to the deafening present. Creative writers have searched for new forms of word communication, methods of greeting more mental and aesthetic than dogs continue to employ so unimaginatively. Bawling creative Babes in the Word continue the struggle to shatter the filmy caul they were born with and get at the rosy nourishing nipples of their mother, the Sphinx-like Reader. Manifestos have been broadcast in all tongues in all times, dating from the one God issued at the Tower of Babble, which carries on today in the Unknown Tongue by which Holy Rollers commune. Maybe when we lift our creative writing heads too high again through the unexpected outlet of the Reading Machine God will come along and pie the type and we'll have to begin all over again. But until then lets be busy at our Tower.

The machine by its very existence makes a need of new words and deletes some worn-out ones. The hackneyed typewriter key-test of "Now is the time for all good men to come to the aid of their party" can be expressed with more interesting optical effect "Nowtime goodmen comeaid their party". No educated reading eye of this age catches the little, useless conventional conjunctions, articles, prefixes, suffixes, etc. unless they are needed for emphasis. The up-to-date eye scarcely sees the "thes," "ands", "buts," "tos", "fors," "fromits", but picks out the meaty nouns and verbs and only qualifying words so placed as to assume importance. Useless, un-

Bob BROWN

important sentence-encumberers will be skipped and never moving missed at all by the eager eye in its excitement at witnessing a type spectacle, a READIE, performing before its Mind's Vision and the sensitive Inner Ear.

Already there is a tendency to do away with quotes in the French fashion and useless capital letters at the beginning of columns of poetry. All modern movements toward more effective simplicity are in the same sure direction, even the poet laureate of word-bound England at the end of his life has done his bit to loosen up the language. Let's see words machine-wise, let the useless ones drop out and the fresh Spring pansy ones pop up.

Without any whirr or splutter writing is readable at the speed of the day — 1930 — not 1450, without being broken up by conventional columns, confined to pages and pickled in books, a READIE runs on before the eye continuously — on forever in-a-single-line-I-see-1450-invention-movable-type-Gutenberg-Wynkyn-de-Worde-Jimmy-the-Caxton-though-Chinese-centuries-before-printed-thousand-page-books-on-silk-leaves-furnished-by-local-silk-worms-no-two-leaves-tinted-alike-printing-from-dainty-porcelain-type-same-stuff-makes-teacups-dreams-Shakespeare-bending-over-workbench-making-language-laboriously-bellowing-blacksmith-turning-out-grotesqueries-at-forge-all-onhisown-to-keep-UP-interest-in-job—Spenstream-of-lusty-steamy-bigfisted-word-moulders-flit-by—Rabelais-BenJonson-DanDefoe-Sterne-WaltWhitman-GertStein-JimJoyce—Stephen-Crane's-Black-Riders-Crash-by-hell-bent-for-leather-uppercase-LOWERCASE-both-together-chanting-valorously-Print-in-action-at-longlast-moveable-type-at-breakneck-gallop—Carl-Sandburg-flashes-through-daredevil-commaless-Cossack-astride-mustang-bronco-vocabulary-leaning-farout-into-inky-night-picking-upcarefully-placed-phrases-with-flashing-Afric-teeth—Myself-I-see-motherfather-newscope-Optical-Writers-running round-rims-rhythmically-Eye-Writers-writing-endless-lines-for-reading-machines-more-optical-mental-more-colorful-readable-than-books—simple-foolproof-Readie-Machine-conveying-breathless-type-to-eager-eyereaders-tickling-Inner-ears-dumping-Inner-Ear-eyefuls-of-writer-right-before-receptive-ocular-brainportals-bringing-closer-hugging-readerwriter-now-there-is-more-mental-necking-radio-reaction-television-readievision-going-on-more-moving-reading-more-moving-writing.

The above is neither telegraphese nor a stab at writing modernly. It is but a crude attempt to convey the optical continuity of reading matter as it appears spinning past the eye out of a word-machine. It is hampered by the connecting hyphens and columns and lacks MOTION, the one essential of the new reading principle.

With written matter moving before the eyes new forms of expression will develop naturally, and surely more expressive ones, at least a technical eye-lingo of the Readie will result. They eye refreshed will ask for more, bawl for occasional tickling eye-Bawl, even tinted paper could be used to help along the flow of words and thoughts; and surely colored lighting effects on the reading tape.

Useless words will go out for a long walk and never come back into the reading language again, they will just walk out, drop out, dim out, fade out – OUT. Writing will recover its earlier naiveté, its Rabelaisian, Shake-spearean charm, its art quality; our reading vocabulary will be circumcised and circumscissiled. For the first time in the History of mental optics there will exist a visual Literary Language sharply separated from the Speaking Tongue. Literary language is Optical, speaking language Vocal, and the gap between them must spread till it becomes a gulf. My reading machine will serve as a wedge. Makers of words will be born; fresh, vital eye-words will wink out of dull, dismal, drooling type at startled smug readers. New methods crave new matter; conventional word-prejudices will be automati-cally overcome, from necessity reading-writing will spring full-blown into being. The Revolution of the Word will be won. Reading-writing will be pro-duced not so much for its sonorific sleep-producing qualities as for its mental-eye-provoking pleasures.

I have lived with five hundred years of printed books and have felt the same papyrus that Nebuchadnezzar might have touched, and all this time I have lived in loving wonder, a great want-to-know about words, their here and their there, their this and their that, and the most efficacious manner of administering the written word to the patient. The monks in the begin-ning didn't do it so badly in their illuminated manuscripts, they retained a little of the healthy hieroglyphic, all Oriental books in ideogramatic character are delights, early colophons splendid. But what have we got in this machine age, only Bruce Rogers and waste-baskets full of glittering comely type to make into beautifully commonplace words which can't tell us much more than the labored chisellings of the stone age, beautiful but dumb books as clumsy in their way as the Rozetti Stone.

Let's let writing out of books, give it a chance and see what it does with its liberty. Maybe there are butterflies in the core of those cloth-cased cocoons stacked away in libraries. Let's let them out and have a look. With reading words freely conveyed maybe books will become as rare as horses after the advent of the auto, perhaps they will be maintained only for personal pleasure or traditional show, as the gorgeously-trapped brewery steeds of Munich.

Let's look for literary renaissance through the Readie; a modern, mov-ing, word spectacle. Let's have a new reading medium in time with our day, so that industrious delvers in the Word-Pile may be rapidly read and quickly understood by their own generation at least.

The Readies are no more unusual than the Talkies, and not a scratch on television. As soon as the reading machine becomes a daily necessity cer-tainly it will be out of date. Pocket reading machines will be the vogue then; reading matter probably will be radioed and words recorded directly on the palpitating ether. But the endless imaginative possibilities of the new medium need not lead us astray. The low-brows are presently revelling in their Movies and Talkies while the almost extinct high-brow is content to sit at home sipping his thin alphabet soup out of archaic volumes of columns, mewling a little like a puling baby taking mush from the tip of an awkward wooden spoon too gross for his musical rose-buddy tempera-mental mouth.

Those Mental Obfuscates who can't make out the Readies on the dim lit-erary horizon of the day will be the first to accept them as a commonplace tomorrow and they will be the loudest in grumbling if anything happens to the Readie mechanism to interrupt the eager optical word-flow as for as much as a *billimeter-augenblick*.

[JUNE 1930]

LA BARBE ! ! !

This space is subscribed by an anonymous advocate of:

Franco-American friendship
Lafayette
Pure (French) Womanhood
     (American)
Clean (American) Manhood
      (French)
Veteran's Crusades
Law and Order
Government of, by or for the people
Unmarried War Mothers
The S.-S. Banner
Trans-Atlantic flights (either successful or unsuccessful)
Etc. etc.

LA BARBE ! ! !

[OCTOBER 1927]

THREE POEMS

by Bryher

DIFFERENT FOCUS

IT'S NOT YOU,
it's everything you were,
lights reflected from a skyscraper,
lights from revolving disks,
words so of this day,
un-told, untold.

Sounds of your voice,
your brain,
your asthenic modern head,
ears,
picking up the wireless of the world,
transmitting it again.

Shells inland
on the bed of a long forgotten dried up sea,
so old that they are young,
prehistoric things,
pterodactyl wings,
stride of dinosaurs in sand;
if you are brittle and dry
and needing
something I cannot even understand,
to be carried by the wind
from the sea,
detached and unrelated,
it is for you to decide this,
not me.

II

YOU SAY THROUGH.
I answer —
there is nothing else to do —
"through."

I never loved you
as I loved the rain;
you never cared,
preferring reindeer
that range from icy water
to browze black willow
on a frozen plain.

Only your brain,
in words reflected,
was a humming bird,
parting blue leaves
that first and sudden time,
to no one else
mysterious —
to me strange.

III

IF I AM A NEEDLE ON A DISK,
   got to play the record out,
got to go on,
whatever voices break across me
or what shadows,
knees or shoulders,
silverpoint the blackness;
got to play the record out
till I break or am lifted,
I dont choose the sound I make,
you don't choose the groove.

No good saying,
take a knife and cut me from the past,
If I am a needle on a disk,
I'm not the new record
nor the old silence.
There is nowhere that we join together,
nowhere . . .
   And it's not your job to lift me at the finish.

[JUNE 1927]

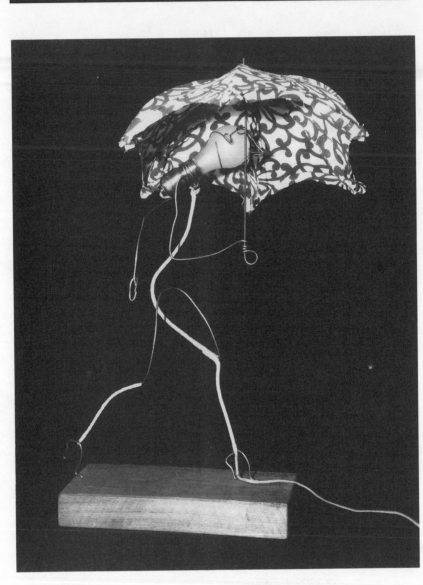

Alexander Calder

Wire Sculpture

*The wire sculpture and artistic toys of
Alexander Calder, a young American who
recently has settled in Paris, have won him
immediate recognition.*

[JUNE 1929]

JULY

by Erskine Caldwell

MIDDLEAGED BEN HACKETT WITH CROMWELL AND JULIA WAS HAYING TO BEAT hell when the thunderstorm broke on the eastridge. Ben knew it was coming, because all morning thunder rumbled up and down the river; but Ben didnt want it to come while most of his firstcrophay was cocked, and he didnt like it at all. Ben was hot and Ben was mad, but the rain cooled him down and took some of the anger out of him. Cromwell and Julia didnt like the heat, and now they didnt like the rain and thunder. Ben swore to them soothingly about the weather and they stood all right.

When the storm was over the hay was too wet to draw, and Ben had to pitch off his load because that too was wet. Swearing and sweating Ben unloaded, and drove Cromwell and Julia across the field and through the gap in the rock wall at the lane. In the lane Ben filled his pipe and perched himself on the hayrack. The sun was out, and it was hot again. But the hay was wet.

"If the weather knows all about making hay it ought to have to get it in itself, by Jesus," Ben told Cromwell and Julia.

Cromwell snorted some thistledown out his nose and Julia swished her horsehairs in Ben's face.

While he was getting his tobacco aglow the team stopt. Ben took five or six deep sucks without looking up.

"Get along there, Cromwell," he urged puffing. "What's ailing you, Julia!"

The team moved forward a pace and again halted. Ben stood up balancing himself on the rack.

"By Jesus!" he grunted masking his face.

An automobile, unoccupied, blocked the narrow lane.

Ben climbed down, swearing to Cromwell and Julia. He walked around the automobile uncertainly, stopt studying it, and walked around it again. No one was in sight. Going closer Ben laid his hand on the door taking from his teeth the pipe with his other hand.

"Damn a man who'd stand his auto abarring the lane," he pronounced, glancing around at Cromwell and Julia for confirmation. "I guess I'll have to push the thing out the way myself. By Jesus, if whoever left it here was here I'd tell him something he wouldnt forget soon!"

But Ben couldnt move the car. It creaked and squeaked when he pushed and when he pulled, but it wouldnt move. Knocking out his pipe and wiping his face Ben backed up to Cromwell and Julia grasping their bridles in his hands. He led his team around the automobile all right. When he got in the lane behind the car he stopt his horses and went back, looking at it and putting his hands on the doors and mudguards.

"By Jesus!" Ben exclaimed highpitched looking in the tonneau. He pulled out a creamsilk stocking and a pair of black patent leatherpumps.

He was too excited to say anything or to do anything with the stocking and shoes. He looked in the driver's seat, and there under the steering-wheel sat a gallonjug of cider almost empty. Ben pulled the cork to smell if it was hard. It was. He jabbed his thumb through the handlehole and threw the jug in his elbow. It was hardcider all right, but there was very little of it left.

"By Jesus", Ben smacked his lips, wiping them with his hand, "that's pretty good cider for a windfall".

He replaced the jug under the steeringwheel. Before he screwed his finger out the handlehole his eyes discovered a garment lying on the floor beside it. He pulled out the garment and held it up before his eyes. It was a pair of lavendersilkdrawers. Ben stared open-mouthed and wildeyed.

"By Jesus, Cromwell," he licked his mustache lip, "what do you know about that!"

Cromwell and the mare nibbled at the roadgrass unconcerned.

Ben handled the drawers a little more intimately. He turned them slowly around looking at all sides. Then he looked inside. Then he smelled them.

"By Jesus, Cromwell," he declared triumphantly, "this is a woman's thing, or else I'm a redheaded tadpole!"

Holding the drawers in his hands tenderly Ben climbed on the hayrack and drove down the lane into the road. They were nice and soft in his hands, and they smelled good, too.

He went down the road homeward thinking about the drawers. They made him want to do something but he didnt know what he could do. When he reached Fred Williams' place he drew up his team. Fred's wife was stooping over in the garden. Ben stuft the drawers in his pocket.

"Nice day, today, Mrs. Williams," he called unsteadily. "Where's Fred?"

"Fred's gone to town today," she answered looking around bent over her knees.

Ben's hand went in his pocket and felt the lavendersilkdrawers. Even in his pocket outofsight they made him feel like a new man trying himself out. He hitched the team to the horserack and went in the garden where Fred's wife was. She was picking peas for supper. Watching her pulling the long round pods and putting them in her apron Ben strode around her in circles putting his hand in the pocket where the lavendersilk-drawers were. Walking around her he spat behind him every other step. The woman didnt say much, and Ben said nothing at all. He was getting so now he could feel the drawers without even putting his hand in his pocket.

When he was behind her the next time Ben clutched her around her waist with his arms and held to her.

"Help!" she yelled at the top of her voice diving forward: "Help!"

When she jumpt forward both of them fell on the peavines tearing them and uprooting them. She yelled and fought but Ben was determined, and he held on to her waist with all his strength. They rolled in the dirt and on the peavines. Ben jerked the drawers out. He got one of her feet through one drawersleg but he couldnt get the other foot in. They rolled some more in the dirt tearing up the peavines. Ben was panting. But he couldnt get the lavendersilkdrawers on Fred's wife's other foot. He was determined to put the drawers on her. Presently she stopt struggling and Ben glanced around at her. She was sitting up looking down at him in the dirt. Both of them were brown with the garden soil, and Ben was sweating through his mask.

"Ben Hackett what are you trying to do?" she sputtered through the earth on her face.

Ben released her legs and looked up at her. He didnt say anything. She stood up and stept in the drawersleg and pulled them up under her dress. That was where he had been trying to put them all the time.

Ben got up dusting his clothes. He followed her across the garden into the frontyard.

"Wait here," she told him.

He waited, and when she came back she carried a basin of water and a towel.

"Wash the dirt off your face and hands, Ben Hackett," she directed standing over him wearing the lavendersilkdrawers.

Ben did as he was told. Then he slapt some more dirt out of his trousers.

When he finished cleaning himself Ben handed her the emptied basin and soiled towel.

"It was mighty nice of you to bring the towel and water," he thanked her.

"You are halfway fit to go home now," she approved.

ALMOST A FABLE

by Emanuel Carnevali

THE SUN JUMPED OUT OF THE LAKE AND THE GODDESS OF THE WATERS PULLED at a thousand horses of light. The Goddess ran on the lake leaving behind her gold coins marvelously big and bright.

The Goddess entered children's rooms and children's dreams, while they lay on their little beds like flowers that have been cut.

Dawn was cool in the sky and the lake was in full uniform, green and red. The bubbles on the crest of the waves were kisses from an angel descended on purpose from heaven.

Children's feet caressed the sand that was mighty around the lake. These little children loved the lake unconsciously as they did once in the times that are past.

Thru the children's toes the fine sand ran, like a liquid of portent and marvel. Children were like instruments of joy. Joy that went beyond life and beyond death.

When the children went to the country they found armies of little daisies. Little white daisies, pure and sweet, simple and sweet, joyous and sweet.

Destiny weights upon you, children, like a hawk or an eagle on a little bird. Alas it is your fate to become old as it is everybody's fate. And then you too shall die and like persons of novels one reads about you saying: he who wrote the book is dead and they whom he wrote about are dead too. For death is the eternal intruse and importunate.

Children walked and the sun followed them slowly slowly. And at the end of their walk death was smiling falsely. And at the end of their walk death awaited them. Children that are dear die too, as well as children who are not dear. These children I speak of are common children not special children of a special tale. These common children wear the smile of the world, for at times the world, this awful old hulk, smiles too.

Children run about quickly enough but death is faster than they. And it seems impossible that that old God who was in the sky should allow them to die. But the world is sad and the world is weary, so weary as to allow children to die while the world stands by sad and weary and it watches and says nothing, afraid of fatigue, afraid of struggle, afraid of contrast and disturbance and change of opinion, and change of habit.

My children (common, I repeat) never wake early enough to give us the spectacle of their meeting the dawn.

My children walked and the sun followed them slowly slowly. And their walk has no end it is eternal and terrible.

[JUNE 1930]

CAN YOU HELP ?

Emanuel Carnevali
is incurably ill, and
entirely dependent
on public charity.
Can you help to
make his suffering
more tolerable ? His
address is

Trattoria di Porta Castello
Bazzano (Bologna)
Italie

[NOVEMBER 1929]

SEVEN O'CLOCK

by Malcolm Cowley

AT SEVEN O'CLOCK WHEN TABLES HAVE BEEN CLEARED
brushed free of crumbs and chairs set back
the dishes scraped and washed and put away

at seven o'clock the wives of Cherry Tree
come to their porches, take a rocking chair
and sway in rhythm, one, two, slippers tap
symmetrically, one . . . two . . . one . . .

Today the house was very hot she said
and Mabel said the house was hot today
and not a cloud in the sky, but a stormy moon
with the horns turned down, so maybe rain would fall
during the night. July, the windless month
when only the hot breath of growing corn
seeps imperceptibly through the dusk, July
in the eighteen-seventies or nineteen-ten
or fifty years from now. Their chairs creak on
one, two, and slippers tapping on the floor

till at half-past nine
there is a sound of closing doors, of bolts
shot, and the sudden glow of lamps.

In all the valley houses at half-past nine
shadows go crawling through the flowered hallways
and gingham rustles up a narrow stair.

[SUMMER 1928]

THE CHESTNUT TREES ARE DEAD

by Malcolm Cowley

WE WILL MAKE OUR WAY OUT OF THE CITY: COME!

It is too late now.

I know a place where blue grass, orchard grass
red clover, timothy and white clover
are tangled in an orchard, and juneberries
ripen and fall at the deep edge of the woods.

Crowds, turbines, unremembered time
it is too late now.

Since unremembered time the ferns have grown
knee-deep, and moss under the chestnut trees
hiding the footprints of small deer. We ran
do you remember, trampling ferns to reach
a spring that issued from the chestnut roots
in a bright stream (we traced it through the laurel
crossing burned ground where briars held us back
with their skinny hands, then crashing down a hill
headlong to find...)

It is too late now, too late
we have lived a great while here and no moons rise
the juneberries will be rotted on the branches
the chestnut trees are dead.

[JANUARY 1928]

RACE BETWEEN A SUBWAY LOCAL AND THE SUBWAY EXPRESS

by Malcolm Cowley

THE DOORS ROLLED NOISILY SHUT, THEN, FOR A MOMENT, THE TWO TRAINS stood side by side, motionless, like panthers gathered for a leap. It was a moment of depth and calm. The platform stood empty under the electric lights. A dozen flakes of snow, which had drifted in through the ventilator, hung briefly in the still air. From the men's toilet a solitary traveler came rushing with long strides. He banged on a door, found a crack, slipped his hand into it, widened the opening, squeezed through. The guard cursed him indifferently. The late traveler, he wore a flat-brimmed Stetson shining with melted snow, went stumbling down the aisle toward the front of the car. There was the rumble and squeak of wheels. With majesty the Express rolled out of the Fourteenth Street station, eight seconds ahead of our Local.

Soon we recovered most of the lost advantage. The Express is a lumbering beast, slow to start, gathering immense speed through momentum only; the Local is a dog yapping at its heels, officious, running quickly, tiring quickly, less popular, vastly more sympathetic. The disease of paradox affects my friends. They know the folklore of the skyscraper, the romance of the girder, the ballad of the pneumatic riveter. They despise the crowd of those who despise the crowd. Each morning they travel in the Local, staring through the windows to watch its almost hopeless race.

The seconds passed. Our train was marching step by step with the Express, at a handicap of maybe half a dozen cars. From the front platform of the first Local car, where we were standing a few feet from the silent engineer, we could watch the seventh car of the Express: an ambulant domestic scene with Papa reading the morning *Times*, Alfred yawning, Joseph and Charles smiling toward Estelle, who was publicly cleaning her fingernails. They were long and pink; her mouth puckered; her eyes were bright. I wanted to pinch her chemical cheeks, and made a forward movement, imagining . . . an opened window, a prayer, my arms stretched out toward her, then torn from my shoulders by the iron posts, sole fixities in a moving world, past which we glided.

In the morning, after black coffee, the time is favorable for mathematics. I estimated the distance between the posts as 5 feet. Since the length of a New York city block is 260 feet, there must be 208 posts between 14th and 18th streets. If we were traveling at the rate of 20 miles an hour, we should pass — I stopped to estimate — about six posts every second. Distance and time are interchangeable. I tried to count the posts, but they had become a blur, a line of shadows marching to the rear, while the hum of the wheels had climbed to a higher octave.

Our sister car was moving beside us still, but we had gained three windows, four . . . And now the stranger, the man in the flat-brimmed Stetson, offers to bet one dollar against three that we beat the Express into the Pennsylvania Station. Five dollars against ten (we have gained another window). Ten dollars against fifteen. It was a desperate wager, yet we could all remember instances, perhaps one in a hundred, perhaps one in fifty, where the Express had been delayed by other trains; where the Local, in spite of its handicap of three stations, had marched ahead into the Terminal. We hope for such a victory today.

We gain another window. Behind us, in the car, a mild interest is creeping over the passengers. Two of them peer through the dirty panes. A thin man in black lays down his newspaper, folds his glasses and slips them into his vest; he fumbles in his coat-pocket for another pair. A woman with a high forehead and crazy eyes writes UP DE VALERA! in the dust of the window; then she stares at the Express. We are gaining continually. The car which carries Estelle is left behind; we gain; and, window after window, we are given a panorama of the train.

It is wrong to believe, as most of us do, that one subway car resembles another. Their personality, which is that of their passengers, changes from end to end of the train. Adventurous people, in general, seek a place at one of the extremes; here also sit the calculating; while those of little energy, of no imagination, are content to be crushed into the center cars, where they are embalmed upright in coffins of eternal glass. I have imagined subways filled with poison gases, and every creature dead on the trains; yet, with a dead hand on the lever, they proceed in haste to reach no destination. I have imagined cars in which sheep, monkeys, fish, were packed together. Watching the West Side subway, I have observed that business men and stenographers crowd the front of the train, since their destination is north of 42d Street; while the cars behind are filled with garment workers, pushing, stinking, gesticulating, reading the scandals of yesterday in the only Yiddish morning news-paper. We have left them far behind, and now, in his dark alcove, we are watching the engineer of the Express.

I must have been holding my breath; it escapes with a gasp; my head is dancing with noise; my hand trembles a little. Beyond the Express I can see another Express, another Local, racing like our two trains, but toward a different goal.

There is a moment in the race, in every true race, when destinies are balanced, when the two contestants are side by side, a second, an instant only, when, through extremes of speed, everything grows still. Perhaps one hears the sound of church bells in the valley. A little smoke drifts in the air that precedes a storm. A yellow light is seen – in the midst of the clouds; on earth, all colors are preternaturally clear. The storm breaks. The thin man in black changes his spectacles again and returns to the morning *World*. A girl's laughter sounds above the screech of the wheels. Suddenly I discover that the Express is marching ahead.

It gains, window by window; it gains, and the panorama of cars is again unrolled: the stenographers and office executives, the nondescripts of the center cars, the piled garment workers, the half-empty car where Estelle has just finished the nails of her left hand. She turns to the nails of her right, smiling secretly. The man in the flat-brimmed Stetson bursts into tears. I lean against the door, tired as the calendar. With a shrug of its red tail-light, the Express bounds northward, to 72d and 96th, the Harlem River with its tugs and barges, the heights beyond the river, scattered apartment houses, schoolboys skating in Van Cortland Park, and toward those final yards where Express and Local are equally disassembled, their identities lost, their cars recoupled into other trains.

[JANUARY 1928]

SOME OPINIONS [1929]

... All unsuspecting in his mad whimsicality, Lewis Carroll discovered the new tenets of writing which were to be hailed in 1929 as the ne plus ultra of artistic creation, hailed upon the first page of the current issue of transition as the revolution of the word. To show proper respect for their predecessor the rebels ought certainly to acknowledge their debt and establish Humpty Dumpty as their prophet ... With the reader thus disposed of, it remained only for these pioneers to begin their process of disintegrating the language, and a good deal of the resultant shambles may be read in the present transition ... Joyce, in his 'Work in Progress' has been consistently practicing the disrupting and rebuilding of words, and Stuart Gilbert interprets a part of this for us in old-fashioned English ... Part of Theo Rutra's contribution is as close a rival to "Jabberwocky" as modern writing can produce. Carroll would have been proud of it ... One can observe the phenomenon with that species of watchful curiosity which is usually accorded a biologic sport, trusting always in the reversion of natural law ...

– New York Sun.

SUMMER TIME

by Archibald Craig

THESE EVENINGS STAY ON LONG
Old women talking in the dusk
Until their voices sink
Hard as the cold tea in the cups.
Its too dusk to write.
The current has'nt come on yet
When the switch makes a hollow click
*   in my fingers.*
These evenings sit on me like old clothes
The sweat cannot penetrate.
They move slowly in the street
Coming along with lunch bags
*   afire with dandelions.*
Their voices leaden against the blocks.
Why is the electric company fooled
Because the papers say lighting up time is 6:45?
There are no lights in the laburnum trees.

They drone around the table
*   the old women's voices...*
"We are young... We are young still and there's
Sun on the dandelions"
And I must listen and curse
*   quietly in the dark.*

[SUMMER 1928]

MOMENT FUGUE

by Hart Crane

THE SYPHILITIC SELLING VIOLETS CALMLY
   and daisies
By the subway news-stand knows
               how hyacinths

This April morning offers
   hurriedly
In bunches sorted freshly
           and bestows
On every purchaser
     (of heaven perhaps)

His eyes —
      like crutches hurtled into grass
Fall phantom-sudden (counting change
   for lilies)

Beyond the roses that no flesh can pass.

[FEBRUARY 1929]

PLEASING TO THE EYE [1927]

"Attractive in form – small, thick, with uncut leaves, a dull blue cover, and its name lettered in silver."

Louisville *Courier Journal.*

THE HARBOR DAWN

by Hart Crane

Brooklyn Heights.

IN SLEEP, — AS THOUGH A SHADOW BLOOMED ALOUD, —
They meet you listening midway in your dream,
The long tired sounds, creeping in grey reefs:
Gongs in white surplices, pursuant wails,
Chugs, whistles . . . signals dispersed in veils.

And then a truck will lumber past the wharves,
Steel clank on some passing tanker deck;
Or a drunken stevedore's howl and thud below.

And if they take your sleep away sometimes
They give it back again . . . Soft sleeves of sound
Wistfully wind the darkness, the pillowed Bay.
Somewhere out there in blankness steam

Spills into steam and wanders, washed away,
— Flurried by keen fifings, eddied
Among distant chiming buoys, drifts . . . The sky,

Cool, feathery fold, suspends, — distils
This wavering slumber . . . Slowly,
Immemorially the window, the half-covered chair
Ask nothing but this sheathe of pallid air.

It is the hour we need not speak. Sirens
Hold us now, stealthily weave us into day.
Let hidden river music summon us gradually —
Fog surges, vague calliopes of morn . . .

While myriad snowy hands are clustering at the panes —

> *your hands within my hands are deeds;*
> *my tongue upon your throat — singing*
> *arms close; eyes wide, undoubtful*
> > *dark*
> > > *drink the dawn —*
> *a forest shudders in your hair!*

The window goes blond slowly. Frostily clears.
From thaumaturgic heights across the river
— Two — three bright Cyclops eyes aglitter, disk
The sun, released — aloft with cold gulls hither,

The fog leans one last moment on the sill.
Under the mistletoe of dreams a star,
As though to join us at some farther hill,
Turns in the waking west and goes to sleep.

[JUNE 1927]

POEM

by Hart Crane

LET NOT THE PILGRIM SEE HIMSELF AGAIN
bound like the dozen turtles on the wharf
each twilight, — still undead, and brine caked in their eyes,

huge, overturned: such thunder in their strain!
And clenched beaks coughing for the surge again!

Slagged of the hurricane, — I, cast within its flow,
congeal by afternoons here, satin and vacant . . .
You have given me the shell, Satan, — the ember,
Carbolic, of the sun exploded in the sea.

Grand Cayman, West Indies.

[APRIL 1927]

THE STRANGER

by Caresse Crosby

A SILVER BIRD AND A BIRD OF GOLD
I harnessed to my chariot of hope
The silver bird wore bells on silver wings
The gold one yoked with filaments and strings of gold.

Myself the charioteer, with whip and lash
Urged on the upward pair
And drove the flashing team
To where a hilltop rose beyond the utmost slope.

Down-lighting there beside an emerald fire
I poured from swift hands out upon the day
A freight of Tyrian Sapphires and a bright display
Of crimson beads —

The silver bird arose and belled soft wings,
The golden bird slipped from his golden strings.

But once my treasures spilled upon the ground
I stilled my heart, and warrior-fashion found
Against my chariot wheels of beaten bronze
Warm sleep—
Deceiving phantom for my eyes were strung
With visions winter-cold
And from the Towers of Thenalia
Swarmed a mistral fold of sheep —

One here, one there, one everywhere
And over all soft snow and crystal sleet —

(I felt the golden feathers nearer creep)

The fire dwindled and the hill and sky
  rekindled
While the snowfall, hardly falling, softly fell —
Upon the sea, and on the distant shore.

Hail land that never was!
The air is stilled once more
and I —

*
* *

No more O Father
from your hands
The Gift of Love.
Once only and forever all of love
Was given
Crimson ribbons, damson grapes,
with tears above.

*
* *

Unavail us the tears of the heart
And the heart-beats that count
Are the shears as they swing
With the weight of the robe —

You have girt us with wool that
is shorn of the sheep
And the perilous breasts of our youth
You have folded in fleece,
O my Father
Our mouths you have stopped
with the harvested herbs of the wood,
And your tent was of flax and
of hemp were the seams of
its pattern!

*
* *

Now the far lands draw near,
Since the speed and the force of our
travel is heat,
Heat born of the forest and hill —

Far lands drawing near!
O freshets of earth give us life for our flight
And the drip and the dole of our loins
We will leave you as wage for our thirst.

*
* *

The golden bird is sleep beneath my hand
No measured circuit
Or fixed limit planned.

The bird of silver thrusting at my side
Is steed to mount,
And so astride
To beautiful and endless otherwheres
Away!
Below me on the plain ten lovers kneel
Above, around, about
The wheeling endless wheels

> *
> * *

Behind the sun a stranger hides
I will show him the sweet in the
curve of my side —
And a rhythm unsung we will sing —

> *
> * *

Against the sun
O my lover you stand
And I
against the sun and the hills
and the world.

Infinitesimal pause of the cycle
Swift prick of Time Past

and the mountains the sea
And my love
O my lover around me and over
and in me forever

> *
> * *

But forever the primary sigh of the flesh
and the womb that is caught
in the turn of the plough
O fertile device in the circle of
how and of how

O steed made of silver what hope have we now!

Sink back to the hilltop and back
to the plain
We must lie with the cattle as
others have lain.
We must yield to the rain.

Intentional kiss for intentional pain —

Will the Stranger still linger there
back of the Sun!

                    *
                  *   *

I rise again
My feet are tangled now.
About me now the clinging
lace of hands
The hardly-heard triumphant
weak commands
of tendrils draining deep for sap —

What if the silver bird and gold
Should wait and wait and I grow old?

O wait!
for I have been
and I have guessed
and I have seen
and I must wholly something know.

The golden bird: "Arise, and we will go."

                    *
                  *   *

But our linen is tinged
with the shame of our sex
and the stain of our rose
is a wound to be hid.

I have bartered with youth
For a cycle of fears
O my son
You are young
You are youth without years.

And I moulded you, I, in the long of a day.
In the morning with pain
In the evening with shame
And at night with a prayer —

I have fashioned you fair?
Is it true, is it true —
Put your feet to the fields
Give your strength to your play
I am free — I am through.

The golden wings are tremulous
and I
(while arms lean earthward)
yearn,
      and we must fly —

               *
           * *

A drift of dust
and our shadow gone over
Erased from the fields
lost into the sun
O my bird of gold
You are wax to flames
and your wings unmould.
Only flight remains.

How your speed is cold!

               *
           * *

Must it be to the heart of the sun bright through
Shall eyes see — Can I tell it is you?

O stranger so masked by such light
If I knew — if I knew.
Your burning is dont to my flesh and O dont
I am tortured with flame.
Your fire about and above and below me
and through me again

Whereby shall I find you
or shall I go —

And Stranger your name?

               *
           * *

A silver bird and a bird of gold
I harnessed to my chariot of hope
The silver bird wore bells on silver wings
The gold one yoked with filaments and strings of gold,

And I the charioteer with word and song
Urged on the upward pair!
The moon was with us —
But the sun was yonder
Ever beyond and always otherwhere!

[NOVEMBER 1929]

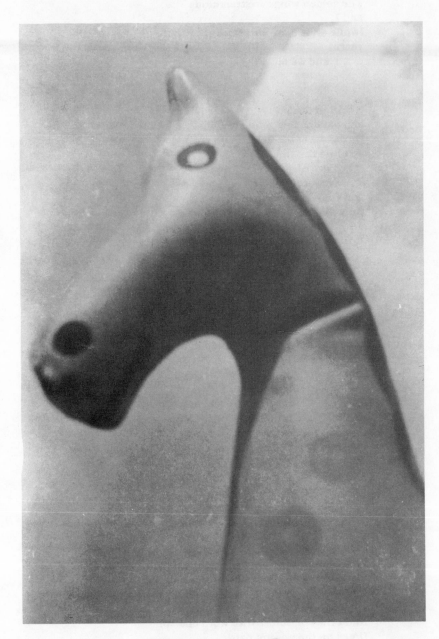

Harry Crosby

Apparition

[JUNE 1929]

Harry CROSBY

THE NEW WORD

by Harry Crosby

THE NEW WORD IS THE SERPENT WHO HAS SLOUGHED OFF HIS OLD vocabulary.

The New Word is the stag who has rid himself of the old wood of his antlers.

The New Word is the clean piercing of a Sword through the rotten carcass of the Dictionary, the Dwarf standing on the shoulders of the Giant (Dictionary) who sees further into the Future than the giant himself, the Panther in the Jungle of Dictionary who pounces upon and devours all timid and facile words, the New Word is a Diamond Wind blowing out the Cobwebs of the Past.

The New Word is a direct stimulant upon the senses, a freshness of vision, an inner sensation, the egg from which other words shall be produced, a herald of revolt, the new tree thrusting above the dreary court-yard of No Change, a jewel upon the breast of Time, the Eve that stands naked before us, the challenge flung in the face of an unadventurous public, the reward of the discoverer, the companion of the prophet, the simplicity of the unexpected, the girder bridge towards a splendid future, the tremendous concentration and internal strength of a Joyce, the defiance of laws.

[JUNE 1929]

PROFUSELY ILLUSTRATED [1927]

"The pictures look to the vulgar eye like the other crazy modernist stuff."

New York *Sun*.

SUITE

by Harry Crosby

Aeronautics

A PROCESSION TO THE HILL OF MONTMARTRE (WHERE STAND THE FAMOUS windmills) in the midst of which is a large Balloon, mounted on wheels and drawn by two donkeys. Behind comes a monkey standing on its hind legs, in clerical garb, and a donkey both of them with trousers on, and looking happy. At the back is the personification of Fire on a cloud, holding a scroll in her hand on which are depicted two Balloons. The Balloon is in mid-air and is encircled by monkeys and donkeys waiting for the Ascent. A blind Man leaves the scene saying, I can see nothing. The Balloon is rising from the platform, in front of which is an enormous crowd of spectators. The Balloon has ascended into the atmosphere. The Balloon moves off in a horizontal direction. The Balloon has disappeared into space. An Explosion is heard. The Balloon has Exploded. The Balloon is on the ground and Peasants are attacking it with pitchforks. Landscape with cottage and hay barn and old white timber inn with thatched roof, men seated drinking, to left a farm-girl feeding pigs, waggoner with his horses at watertrough. The inn stands on the banks of the river behind spreading trees. A cow is drinking. The Virgin seated by the Tree. The Virgin with the Rabbits. Saint George with the Dragon. The Circumcision in the Stable. The Betrothal of the Virgin. The Wondrous Hog. The Brood Mares. The tiled buildings of the mill are seen on the further bank of the river. In foreground to right two women washing clothes. In centre soldiers firing. To left spectators with the American Flag above in various attitudes of alarm. A vixen sits on the ledge of the bank and looks toward five cubs, a sixth cub peers out of a hole in the bank. Enter the Blind Man. Enter an Aardvark. Enter a man with a knife left hand raised to his face (female figure partly nude floating in the air beside him). He is followed by a young woman plucking a fowl. Her hair is in curls she has pearls round her neck and she is wearing an ermine cloak with jewels. Enter a young peasant girl carrying basket rejecting the advances of a young man in uniform (female figure partly nude floating in the air beside him) Enter mother and child (the child has pyelitis). Enter Elsa de

Brabant. Enter an Augur observing Birds. Enter a Flying Fox. Enter a Stork and a Pelican. Enter a Black Hawk. Enter a Red Swan. Enter Santa Claus with a portion of caviar. Enter Tilden. Enter Walter Hagen in a knitgrip knicker (no buckles to buckle). Enter the Tenth Plague of Egypt. Enter the Madonna of the Sleeping Cars. Enter Anna Livia Plurabelle. Enter La Mère Gérard. Enter La Vieille aux Loques. Enter La Marchande de Moutarde. Enter the Red Dress. Enter two girls one combing her hair. Oh! Why! – I don't know about loving him very much. Enter Daniel Webster. Thank God! I – I also – am an American! Enter Christ and the Woman of Samaria. Enter the Man in the Moon. Enter Champagne Charley. Enter the Monkey in clerical garb (female figure partly nude floating in the air beside him) fur cap coat with fur cuffs reading aloud a book of common prayer. Come Holy Ghost our souls inspire. Lightening flashing in the background. Enter old red man with red helmet on his head. Enter old bearded man in a high fur cap with closed eyes. Enter an Animal of No Importance. Enter a Virgin making much of time. Enter Renoir (female figure partly nude floating in the air beside him) If women had no breasts I would not have painted them. Enter H. D. wrapped in a palimpsest. Enter a welldressed man in everyday attire arm in arm with a Follies Girl in a modish three-color one-piece club-striped combination travelo swim-suit. I've simply nothing to wear. Enter Prufrock in a Rock Fleece Overcoat. Enter Miss Everis. I am five months pregnant. The other day I felt a pain in my abdomen. Enter Steve Donoghue. Enter Kefalin winner of the Grand Prix. Enter an Onanist. Enter a Masochist. Enter Europe's Greatest Lover. Enter Antony and Cleopatra. Enter the Harvard Track Team. Enter Standard Oil Bearer right hand holding gloves left grasping staff of standard, so safe so sure so easy to handle. Enter Porphyria's Lover. Enter Mr. and Mrs. Lingam with an attendant behind. Enter a Jury of Annoyance. Enter Sportsman holding up a hare in his right hand. Enter a Feudal Ladye amorous to be known. Enter a Knight Errant. Enter T. Noorderquartier (halitoxio) Enter Nicolas Alfan de Ribera Marquis de Villanneva de las Torres de Dugnes d'Alcala Grands d'Espagne. Enter Lindberg with a Lion-Tamer. Enter Vandals and Visigoths. Enter the Pancake-Woman reading aloud What Every Girl Should Know. Enter Joseph telling his Dreams. Enter Blasus de Manfre, the Waterspouter. Enter Roman Youth Swallowing Stones (burst of applause from a London whore who appears standing between a lion and a unicorn). Enter an ignorant Physician. Enter a Fair Lady in Revolt. Enter Mr. Guy Holt with a flair for civilized fiction. Enter a Magician. Enter a Fawn dressed up as a Girl. Enter Queens in Hyacinth. Enter Jamaica God of Rum. Enter His Excellency Kno Sung Tao holding a jar (black idol) in both hands. Enter the Donkey Ambassador holding a lemon in both hands, very rare in this undivided state. Enter a Pederast holding a lipstick in both hands. Enter John Paul Jones supported by an officer of the law white cravat hat and sword in right hand. Enter Marie

Antoinette powdered hair lace silk combination pyjamas. Enter Shep-
herdesses pursued by Illustrious Americans. Enter Miss Atlantic
Monthly. Brekete ex Kotex Kotex pursued by the Earl of Fitzdotterel's
Eldest Son. I reflect with pleasure on the success with which the
British undertakers have prospered this last summer. Enter the Ghost
of Hamlet. Enter a Temple Boy. Enter Alpha and Omega. Enter the Soul
killed by the Explosion. Enter Rimbaud. Enter Van Gogh. Enter Amon
Ra. Enter the Star of the East. Enter the Stars. Enter the Youngest
Princess. Enter the Queen of Peking, Enter the Moon. Enter Death
stabbed in the Back. There is a Circle in the Centre. Enter the Grey
Princess. Enter the Cramoisy Queen. Enter the Mad Queen. Enter the
Sun.

The Blind Man leaves the scene, saying, I can see nothing.

The Sun

WHEN I LOOK INTO THE SUN I SUN-LOVER SUN-WORSHIPPER SUN-SEEKER
when I look into the Sun (sunne sonne soleil sol) what is it in the Sun I
deify!

His madness : his incorruptibility his central intensity and fire : his
permanency of heat : his candle-power (fifteen hundred and seventy-
five billions of billions 1,575,000,000,000,000,000,000,000,000) : his
age and duration : his dangerousness to man as seen by the effects
(heatstroke, insolation, thermic fever, siriasis) he sometimes produces upon the nervous system : the healing virtues of his rays (re-
stores youthful vigor and vitality is the source of health and energy,
oblivionizes ninety per cent of all human aches and pains) : his purity
(he can penetrate into unclean places brothels privies prisons and not
be polluted by them) : his magnitude (400 times as large as the moon) :
his weight two octillions of tons or 746 times as heavy as the combined
weights of all the planets) : his brilliance (5300 times brighter than the
dazzling radiance of incandescent metal) : his distance from the earth
as determined by the equation of light, the constant of abberation, the
parallectic inequality of the moon (an aviator flying from the earth to
the sun would require 175 years to make the journey) : his probable
union in a single mass with the earth in the far-distant past : the probability that in some remote future he will begin to grow colder (there is
a turning point in the life of every star) : his allotropic variations : his
orbital motion : his course through the zodiac : his motion among the
stars : his path along the ecliptic : his wingéd disk : his chariot : his
diameter and dimensions : his depth and density, his rotation : his
contraction : his daily appearance and disappearance : his image tat-
tooed upon my back : his image formed in my mind : the colors of his

spectrum as examined with special photographic plates, with a spectroheliograph, with an altazimuth, with a pyrheliometer, with an actionometer, with the bolometer, the radiomocrometer, the interferometer : his uninhabitability : the festivals held in his honor : the horses sacrificed in his honor : the obelisks dedicated in his honor : the verses recited in his honor : the dances danced by the Red Indians in his honor : the masks worn by the Aztecs in his honor : the self-torture endured by the Incas in his honor : his importance to the life of the earth, cut off his rays for even a single month and the earth would die : his importance to the life of the soul, cut off his rays for even a single hour and the soul would die : his disturbing influence on the motions of the moon : his attraction for Venus : his turbulence during a Transit of Venus : his contacts with Venus (internal and external) : his cosmical significance : his splendor and strength as symbolised by the seminal energy of the ox : his gold-fingered quietness in late Autumn : his whiteness in the Desert : his cold redness in Winter : his dark and sinister appearance before a Storm : his solid rotundity : his definiteness of form : his politeness in stopping for Joshua : his fascination for Icarus : his importance to the Ancient Mariner : his momentousness to the Prophet : his affiliation with Heliogabalus who married him to the moon : his mad influence over Aknaton : the reproductions of him by Van Gogh : the reproductions of him on old coins, on the American twenty-dollar gold piece, on the jackets of jockeys, on soap advertisements, in old woodcuts, on kindergarten blackboards, on the signs of old taverns : his tremendous influence on religions (among the Vedic Indians, among the Ancient Persians, among the Ancient Greeks, among the indigenous Americans, among the Ancient Romans, among the Babylonians and Assyrians, among the Ancient Egyptians, among the Hindoos among the Japanese) : the temples erected to his glory (in particular the great sun-temple of Baalbek) : his power of consuming souls : his unconcealed love for sun-dials (true as the dial to the sun) : the height he attains at the meridian : his family of asteroids : the occurrence of his name in ornithology, witness the sun-bittern (eurypyga helias) : among the vertebrates, witness the sun-fish or basking shark : in horticulture witness the tournesol, the heliotrope, the sunflower (helianthus annus) the marigold and the solsaece (from the word solsequium – sun-following) : his light – an uninterrupted continuance of gradation from the burning sunshine of a tropical noon to the pale luminosity that throws no shadow : his faculae and flocculi : his pederastic friendship with the Man in the Moon : the smallness of the target he offers to a meteorite (soul) arrowing toward him from infinity : the different behaviour of his spectral lines which are believed to originate at different levels and the relative Doppler displacements of the same spectral lines as given by his receding and avancing limbs : his importance in the Nebular Hypothesis : his personification in the form of a mirror in Japan : in the form of Ra in Egypt : his halos, rainbows and mirages : his eclipses, in particular the great Egyptian Eclipse of May 17 1882 : his nakedness : his red effrontery : his hot-tempered intolerance : his attraction for the earth (equal to the breaking strain of a steel rod three thousand miles in diameter) : his temperature (if he were to come as near as the moon, the solid earth would melt like wax) his reflection in the eyes of a girl (perihelion and aphelion) his mountains of flame which thrust upward into infinity : the fantastic shapes of his eruptive prominences (solar-lizards sun-dogs sharp crimson in color) : his brilliant spikes or jets, cyclones and geysers vertical filaments and columns of liquid flame : the cyclonic motion of his spots : his volcanic restlessness : his contortions : his velocity of three or four hundred miles an hour : his coronoidal dis-charges : his cyclonic protuberances, whirling fire spouts, fiery flames and furious commotions : his tunnel-shaped vortices : his equatorial acceleration : his telluric storms : his vibrations : his acrobatics among the clouds : his great display of sun-spots : his magnetic storms (during which the compass-needle is almost wild with excitement) : his prominences that have been seen to rise in a few minutes to elevations of two and three hundred thousand miles : his frenzy of turmoil : his periodic explosions : his madness in a lover's heart.

[FEBRUARY 1929]

SOME OPINIONS [1929]

– I find the Proclamation much the most unintelligible piece of writing in the volume (which includes Gertrude Stein and A. Lincoln Gillespie Jr.) and I wish that admirable writer, Hart Crane, whose name appears among the signatories, had taken the Proclaiming in hand. Only one thing to me is clear: after proclaiming their absolute independence of dictionaries and grammars, and their faith in a fabulous world, nine-tenths of the writers re-sume their normal regard for the reader and their unconquerable high-school standard; the remaining tenth immediately become the absolute dependents of James Joyce. This imitativeness is deplorable . . .

Peter Monro Jack in *Manuscripts*.

Stuart Davis

Gasoline Pump

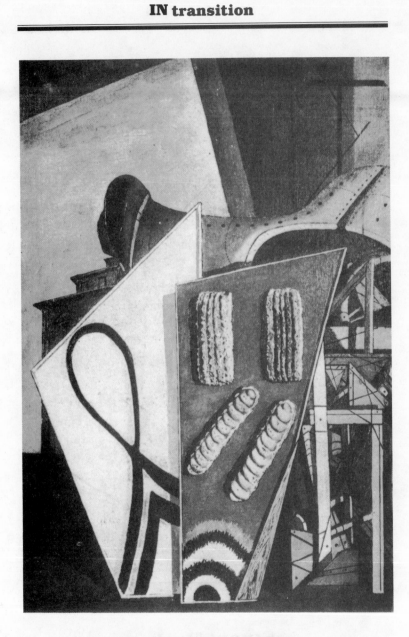

Giorgio de Chirico

Painting

Giorgio de Chirico is of Sicilian origin, although he has made Paris his headquarters for several years. He was born in Athens in 1888. His works began to appear in various exhibitions about 1910, but his career was interrupted by the war, during which time he served for Italy. [MAY 1929]

[JANUARY 1928]

THE DOVE OF THE ARK

by Robert Desnos

CURSED
Be the father of the wife
of the blacksmith who forged the iron of the hatchet
with which the wood-cutter hewed down the oak
in which someone carved the bed
where the great-grandfather was engendered
of the man who drove the wagon
in which your mother
met your father!

[APRIL 1927]

LA BARBE ! ! !

This space is subscribed by an anonymous advocate of:

The last interpreter of the ideas of Paul Valery.
The next to the last interpreter of the ideas of Paul Valery.
The last interpreter of the last interpreter of the ideas of Paul Valery.
The next to the last interpreter of the last interpreter of the ideas of Paul Valery.
The last interpreter of the next to the last interpreter of the ideas of Paul Valery.
The next to the last interpreter of the next to the last interpreter of the ideas of Paul Valery.

LA BARBE ! ! !

[DECEMBER 1927]

MIDNIGHT AT TWO O'CLOCK
An Experiment in Modern Magic

by Robert Desnos

[Silent Film Scenario]

1. A villa in the country. View of the country. Hills, fields, woods. A river. A bridge over this river.

2. The occupants of the villa. A man (35 years old) and his mistress.

3. They walk out of the villa. The road.

4. Arrival at the station. Arrival of the train.

5. The person they came to meet. A man, rather young (28 years old). Getting off the train. Shaking hands.

6. Towards the villa.

7. The garden. All three around a table laden with glasses and bottles.

8. The lover goes out.

9. Exchange of kisses between the woman and the new arrival.

10. The next morning. Departure of the three characters on a fishing expedition.

11. The bridge seen at the beginning. All three are fishing.

12. The woman and the young man are bored: *"We are going for a stroll."*

13. The lover keeps on fishing. The cork in the current.

14. The stroll of the woman and the young man. Kisses up till the moment when they near the bridge hidden by brushwood.

15. The lover tries to disengage his line which is caught in the weeds.

16. He leans towards the parapet. Leans over still further and falls.

17. Circles in the water.

18. At the top of a hill a peasant who saw the fall. He runs.

19. Arrival of the two other characters at the bridge. They call their companion. They lean on the parapet: circles in the water.

20. The sun. Dizziness of the two strollers. White circles dance around them.

21. The fishing line in the current, down the river.

22. Arrival of the peasant. Explanations.

23. Circles in the water.

24. A barge. Attempts at recovery with a boat-hook.

25. The bank of the river, downstream. The body of a drowned man at the foot of a tree.

26. Evening. The woman and her young lover pensive at a window.

27. The round setting sun.

28. Kisses.

29. Their eyes in the foreground. The round pupils.

30. Night. The lighted lamp. The circle of light on the ceiling. The circle made by the lamp-shade on the floor.

31. Separation to go to bed.

32. Night. The big round moon seen through the window of the bedrooms.

33. The next day. Breakfast. The round plates. The round table mats.

34. The lovers look at each other in silence.

35. Circles in the water.

36. The round knob of the door turns slowly. The door opens. The two lovers watch it open. Nobody comes in.

37. Through the door can be seen the road along which there passes a little boy playing with his hoop, and a cart with large wheels (in the foreground).

38. Circles in the water.

39. One evening at bedtime.

40. The lover sleeping in his bed.

41. The woman sleeping in her bed.

42. Dream of the lover. The place Vendôme, quite deserted, where he is walking, then the Place de la Concorde.

43. Then the Tour Eiffel. First pale then very clear vision of the "Big Wheel" in the background.

44. Then the Place des Victoires.

45. The woman's dream: She is jumping through a succession of paper-covered hoops. She finds herself in a deserted church.

46. The priest is officiating, the host in his hand, just about to be elevated.

47. The host increases in size out of all proportion as he holds it.

48. A halo appears behind the head of the priest who takes on the conventional appearance of a saint.

49. Fear of the woman who leaves the church.

50. A beggar at the Church door. She gives him two pennies.

51. The beggar drops his hat out of which falls a multitude of coins, a real torrent, before which the woman flees.

52. She arrives at the Place des Victoires. Meeting with her lover.

53. As they are about to embrace, the torrent of pennies appears from the rue Vide-Gousset.

54. It submerges the Place.

55. The lover in a torrent which carries him off. He lands on a narrow beach. As he is about to rise the water seizes him again. Impression of drowning. Awakening.

56. The woman under a mass of coins, in a cellar. Oppression. Awakening.

57. Calm night outside. The round moon.

58. The staircase of the villa. The landing of the third and top floor. The lovers have their rooms on the second floor.

59. Appearance of a ball the size of a croquet ball.

60. The ball goes down the stairs, step by step, slowly.

61. The ball passes the landing of the floor where the two lovers are sleeping.

62. It keeps on going down.

63. Awakening of the man. He listens. He gets up.

64. The ball which has reached the ground floor goes out the door.

65. It gets lost in the garden.

66. The man on the stairs, then on the first floor. He looks about, opens the doors. Nothing.

67. The woman leaves her room. *"What is the matter? I thought I heard a noise — I too."*

68. The next day. Both seated in the garden. A round balloon in the sky over their heads.

69. Then tennis players at the side of the garden. A stray ball falls on the table.

70. Uneasiness.

71. Walk out in the country.

72. In a clearing, croquet players.

73. On the road the cart with the big wheels (in the foreground): the little boy with the hoop.

74. Further on, a worker in a field. Just as they pass, he stops ploughing and digs in the earth. The two walkers watch him. He uncovers a cannon ball, the vestige of a former war.

75. Return, both thoughtful.

76. At home. The cat.

77. The woman wants to caress it. Suddenly the cat turns into a ball. Cry of the woman, the man turns around. Fright.

78. Slowly the ball becomes a cat again.

79. He. He caresses the cat which rubs against his legs.

80. Night.

81. Same as 58.

82. Same as 59.

83. Same as 60.

84. He awakens, listens, rises and goes out with an electric lamp in his hand.

85. He meets the woman on the landing.

86. The ball continues on down.

87. He turns the light on the step. The ball rolls down lighted up.

88. Fright of the two lovers on the stairs.

89. The next day at lunch.

90. The door-knob.

91. It turns. The door opens. The two lunching together turn about.

92. Entrance of the ball.

93. The two heroes rise, knocking over a chair.

94. The ball turns around them, then leaves.

95 to 112. Repetition of 89 to 94, with only a few differences in detail, each time on a different day. The ball lingers more and more.

113 to 116. Same as 89, 90, 91, 92.

117. The two characters do not even rise now. They are as though petrified.

118. The ball jumps on the table.

119. The ball approaches the plates which are emptied.

120. The following days. The ball now has its place set at the table. The food placed before it disappears. The ball has grown bigger. It is like a foot-ball.

121. Through the window. Foot-ball players. A spherical balloon in the sky. A belfry with its clock.

122. The man throws his napkin on the floor, and with hard kicks sends the ball through the window.

123. The ball quite tiny on the road. It rolls along. It passes a grade crossing, a village, a wood, a village, fields, a forest, the toll-gate of Paris. It rolls across the streets in the Place de la Bastille, Place Vendôme, Place des Victoires, Place de la Concorde, from the Trocadéro to the Tour Eiffel, without apparently being noticed, it leaves Paris, the country, the sea: the ball rolls on the waves: boats, an island. The ball rolls along the beach and stops in a luxuriant and equatorial forest.

124. The couple in the villa, delivered from their night-mare.

125. The ball in the forest. It absorbs birds which graze against it, little snakes, rabbits etc. It grows in size becomes as big as a drum, then a bass drum, then a house. Soon it absorbs whole trees.

126. The couple in the villa. It is winter. The trees bare. Snow on the ground.

127. One night: the villa. The round moon.

128. The forest of the ball.

129. The ball starts to move.

130. It retraces exactly, in the opposite direction, the road it came on, only at night. Its enormous but almost immaterial mass passes

over the sea, then through Paris: then the country. It casts an immense shadow against the sky.

131. The villa.

132. The ball at the top of a hill dominating the villa.

133. The villa.

134. The ball rolls down the hill.

135. It arrives at the house.

136. Just as it arrives at the house, everything, ball and house, disappears, as though swallowed up.

137. The round moon.

138. Dawn. In place of the house a vast funnel.

139. Arrival of two gendarmes. They look at the funnel, signs of astonishment.

140. A little later, peasants,? Astonishment.

141. Night, the moon.

142. Daytime, a round balloon in the sky. A little boy plays with a hoop along the road. Croquet players. A cart; (the wheels in the foreground).

143 to 154. Night, the moon. Succession of day and night on the deserted funnel (each time the moon grows slimmer until it becomes a slender crescent).

155. One morning. Automobilists stop.

156. A shepherd.

157. Question by the automobilists. Sign of ignorance from the shepherd.

158. The little boy with the hoop.

159. The sphere in the sky.

160. Circles in the water.

161. The sphere in the sky.

Note. – Each time that the ball appears, the orchestra plays, *"La Carmagnole"*. The rest of the time traditional moving-picture music. No artistic music, moving picture music.

Translated from the French by MARIA JOLAS.

Paul ELUARD

A DREAM

by Paul Eluard

I MEET HER ON THE SIDEWALK OF A DESERTED PARIS STREET. THE SKY of an indefinite color gives me the feeling of great physical liberty. I do not see the face of the woman who is the color of the hour, but I find great pleasure in not taking my eyes from the place where she is. Somehow I seem to be passing through the four seasons. At the end of a long moment, the woman slowly unties the knots of the multi-colored ribbons she has on her breasts and body. Then appears her face, white and hard as marble.

Translated from the French by EUGENE JOLAS.

[MAY 1927]

IN COMPANY
(Surrealist Text)

by Paul Eluard

I DO NOT MOURN — BUT MERELY BECAUSE MOURNING IS AN INSUFFICIENT form of despair – the time when I was suspicious, or still hoped to have an enemy to vanquish, some dent to make in human nature, or some sacred hiding place. Suspicion was then still the stop, the delectable substantiation of the finite. A thread drawn by a swallow which, open-winged, forms the point of the arrow, and distorts the appearance of man as well as his reality. The wind will not go where man wants it to go. Luckily. These are the frontiers of error, here are the blind who do not want to put their feet where the step is missing, here are the mute who think with words, here are the deaf who bid the world's noises grow silent.

The tired limbs, my word, do not separate easily. Their ignorance of solitude prevents them from giving themselves up to crafty individual experiences of amusing physique, crumbs of the great rest, so many minute bursts of laughter of the wistarias and acacias in the setting.

The spring of virtue is not dried up. Large beautiful eyes that are wide open serve still for the contemplation of industrious hands that have never done evil and that are bored and bore everyone else. The lowest reckoning closes these eyes each day. They favor sleep only to plunge later on into the contemplation of industrious hands that have never done evil and are bored and bore everyone else. Odious trade!

All this lives: this patient insect body, this loving bird body, this loyal mammiferous body, and this lean and vain body of the beast of my childhood, all this lives. Only its head has died. I had to kill it. My face understands me no longer. And there are no others.

Translated from the French by EUGENE JOLAS.

[MAY 1927]

GEORGES BRAQUE

by Paul Eluard

A BIRD FLIES AWAY,
It throws off the clouds like a useless veil,
It never feared the light,
Enclosed in its flight,
It never had a shadow.

Harvest shells broken by the sun.
All the leaves in the woods say yes,
They only know how to say yes,
Each question, each answer,
And the dew flows in the depths of this yes.

A man with soft eyes describes the sky of love.
He gathers its wonders
Like leaves in a wood,
Like birds in their wings,
And men in their slumber.

Translated from the French by EUGENE JOLAS.

[MAY 1927]

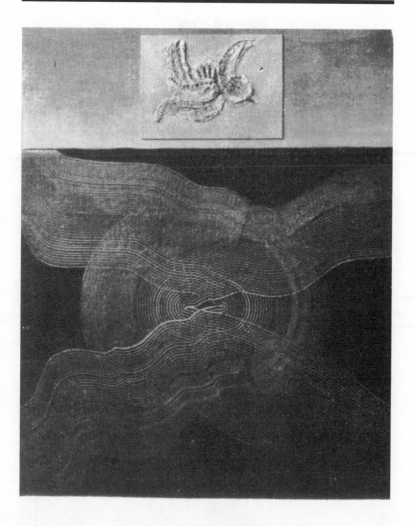

Max Ernst

Mer et Oiseau

The exhibition of the works of Max Ernst, at the
Van Leer galleries, has already proven to be an event
of highest importance. Many of those who had
taken the Surrealistes too lightly have been
brought to a realization of their error.   [MAY 1927]

[APRIL 1927]

POEM

by Serge Essenin

THEN THE MOON WILL SWIM AND SWIM,
Letting the oars fall into the lake;
And Russia will always live like this,
Dancing and weeping at the gate.

Translated from the Russian by GUSTA ZIMBALIST AND EUGENE JOLAS.

[JUNE 1927]

MOST MAGAZINES
ARE WORTHLESS
A MONTH AFTER
THEIR APPEARANCE

TRANSITION IS THE
ONE REVIEW WHOSE
BACK NUMBERS INCREASE
CONTINUALLY IN VALUE

[FALL 1928]

André GIDE

ROUNDELAY OF THE POMEGRANATE

by André Gide

SHOULD YOU SEEK YET A LONG WHILE
The impossible happiness of the soul,
– Joys of the flesh and joys of the senses
May another condemn you, if he likes,
Bitter joys of the flesh and the senses –
May he condemn you – I dare not.

– To be sure, I admire you, Didier, fervent philosopher,
If faith in your thought leads you to believe
That nothing is preferable to the joy of the spirit.
But not in all spirits can there be such loves.

To be sure, I love them, too,
Mortal quakings of my soul,
Joys of the heart, joys of the spirit –
But it is of you, pleasures, I sing.

Joys of the flesh, tender as grass,
Charming as the hedge flowers
Mown or withered sooner than the meadow grass,
Or the sad spirae that sheds its leaves when touched.

Sight – the most distressing of our senses ...
Everything we cannot touch grieves us;
The spirit seizes more easily the thought
Than our hand that which our eyes covet.
– O! may you only desire things you can touch –
Nathaniel, and seek not a more perfect possession.
The sweetest joys of my senses
Have been quenched thirsts.

To be sure, the mist at sun-up on the plains is lovely –
And lovely the sun –

Lovely under our bare feet is the damp earth,
And the sand made wet by the sea;
Lovely was the water of springs when we wanted to bathe;
Lovely it was to kiss the unknown lips touched by mine
    in the shadow . . .

But of fruits — of fruits — Nathaniel, what shall I say?

— O! that you have not known them,
Nathaniel, drives me to despair . . .
. . . Their pulp was delicious and juicy,
Savory as bleeding flesh,
Red as blood trickling from a wound.
. . . These, Nathaniel, did not require a special thirst;
They were served in golden baskets;
At first, incomparably flat, their taste was sickening,
Unlike that of any other fruit on earth;
It recalled the taste of over-ripe Indian pears,
And the pulp seemed lifeless;
It left a bitter after-taste in the mouth,
Which only the eating of another one would heal;
Its thrill hardly lasted longer
Than the moment of tasting the juice;
And the nicer that moment seemed,
The flatter and more nauseating became the after-taste.
Quickly the basket was emptied . . .
And we left the last one therein
Rather than divide it.

Alas! Nathaniel, who can say of our lips
What made them burn so bitterly?
No water could wash them —
The desire for these fruits tortured our very souls.

For three days, on our walks, we sought them;
Their season was over.
Where shall we find, Nathaniel, in our wanderings,
New fruits to give us other desires?
There are those we shall eat on terraces,
Before the sea and the sunset.
There are those preserved in sugared glaze
With a drop of brandy inside.

André GIDE

There are those to be picked from the trees
Of private gardens with walls around,
Which one eats in the shade during the tropical season.
We will arrange little tables —
The fruits will fall about us,
When we shake the branches,
And the torpid flies will wake.
The fallen fruits will be gathered into bowls,
And even their fragrance will be enough to enchant us . . .

There are those the rind of which stains the lips
    and which we eat only when we are very thirsty.
We found them along sandy roads;
They gleamed through the thorny foliage
Which tore our hands when we tried to pluck them;
And our thirst was hardly quenched.
There are those from which jellies are made,
Merely by letting them cook in the sun.
There are those the flesh of which, in spite of winter, remains sour;
Our teeth are on edge, when we bite into them.
There are those the flesh of which, even in summer,
    seems always cold.
We eat them, squatted on rush-mats,
In little inns.
There are those the memory of which equals a thirst,
When we can find them no longer.

Nathaniel, shall I speak to you of pomegranates?
They were sold for a few pennies, at that Oriental fair,
Upon reed crates in which they had tumbled about.
We saw some of them roll far into the dust,
And naked children gather them.
— Their juice is bitter-sweet like that of unripe raspberries.

Their blossoms are like wax,
Having the color of the fruit.
Guarded treasure, hive-like sections,

Abundance of savor,
Pentagonal architecture.
The rind bursts, the seeds fall —
Seeds of blood in azure cups;
And others, drops of gold, in dishes of enameled bronze.

Now sing of the fig, Simiane,
Because its loves are hidden.
I sing of the fig, she said,
And its beautiful hidden loves.
Its blooming is deeply enfolded.
Fig! Secret room where nuptials are held:
No perfume carries their tale outside.
Since none of it escapes,
All the fragrance becomes succulence and savor.
Flower without beauty; fruit of delights;
Fruit which is only its ripened blossom.

I have sung the fig, she said.
Now sing all the flowers ...

The acid wild plum of the hedges,
Which the cold snow sweetens.
The medlar eaten only when rotten;
And the chestnut, the color of dead leaves,
Which we set to burst before the fire.

(Authorized translation from the French by EUGENE JOLAS.)

[APRIL 1927]

SOME OPINIONS [1929]

– Foremost in leading ... the present-day effort to re-make the English language is the periodical called *transition* (Paris), Don't accuse us of a blunder; the lower case is elevated and capitals, as may be observed in much modern poetry, are left moldering in their cases ...
                    – *The Literary Digest* in "Lewis Carroll Redivivus."

André GIDE

FOOD OF THE EARTH

by André Gide

NATHANIEL, I SHALL TALK TO YOU ABOUT WAITING.

I have seen the plain wait after summer; wait for a bit of rain. The dust of the road had become too light and each breath of air whirred it upward. It was not even a desire anymore; it was an apprehension. The earth was cracking with dryness, better to welcome the water. The smell of the flowers on the heather became wellnigh unbearable. Everything swooned beneath the sun. Every afternoon we rested on the terrace sheltered somewhat from the extraordinary brilliance of the day. That was the time, when the conetrees, charged with pollen, stir their branches lightly in order to scatter their fruitfulness far and near. The sky had become stormy and all nature was waiting. The moment was too oppressingly solemn, for all the birds had become mute. There rose from the earth such a flaming breath that one almost fainted, and the pollen of the fir-trees came like a golden smoke from the branches. – Then it rained.

I have seen the sky tremble with waiting for dawn. One by one the stars went out. The meadows were flooded with dew; the air had only icy caresses. It seemed for some time that life dimly outlined wanted to linger for sleep, and my head, still tired, became filled with torpor. I walked to the edge of the wood; I sat down; each beast took up its work once more, and its joy in the certainty that the day would come, and the mystery of life began to stir again in every indentation of the leaves. – Then came the day.

I have also seen other dawns – I have seen the waiting for night.

Nathaniel, may every act of waiting in you be not even a desire – but simply a disposition for welcoming it. – Await everything that comes to you – but desire only that which comes to you – Do not desire anything save what you have . . . Understand that at each moment of the day you may possess God in his totality. – May your desire be love, and your possession amourous . . . for what is a desire that is not efficacious?

Really, Nathaniel, you possess God and you had not noticed it! – To possess God is to see him; but one does not look at him. Did you not, along any path, Balaam, see God, when your ass stopped before him? – because you, you imagined him differently. – But, Nathaniel, it is only God one cannot wait for. – To wait for God, Nathaniel, means not to understand that you already possess him. – Do not distinguish God from happiness and put all your happiness into the moment.

I have carried all my belongings in me, like the women of the pale Orient who carry their entire fortune with them. At every little moment of my life I have been able to feel in me the totality of my belongings. It was not by the accumulation of many special things, but merely by worshipping them. I have constantly kept all my belongings within my power.

Look at the evening as if the day were to die there;
And at the morning, as if everything were being born there.
May your vision be new at every moment.
The wise man is he whom everything astonishes.

All the fatigue of your head, Nathaniel, comes from the diversity of your goods. You do not even know which one *among all others* you prefer and you do not understand that the only good is life. The smallest moment of life is stronger than death, and denies it. Death is only the furlough for another life – so that everything may be cease-lessly renewed – so that no form of life retain *that* longer than it needs to say this. Happy the moment, when your word echoes. All the rest of the time, listen – but when you speak, do not listen anymore.

You must burn all books in you, Nathaniel.

[NOVEMBER 1927]

SOME OPINIONS [1929]

– *transition*, the official organ of revolt in America today . . .
– Horace Gregory in the *New York Sun*.

POEMS

by Claire and Ivan Goll

Ivan to Claire

SOMETIMES MY DEAD HEART CRIES IN THE NIGHT
Like an old press that creaks
And recalls the time of the pink cherry-trees
An old need to complain
To write your name on a passing cloud
To look at a meadow whose willows you once sang
Sometimes still I open my eyes
Behind myopic blinds
Like bungalows for rent by the sea
The owner of which is unknown

Claire to Ivan

I am afraid when you sleep
When you put out the search-light of your eyes
I fear the end of the world
When you are not on watch
Last night I drank the moon from your hand
You gave me the nocturnal wind
In small doses
To calm my fever
But now that you travel among the stars
I tremble in the outer hall
All my tears in my satchel
And the photo of your heart
And a nose-gay of withered smiles
And I fear stellar catastrophy.

Ivan to Claire

39 degrees
A carnaval of fever and scarlet
Bursts in your head,
A wild feast goes on there,

Flaming shadows kiss you,
The drunken gods carry you off
Towards the mountains of death!
And I, in my prison of flesh,
Suffering from normal health
In the cold of every day
Captive behind the bars of rain
I attend your orgy
Like a poor man before a mystery booth
His feet sunk in the mire

Claire to Ivan

Tear me into a thousand pieces,
Royal tiger of my heart!
Mutilate my smile,
Wrench from me cries greater than my body,
Plant in place of my red hair
The white hair of sorrow,
Make my feet grow old
As they wait for you in vain,
And waste all my tears in an hour:
I can only lick your hand.

Translated from the French by EUGENE JOLAS.

[JUNE 1930]

SOME OPINIONS [1929]

The revolution of the English word having been accomplished, that revolution is now proclaimed. The proclamation appears in the spring-summer number of that generally unintelligible periodical called *Transition*. Its unintelligibility is the result of intention not accident. The proclamation appears in a type format suggesting the chorus of trumpets in «Aida» just before the conquering Rhadames appears on the scene. Hear ye, hear ye! ... It will be observed that the proclamation against grammar and syntax is grammatically correct and that the signers of the proclamation continue to be designated by conventional names – two of the signers have middle initials – instead of by esoteric numbers.
– Harry Salpeter in the *New York World*.

Claire and Ivan GOLL

POEMS

by Claire and Ivan Goll

Ivan to Claire

COME BACK;
I shall invent a fifth season for us alone,
Where the oysters will have wings,
Where the birds will sing Stravinsky,
And the golden hesperides
Will ripen to fig-trees.

I shall change all the calendars,
That lack the dates of your vanished trysts,
And on the maps of Europe
I shall efface the roads of your flights.

Come back:
The world will be born again,
The compass will have a new North:
Your heart.

Claire to Ivan

MAY WEEDS GROW UNDER YOUR STEPS;
May the poisonous saffron pursue you,
May hemlock border the roads
Of your slumber!

I am preparing a celestial apéritif for you:
The strychnine of my thoughts,
And my tears – drops of belladonna.

Soon I shall wait no longer for the night
To sob like the owl.

Translated from the French by MADELEINE REID.

[JANUARY 1928]

O JORROCKS, I HAVE PROMISED

by Robert Graves

SPRUNG OF NO WORTHIER PARENTAGE OF SUN
In February, and fire-side and the snow
Streaked on the north side of each wall and hedge,
And breakfast, late, in bed, and a tall puppy
Restless for sticks to fetch and tussle over,
And Jorrocks bawling from the library shelf,
And the accumulation of newspapers
And the day-after-judgement-day to face –
This poem (only well-bred on one side,
Father a grum, mother a lady's maid)
Asked for a style, a place in literature.
So, since the morning had been wholly spoilt
By sun, by snow, breakfast in bed, the puppy,
By literature, a headache and their headaches;
Throwing away the rest of my bad day
I gave it style, let it be literature
Only too well, and let it talk itself
And me to boredom, let it draw lunch out
From one o'clock to three with nuts and smoking
While it went talking on, with imagery,
Why it was what it was, and had no breeding
But waste things and the ambition to be real;
And flattered me with puppy gratitude.
I let it miss the one train back to town
And stay to tea and supper and a bed
And even bed-in-breakfast the next morning.
More thanks.
                    The penalty of authorship;
Forced hospitality, an impotence
Expecting an impossible return
Not only from the plainly stupid chance
But from impossible caddishness, no less.
I answered leading questions about Poe
And let it photograph me in the snow
And gave it a signed copy of itself

And "the nursery money-box is on the shelf,
How kind of you to give them each a penny."

> O Jorrocks I have promised
>   To serve thee to the end,
> To entertain young Indians,
>   The pupils of my friend,
> To entertain Etonians
>   And for their sake combine
> The wit of T. S. Eliot,
>   The grace of Gertrude Stein.
> Be thou forever near me
>   To hasten or control,
> Thou Literary Supplement,
>   Thou Guardian of my soul.
> I shall not fear the battle
>   While thou art by my side
> Nor wander from the pathway
>   If thou shalt be my guide.

Amen.

[OCTOBER 1927]

SOME OPINIONS [1929]

– Very personal, although eclectic, *Transition* asserts itself more and more
... as the exchange *par excellence* between France-Europe-America.
– Regis Michaud in *Littérature Américaine*, Kra, Paris.

Juan Gris

Painting

From the collection of Miss Gertrude Stein

Juan Gris

Still Life

Georg Gross

The Little Agitator

[JUNE 1930]

GIFT

by H.D.

ARDENT
yet chill and formal,
how I ache
to tempt a chisle
as a sculptor, take
this one,
replacing this and this and this
for some defect
of point, of blade, of hilt;

in answer to my thwarted fingers, make
as from the clear edge of some glacier-drift,
a slim amphora,
a most gracious vase;

instead of ranging
from your shoulders' straight
clear line, uninterrupted stretch
of snow, with light
of some dawn-cloud on it,
I'd calm my hands
against this priceless thing,
chisle it, circumscribe
set pattern, formal-wise,
inset with stiff acanthus leaves and bays;

and where some boulder
shelves out in some place
where ice curves back
like sea-waves with the crest
of each green ripple
frozen marble wise,

under that rock that holds
the first swift kiss
of the spring-sun's white, incandescent breath,
I'd seek
you flowers:
(ah flowers
that sweetly fall and rest
softly and smoothly
on an icy bed,
the cyclamen white and red,
how sweet, how fiery,
lovers could only know,
bled in some ice of fire,
or fire of snow);

so I might set
about the Parian throat,
delicate tendrils
of the scented host,
slight fronds
with irridescent shell-like grace,
smooth like the alabaster,
thin and rare.

[JULY 1927]

SOME OPINIONS [1929]

– The Spring-Summer number of *Transition* prints one piece taken from the *New York World* that will prove highly illuminating to those who wish to translate Walter Winchell ... *Transition* has at least performed a public service in printing some of the newer obscurantisms that have at least more vitality than those invented by James Joyce.

– New York Times

PSYCHE

by H.D.

"Love drove her to Hell."

CYTHERA'S PEARL WERE DIM,
had I not won from him
this ruby, cut of fire;
my quivering lamp were dark,
but for its spark to light
the alabaster white shell
with his life and power.

The pearl were cold and dark
had I not won the spark
of love's intensest flame;
men speaking name no name
to tell the King I hold,
lord not of lands nor gold.

His kiss no poets tell;
Persephone in hell
might best describe his look,
and yet the flowers she lost,
lilies and myrtle tossed
by Aetna's fire-scarred rim,
were nothing to the few
iris and single blue
violets my starved hands took
when he invited me
to taste eternity.

You count your lover fair,
your bride or your bride-groom,
yet you would shun the room
where their enchantments are;
if I could prove how I

met ecstasy you'd choose
the very beggar's rod,
with poets sing or die.

If I could sing this god,
Persephone in Hell
would lift her quivering lids
and smile, the mysteries hid,
escaping all the years
alike both priest and cynic
would smilingly prevail;
dead men would start and move
toward me to learn of love.

[JULY 1927]

SOME OPINIONS [1929]

— I have just joined the ranks of the "transition" group. I think I must go to Paris and climb aboard the band-wagon which the editors of the insurgent periodical "transition" have started on its way . . . It seems that Eugene Jolas and Elliot Paul and all the other members of the James Joyce Adulation and Interpretation Union, Local 69, have decided that the revered Joyce is not sufficient unto himself. Let Joyce be unconfined, is the slogan of the new movement, with the result that not only does the present number of "transition" overflow with disintegrated and newly synthesized words from lesser Joyces, but it also contains a proclamation which endeavours to state explicitly and with appropriate pomp the tenets of the latest revolution in the English language . . .
— William Sloskin in the *New York Eve. Post.*

HILLS LIKE WHITE ELEPHANTS

by Ernest Hemingway

THE HILLS ACROSS THE VALLEY OF THE EBRO WERE LONG AND WHITE. ON this side there was no shade and no trees and the station was between two lines of rails in the sun. Close against the side of the station there was the warm shadow of the building and a curtain made of strings of bamboo beads hung across the open door into the bar to keep out flies. The American and the girl with him sat at a table in the shade outside the building. It was very hot and the Express from Barcelona would come in forty minutes. It stopped at this junction for two minutes and went on to Madrid.

"What should we drink?" the girl asked. She had taken off her hat and put it on the table.

"It's pretty hot," the man said.

"Let's drink beer."

"Dos cervezas," the man said into the curtain.

"Big ones?" a woman asked from the doorway.

"Yes. Two big ones."

The woman brought two glasses of beer and two felt pads. She put the felt pads and the beer glasses on the table and looked at the man and the girl. The girl was looking off at the line of hills. They were white in the sun and the country was brown and dry.

"They look like white elephants," she said.

"I've never seen one," the man drank his beer.

"No you wouldn't have."

"I might have," the man said. "Just because you say I wouldn't have doesn't prove anything."

The girl looked at the bead curtain. "They've painted something on it," she said. "What does it say?"

"Anis del Toro. It's a drink."

"Could we try it?"

The man called "Listen" through the curtain. The woman came out from the bar.

"Four reales."

"We want two Anis del Toro."

"With water?"

"Do you want it with water?"

"I don't know," the girl said. "Is it good with water?"

"It's all right."

"You want them with water?" asked the woman.

"Yes, with water."

"It tastes like licorice," the girl said.

"That's the way with everything."

"Yes," said the girl. "Everything tastes of licorice. Especially all the things you've waited so long for like absinthe."

"Oh cut it out."

"You started it," the girl said. "I was being amused. I was having a fine time."

"Well let's try and have a fine time."

"All right. I was trying. I said the mountains looked like white elephants. Wasn't that bright?"

"That was bright."

"I wanted to try this new drink. That's all we do, isn't it? Look at things and try new drinks."

"I guess so."

The girl looked across at the hills.

"They're lovely hills," she said. "They dont really look like white elephants. I just meant the colouring of their skin through the trees."

"Should we have another drink?"

"All right."

The warm wind blew the bead curtain against the table.

"The beer's nice and cool," the man said.

"It's lovely," the girl said.

"It's really an awfully simple operation," the man said. "It's not really an operation at all."

The girl looked at the ground the table legs rested on.

"I know you wouldn't mind it, Jig. It's really not anything. It's just to let the air in."

The girl did not say anything.

"I'll go with you and I'll stay with you all the time. They just let the air in and then it's all perfectly natural."

"Then what will we do afterwards?"

"We'll be fine afterwards. Just like we were before."

"What makes you think so?"

"That's the only thing that bothers us. It's the only thing that's made us unhappy."

The girl looked at the bead curtain, put her hand out and took hold of two of the strings of beads.

"And you think then we'll be all right and be happy."

"I know we will. You dont have to be afraid. I've known lots of people that have done it."

"So have I," said the girl. "And afterwards they were all so happy."

"Well," the man said, "If you dont want to you dont have to. I wouldn't

Ernest Hemingway in Florida
(Loaned by Sylvia Beach)

have you do it if you didn't want to. But I know it's perfectly simple."

"And you really want to?"

"I think it's the best thing to do. But I dont want you to do it if you dont really want to."

"And if I do it you'll be happy and things will be like they were and you'll love me?"

"I love you now. You know I love you."

"I know. But if I do it then it will be nice again if I say things are like white elephants and you'll like it?"

"I'll love it. I love it now but I just can't think about it. You know how I get when I worry."

"If I do it you won't ever worry?"

"I won't worry about that because it's perfectly simple."

"Then I'll do it. Because I don't care about me."

"What do you mean."

"I don't care about me."

"Well I care about you."

"Oh yes. But I don't care about me. And I'll do it and then everything will be fine."

"I dont want you to do it if you feel that way."

The girl stood up and walked to the end of the station. Across on the other side were fields of grain and trees along the banks of the Ebro. Far away beyond the river were mountains. The shadow of a cloud moved across the field of grain and she saw the river through the trees.

"And we could have all this," she said. "And we could have everything and every day we make it more impossible."

"What did you say?"

"I said we could have everything."

"We can have everything."

"No we can't."

"We can have the whole world."

"No we can't."

"We can go everywhere."

"No we can't. It isn't ours anymore."

"It's ours."

"No it isn't. And once they take it away you never get it back."

"But they haven't taken it away."

"We'll wait and see."

"Come on back in the shade," he said. "You mustn't feel that way."

"I dont feel any way," the girl said. "I just know things."

"I dont want you to do anything that you don't want to do – "

"Nor that isn't good for me," she said. "I know. Could we have another beer?"

"All right. But you've got to realize – "

"I realize," the girl said. "Can't we maybe stop talking?"

They sat down at the table and the girl looked across at the hills on the dry side of the valley and the man looked at her and at the table.

"You've got to realize," he said, "that I don't want you to do it if you don't want to. I'm perfectly willing to go through with it if it means anything to you."

"Doesn't it mean anything to you? We could get along."

"Of course it does. But I don't want anybody but you. I don't want anyone else. And I know it's perfectly simple."

"Yes you know it's perfectly simple."

"It's all right for you to say that but I do know it."

"Would you do something for me now?"

"I'd do anything for you."

"Would you please please please please please please please stop talking?"

He did not say anything but looked at the bags against the wall of the station. There were labels on them from all the hotels where they had stopped.

"But I don't want you to," he said, "I don't care anything about it."

"I'll scream," the girl said.

The woman came out through the curtains with two glasses of beer and put them down on the damp felt pads. "The train comes in five minutes," she said.

"What did she say?" asked the girl.

"That the train is coming in five minutes."

The girl smiled brightly at the woman to thank her.

"I'd better take the bags over to the other side of the station," the man said. She smiled at him.

"All right. Then come back and we'll finish the beer."

He picked up the two heavy bags and carried them around the station to the other tracks. He looked up the tracks but could not see the train. Coming back he walked through the bar room where people waiting for the train were drinking. He drank an Anis at the bar and looked at the people. They were all waiting reasonably for the train. He went out through the bead curtain. She was sitting at the table and smiled at him.

"Do you feel better?" he asked.

"I feel fine," she said. "There's nothing wrong with me. I feel fine."

[AUGUST 1927]

SLANGUAGE: 1929

by Theodore D. Irwin

What they mean

1. On the up-and-up.
2. To lay an egg.
3. Kiss-off.
4. Horse-opera.
5. To click.
6. To lam.
7. Puddle-jumper.
8. Flesh and blood angel.

9. Wowser.
10. To frigidaire.
11. To take it on the heel and toe.
12. Sham, Shamos.
13. To make whoopee.

14. In a spot.

15. Ticker-and-tape worm.

16. Flicker.
17. Spanish guitar.
18. Shellacked.
19. Lallygagger.
20. To ankle.
21. To wham.

22. To get the magoo.

23. To tear a herring.
24. Gabbies, squawkies.
25. To be Chicago'd.

26. Welded, sealed.
27. To shelve.
28. Daisy roots.
29. To make snooty.
30. Tidy unit.
31. To angel.

1. In good faith; above-board; true.
2. Collapse; flounder; ruined.
3. Dismissal; farewell.
4. Western motion picture.
5. Impress favorably; up to the mark.
6. Retreat hastily; escape.
7. Automobile.
8. Damsel who clicks; beauteous maiden of charm.
9. Blue-nose reformer.
10. Treat coldly; snub.
11. Depart.
12. Officer of the law.
13. Applied to all varieties of unbridled revelry usually containing joyous ingredients of wine, women and warbling; vide "Garbo-Gilberting."
14. Any dangerous or perplexing situation.
15. Wall Street broker; any one who plays the market.
16. Motion picture.
17. Cigar.
18. Intoxicated condition.
19. Swain who lingers in the vestibule.
20. Walk, amble.
21. Strike forcibly; land knockout blow; smash.
22. Specifically to receive a custard pie in the face; generally, bad luck.
23. To dine.
24. Talking motion pictures.
25. Despatched via machine gun or automatic; any premeditated form of murder.
26. Married.
27. Desert; relinquish; renounce.
28. Feet.
29. Exclusive, snobbish whoopee.
30. See "flesh-and-blood angel."
31. To secretly sponsor; (noun), silent financial backer of an enterprise; often is "sugar daddy."

32. Shive.
33. Gargo-Gilberting.

34. Biggie.

35. Clothesline.
36. Hoofer.
37. To have a yen.
38. Hustler.

39. Everything is copesetty.
40. To scram.
41. Snappy piece of work.
42. Tag.
43. To curdle.
44. Ironsides.
45. Sugar daddy.

46. Weeping willow.
47. To tail.
48. Wind-sucker.
49. Racket.

50. Night bomber.

51. G., grand.

52. Merry magdalen.

53. To gag.

54. Bennie.
55. Jackie Horner.
56. Pan.
57. Egg-harbour.
58. Handcuff.
59. To flop.
60. Yard.
61. Air-bisectors.
62. Big yes-and-no man.
63. To be washed up with.
64. Heap.

65. To be taken for a ride.
66. Palooka.

67. Rock.
68. Platter.
69. Chunk of lead.

70. The stem, Mazda belt.
71. Scanties.

---

32. Knife, particularly stiletto.
33. Indulging in amorous pursuits;
    ardently enamored couple
    minding their own business.
34. Bigwig; personage of importance
    and influence; celebrity.
35. Local gossip.
36. Professional dancer.
37. To yearn.
38. Racketeer; professional criminal;
    also applied to a lady of the
    evening.
39. O. K.; settled.
40. See "to lam."
41. See "tidy unit."
42. Name.
43. See "to lay an egg."
44. Corseted maiden.
45. Gentleman liberal with the shekels;
    patron saint of "merry magdalens."
46. Pillow.
47. Watch closely; follow; spy upon.
48. Braggart.
49. Particular kind of fraud or
    robbery; any shady pursuit.
50. Individual, particularly aviator,
    who sleeps in daytime and visits
    guzzle grottos at night.
51. Thousand, usually applied to
    "sugar."
52. Lady of the chorus or whoopee
    parlor.
53. To achieve a bon mot; (noun)
    witticism; affectation; anything
    humorous or fictitious; unusual
    situation in a flicker.
54. Overcoat.
55. Corner.
56. Physiognomy.
57. Free dance.
58. Engagement ring.
59. Sit; lie down; sleep.
60. Dollar.
61. High-kicking hoofers.
62. Executive; head of firm.
63. Sever relations.
64. Any machine; see
    "puddle-jumper."
65. See "Chicago'd."
66. Fourth-rate pugilist; one of low
    repute.
67. Diamond.
68. Gramophone record.
69. Lass, usually with nutcracker
    face, who disapproves of Garbo-
    Gilberting.
70. Times Square and vicinity.
71. Underwear, particularly
    feminine.

72. Annie Oakley.	72. See "copesetty."
73. Tilted.	73. Drastically changed; upset.
74. Moped.	74. Vanished.
75. Rats and mice.	75. Dice.
76. Sonk.	76. Collapse heavily.
77. Biscuit.	77. Flapper who pets.
78. Canned heat.	78. That which produces the "shellacked" or "snooted;" also known as "giggle water."
79. Smoke eater.	79. Lady who smokes to excess.
80. To gat-up.	80. To hold up a person or place with gun.
81. To reef.	81. Steal; pick a pocket.
82. Twist.	82. Girl.
83. Fakealoo.	83. Fictitious story; yarn intended to deceive.
84. Rag.	84. Newspaper; also see "chunk of lead."
85. False alarm.	85. Divorced woman.
86. Juicer.	86. Electrician.
87. Bell polisher.	87. See "lallygagger."
88. Wire.	88. Pickpocket.
89. Hypos.	89. Drug addicts.
90. To bump off.	90. See "taken for a ride."
91. Cellar smeller.	91. Free drinker; also a Prohibition officer.
92. To tin-ear.	92. To listen; pay attention.
93. Dukes.	93. Hands.
94. Nifties.	94. Witticisms; see "gag."
95. Rap.	95. Any sort of betrayal or indiscretion; nod, greet.
96. To bach.	96. Live in bachelor quarters.
97. Wally.	97. Well-dressed man.
98. Stems.	98. See "daisy-roots."
99. Finish ace-deuce.	99. To fall; defeated; arrive last.
100. To go into the gauze.	100. Rendered unconscious via receipt of a wham.

Theodore D. Irwin in the NEW YORK WORLD.

Eugene JOLAS

ACROBATS

by Eugene Jolas

YOU JUGGLE LITANIES FOR LIGHT.
Your hands tighten over white magic.
You fling our longings into the air.
Proudly you sway on trapezes.

Your muscles ache fanatic adorations.
On lithe feet you dance a Hosannah.
You grow rigid in stigmatic tortures.
You die cruelly in pyramids.

There is a resurrection you await.
Drums beat the dawn of an oak forest.
April blossoms with foam in our hearts —
We are ploughing rain-ravished acres.

[AUGUST 1927]

SOME OPINIONS [1929]

— The double Spring-Summer number of *transition*, the magazine which refuses to pay any respect to capital letters, contains in the foreground of its contents a contribution from the pen of Theo Rutra. We quote it in full, and after you have read it, call in the doctor . . .

— Baltimore (Md.) Sun.

EXPRESS

by Eugene Jolas

WHEELS SCREAM IN FEVERED CRASH OF SPEED.
We hunger for eternity;
We smuggle golden sins in suit-cases;
We have sneers hidden in our pockets;
O villages! O languid smoke over gables!
We tremble with longing for your dusk.

Hiss, locomotive, your rhythms of silver . . .
We droop in nightmares.
Mechanical puppets, we wait for salvations;
Behind us lies darkness of furnace towns,
And leprous faces greedy after sun;
Our pulses roar like pistons.

The roads wind in and out through strange mountains;
Nerves beat time with dreams;
Valleys make us giddy with rotting roses;
Luxurious forests sing their green laughter –
We feel drunken on lonely trails and we sing
Songs about our miseries.
Memories come with shimmer of orgies.
Women stand in flames.
Night spreads films of giant cities;
But luminous landscapes rise to our flight;
Garlands flutter in winds of longing.
We enter the ultimate station flooded in light.

[AUGUST 1927]

James JOYCE

WORK IN PROGRESS
[Finnegans Wake]

by James Joyce

*T*HE LAST FOUR PAGES OF ANNA LIVIA PLURABELLE, BY JAMES JOYCE,
have here been put into Basic English, the International Lan-
guage of 850 words in which everything may be said. Their
purpose is to give the simple sense of the Gramophone Record
made by Mr. Joyce, who has himself taken part in the attempt;
and the reader will see that it has generally been possible to
keep almost the same rhythms.

In places the sense of the story has been changed a little, but
this is because the writer took the view that it was more im-
portant to get these effects of rhythm than to give the nearest
Basic Word every time. Where names of rivers have been used
simply for their sound they are put into the Basic story with-
out any change, and underlined. Words from Latin and other
languages are given in the same way.

The normal process of putting complex ideas by men of
letters into Basic English is through the use of foot-notes,
wherever there would be any doubt as to the sense of the
simpler account. But Mr. Joyce was of opinion that a com-
parison of the two languages would be of greater interest if the
Basic English were printed without the additions necessary to
make the sense more complete. In this way the simplest and
most complex languages of man are placed side by side.
— C. K. Ogden.

[MARCH 1932]

WELL, YOU KNOW OR DON'T YOU KENNET OR HAVEN'T I TOLD YOU EVERY story has an end and that's the he and the she of it. Look, look, the dusk is growing. Fieluhr? Filou! What age is at? It saon is late. 'Tis endless now since I or anyone last saw Waterhouse's clock. They took it asunder, I heard them say. When will they reassemble it? O, my back, my back, my back! I'd want to go to Aches-les-Pains. Wring out the clothes! Wring in the dew! Godavari vert the showers! And grant of Thy grace. Aman. Will we spread them here now? Ay, we will. Spread on your bank and I'll spread mine on mine. It's what I'm doing. Spread! It's churning chill. Der went is rising. I'll lay a few stones on the hostel sheets. A man and his bride embraced between them. Else I'd have sprinkled and folded them only. And I'll tie my butcher's apron here. It's suety yet. The strollers will pass it by. Six shifts, ten kerchiefs, nine to hold to the fire and this for the code, the convent napkins twelve, one baby's shawl. Where are all her childer now? In kingdome gone or power to come or gloria be to them farther? Allalivial, allallu-vial! Some here, more no more, more again lost to the stranger I've heard tell that same brooch of the Shannons was married into a family in Spain. And all the Dunders de Dunnes in Markland's Vineland beyond Brendan's herring pool takes number nine in yangsee's hats. And one of Biddy's beads went bobbing till she rounded up last hister-eve with a marigold and a cobbler's candle in a side strain of a main drain of a manzinahurries off Bachelor's Walk. But all that's left to the last of the Meaghere in the loop of the years prefixed and between is one kneebuckle and two hooks in the front. Do you tell me that now? I do in troth. And didn't you hear it a deluge of times? You deed, you deed! I need, I need! It's that irrawaddyng I've stuck in my aars. It all but husheth the lethest sound. Oronoko! What's your trouble? Is that the great Finnleader himself in his joakimono on his statue riding the high horse there forehengist? Father of Otters, it is himself! Yonne there! Is it that? On Fallareen Common? You're thinking of Astley's Amphitheayter where the bobby restrained you making sugarstuck pouts to the ghostwhite horse of the Peppers. Throw the cobwebs from your eyes, woman, and spread your washing proper. It's well I know your sort of slop. Ireland sober is Ireland stiff. Your prayers. Were you lifting your elbow, tell us, glazy cheeks, in Conway's Carrigacurra can-teen? Was I what, hobbledyhips? Amn't I up since the damp dawn with Corrigan's pulse and varicose veins, soaking and bleaching boiler rags, and sweating cold, a widow like me, for to deck my tennis champion son, the laundryman with the lavender flannels? You won your lim-popo limp fron the husky hussars when Collars and Cuffs was heir to the town and your slur gave the stink to Carlow. Holy Scamander, I saw it again! Near the golden falls. Icis on us! Seints of light! There! Subdue your noise, you poor creature! What is it but a blackburry growth or the dwyergray ass them four old codgers owns. Are you meanam Tar-pey and Lyons and Gregory? I mean now, thank all, the four of them,

WELL ARE YOU CONSCIOUS, OR HAVEN'T YOU KNOWLEDGE, OR HAVEN'T I SAID it, that every story has an ending and that's the he and the she of it. Look, look, the dark is coming. My branches high are taking root. And my cold seat's gone grey. *'Viel Uhr? Filou!* What time is it? It's getting late.

How far the day when I or anyone last saw Waterhouse's clock! They took it to pieces, so they said. When will they put it together again? O, my back, my back, my back! I would go then to Aix-les-Pains. Ping pong! That's the bell for Sachseläute — And Concepta de Spiritu — Pang! Take the water out of your cloths! Out with the old, and in the new! *Godavari* keep off the rains! And give us support! So be. Will we put them here now? Yes, we will. Flip! Put out yours on your side there and here I'll do the same. Flap! It's what I'm doing. Place! It's turning cold. The wind gets high. I'll put some stones on the hotel linen. But that it came from a married bed it would be watered and folded only. And I'll put my meatman's garment here. There's fat on it still. The road boys will all go past. Six undergarments, ten face cloths, nine to put by the fire, and this for the cold, the church house sisters' linens twelve, one baby's overall.

Mother Joseph might give it away, she said. Whose head? Other ways? *Deo Gratias!* Where now is all her family, say? In the land of the dead or power to come or their great name for ever and ever? All have livings! All is well! Some here, more no more, more again in a strange land. They say that same girl of the Shannons was married into a family in Spain. And all the Dunders de Dunnes in Markland's Wineland, the other side of the water, take number nine in American hats. And that threaded ball so loved by Biddy went jumping till it came to rest by religion's order yesterday night with a waxlight and a flower of gold in a side branch of a wide drain of a man's-friend-in-need off Bachelor's Walk. But all there is now for the last of the Meaghers in the round of the years before and between is one knee-ornament and two hooks in the front. Do you say that now? Truly I do. May Earth give peace to their hearts and minds. *Ussa, Ulla,* we're all of us shades. Why, haven't they said it a number of times, over and over, again and again? They did, they did. I've need, I've need! It's that soft material I've put in my ears. It almost makes the least sound quiet. *Oronoko!* What's your trouble? Is that great Finn the ruler himself in his coat-of-war on the high stone horse there before Hengist? Father of Waters, it is himself! Over there! Is it that? On Fallareen Common? You've Astley's theatre now in your head, where you were making your sugar-stick mouths at poor Death-white, the horse of the Peppers, till police put a top to your doings. Take that spider's mist off from your eyes, woman, and put out your washing squarely. I've had enough to do with your sort of cheap work. Flap! Ireland dry is Ireland stiff. May yours be helped, Mary, for you're fullest among women, but the weight is with me! Alas! It seemed so! Madame Angot! Were you lifting your glass then, say Mrs. Redface, in Conway's beerhouse at Carrigacurra? Was I what, loose-in-the-back? Flop! Your tail walk's Graeco-Roman but your back parts are out of the straight. Haven't I been up from the wet early morning, Martha Mary Alacoque, with Corrigan's trouble and my blood-vessels thick, my wheel-rod smashed, Alice Jane at her last, and my dog with one eye two times overturned, wetting engine cloths and making them white, now heated by turns and then again cold, I a woman whose man is no more, that my sporting son may go well-dressed, the washerman with the and the roar of them, that draves that stray in the mist and old Johnny Mac Dougal along with them. Is that the Poolbeg flasher beyant or a fireboat coasting nigh the Kishtna or a glow I behold within a hedge or my Garry come back from the Indes? Wait till the honeying of the lune, love! Die eve, little eve, die! We see that wonder in your eye. We'll meet again, we'll part once more. The spot I'll seek if the hour you'll find. My chart shines high where the blue milk's upset. Forgivemequick, I'm going! And you, pluck your watch, forgetmenot. My sights are swimming thicker on me by the shadows to this place. I'll sow home slowly now by own way, moyvalley way. Tow will I too, rathmine.

Ah, but she was the queer old skeowsha anyhow, Anna Livia, trinket-toes. And sure he was the quare old buntz too, Dear Dirty Dumpling, foostherfather of fingalls and dottergills. Gammer and gaffer we're all their gangsters. Hadn't he seven dams to wive him? And every dam had her seven crutches. And every crutch had its seven hues. And each hue had a differing cry. Sudds, for me and supper for you and the doctor's bill for Joe John. Before! Before! He married his markets, cheap by foul, I know, like any Etrurian Catholic Heathen, in their pinky limony creamy birnies and their turkiss indienne mauves. But at milkidmass who was the spouse? Then all that was was fair. In Elvenland? Teems of times and happy returns. The same anew. Ordovico or viricordo. Anna was, Livia is, Plurabelle's to be. Northmen's thing made south-folk's place but howmulty plurators made eachone in person? Latin me that, my trinity scholard, out of eure sanscreed into oure eryan. *Hircus Civis Eblanensis!* He had buckgoat paps on him, soft ones for orphans. Ho, Lord! Twins of his bosom. Lord save us! And ho! Hey? What all men. Hot? His tittering daughters of. Whawk?

Can't hear with the waters of. The chittering waters of. Flittering bats, fieldmice bawk talk. Ho! Are you not gone ahome? What Tom Malone? Can't hear with bawk of bats, all the liffeying waters of. Ho, talk save us! My foos won't moos. I feel as old as yonder elm. A tale told of Shaun or Shem? All Livia's daughtersons. Dark hawks hear us. Night! Night! My ho head halls. I feel as heavy as yonder stone. Tell me of John or Shaun? Who were Shem and Shaun the living sons or daughters of? Night now! Tell me, tell me, tell me, elm! Night night! Tell me tale of stem or stone. Beside the rivering waters of, hitherand-thithering waters of. Night![1]

(to be continued.)

(1) This piece concludes Part I. of James Joyce's new work. The opening pages of Part III. will appear in the next number of *transition*.

[NOVEMBER 1927]

blue-grey trousers? You got your strange walk from the army diseased when the Duke of Clarence had the run of the town and 'twas you gave the smell to Carlow. Am I seeing right? Yes, I saw it again! Near the gold falls! My blood is ice! Forms of light! See there!

Keep down your noise, you foolish woman! What is it but a black-berry growth or that grey long-ears the old four are owners of. Are you talking of Tarpey and Lyons and Gregory? I am saying now, please all, the four of them, and the cry of them, that sends that go-in-the-mist and old Johnny Mac Dougal among them.

Is that the Poolbeg light-house over there, far, far, or a steamer sailing near the Kish sands or a fire I see in the undergrowth or my Garry come back from Indies? Do not go till the moon is up love. She's dead, little Eve, little Eve she's dead. We see that strange look in your eye. A meeting again, and then a parting. I'll give the place; let the hour be yours. My map is on high where the blue milk's moving. Quick, let me go. I'm going! So long! And you, take your watch, the memory flower. By night your guiding star. So safe to journey's end! What I see gets feebler among these shades.

I'll go slowly now by my way, to Moyvalley. And so will I, to Rathmines.

Ah, but she was a strange little old woman, anyhow, Anna Livia, with drops from her toes. And Dear Dirty Dublin, he, on my word, was a strange fat old father to his Danes light and dark, the female and male.

Old girl and old boy, their servants are we. Hadn't he his seven women of pleasure? And every woman her seven sticks. And every stick its seven colours. And every colour a different cry. Washing for me, a good meal for you and the chemist's account for Joe John. Before! Before! His markets were married, the cheap with the bad, like Etrurian Catholics of hated religion in their light reds, light oranges, light yellows, light greens, and the rest of the seven the rain gives.

But in the animals' time, where was the woman? Then all that was was good. Land that is not? A number of times, coming happily back. The same and new. Vico's order but natural, free. Anna was, Livia is, Plurabelle's to be. Our Norwegian Thing-seat was where Suffolk Street is, but what number of places will make things into persons? Put that into Latin, my Trinity man, out of your Sanscrit into our Aryan. *Hircus Civis Eblanensis!* He was kind as a she-goat, to young without mothers. O, Laws! Soft milk bags two. O, Laws! O, Laws! Hey! What, all men? What? His laughing daughters of. What?

No sound but the waters of. The dancing waters of. Winged things in flight, field-rats louder than talk. Ho! Are you not gone, ho! What Tom Malone? No sound but the noise of these things, the Liffey and all its waters of. Ho, talk safe keep us! There's no moving this my foot. I seem as old as that tree over there. A story of Shaun or Shem but where? All Livia's daughters and sons. Dark birds are hearing. Night! Night! My old head's bent. My weight is like that stone you see. What may the John Shaun story be? Or who were Shem and Shaun the living sons and daughters of? Night now! Say it, say it, tree! Night night! The story say of stem or stone. By the side of the river waters of, this way and that way waters of. Night!

[MARCH 1932]

Several weeks of ill health have seriously handicapped Mr. Joyce in the exacting process of putting Book Three of his new work in its expanded and perfected form. Since he is so painstaking in his writing he has preferred to wait one more month before submitting the text for publication. The editors have gladly accorded him another month of rest and feel confident that the readers of *transition*, understanding the situation, will ungrudgingly postpone a little longer their enjoyment of the ensuing portions of this marvelous literary achievement.

[JANUARY 1928]

C. G. JUNG

PSYCHOLOGY AND POETRY
[Extract]

by C.G. Jung

IT IS INCONTESTABLY CERTAIN THAT PSYCHOLOGY — AS THE SCIENCE of psychic processes — may be brought into relation with the science of literature. The soul is the mother and the receptacle of all the sciences as well as of every work of art. The science of the soul should thus be able to demonstrate and explain the psychological structure of the work of art on the one hand and the psychological postulates of the artistic-creative man on the other. These two tasks are of a radically different nature: in the first case it is a question of an "intentionally" formed product of complicated psychic activities, in the second case, however, it concerns the psychic apparatus itself. In the first case also, the object of psychological analysis and interpretation is the firmly circumscribed, concrete work of art, whereas in the second, it is the living-creative man in the most individual form of his unique personality. Although both objects are in the most intimate relation and are connected in indissoluble reciprocal action, it is impossible for one to explain the other. To be sure, we may draw conclusions from one to the other, but these conclusions are never convincing. Even at best, they are and remain probabilities, or felicitous *apperçus.* Goethe's special relation to his mother gives us indeed a glimpse, when we examine Faust's exclamation: "The mothers, mothers, it sounds so strange." But we do not succeed in discovering just how a Faust can emerge through the connection with the mother, although down deep we surmise that in the man Goethe this relationship somehow existed. Nor can we, reversely, in any way recognize, or deduce conclusively from the Nibelungenring the fact that Wagner was inclined towards feminine "transvestitism", albeit here, too, secret paths lead from the heroic element of the Nibelungen to the morbidly feminine in the man Wagner.

The present state of psychological science which — be it said in passing — is the youngest of all sciences, in no way permits us to establish strict causal associations in this region which, as a science, it ought to do. Psychology gives us positive causalities only in the region of the semi-psychological instincts and reflexes. But where the real life of the soul begins, i.e. in the complex, we must be satisfied with painting vast canvases of events, and colorful pictures of the strange and super-humanly ingenious tissues, and we cannot designate even a single process as "necessary". If this were not the case, and if psychology could show positive causalities in the work of art and in artistic creation, the whole science of art would be deprived of its own ground and become merely a special branch of psychology. Although psychology should never give up its claim to explore and establish the causality of complicated processes, without renouncing itself, it can never attain the fulfillment of this claim, because the irrational-creative, which stands out most distinctly in art, would ultimately mock at all rationalizing efforts. All ordinary expression may be explained causally, but creative expression, which is the absolute contrary of ordinary expression, will be forever hidden from human knowledge. We may continue to describe it, and sense it, but in appearance only, and we will never understand it. The science of art and psychology will be dependent one upon the other, and the principle of the one will not negate that of the other. The principle of psychology demands the appearance of the given psychic element as being deducible, the principle of the science of art demands the consideration of the psychic as something really existent, whether it be a question of the work of art or of the artist himself. Both principles are valid in spite of their relativity.

Translated from the German by EUGENE JOLAS.

[JUNE 1930]

Franz KAFKA

THE SENTENCE

by Franz Kafka

IT WAS BEFORE NOON ON A SUNDAY IN A MOST LOVELY SPRING. GEORGE Bendemann, a young businessman, was sitting in his private room on the first floor of one of those low, lightly built houses, strung along a river in a row, and different from one another in height and color only. He had just finished a letter to a friend of his youth who was now abroad, had sealed it with playful slowness and then gazed from the window, his elbow on his desk, – out over the river, the bridge and the summits on the other bank with their frail green.

He thought of how his friend, discontented with his progress at home, had taken refuge in Russia years ago. Now he carried on a business in St. Petersburg, which had begun under excellent auspices, but for some time had been facing difficulties, according to the complaints he made during his visits which became rarer and rarer. Thus uselessly he worked himself to death abroad. His strange full beard hid but scantily his face well-known from childhood days, and his yellow complexion seemed to point to a progressive illness. According to his story he had no real connection with the colony of his countrymen there, and hardly any social contact with native families. Therefore he had adjusted his life definitely to a batchelor's existence.

What could one write to such a man, who had obviously gone to seed, for whom one could feel sorry but whom could not help? Should one perhaps advise him to come home, to begin his life here over again, to resume all the old friendly relations, – simply to have confidence in the aid of his friends? But that meant nothing more than telling him at the same time, – the more hurtingly the more delicately it was said, – that his attempts heretofore had failed, that he should relinquish them, that he should return and let himself be stared at as one who had come back to stay, that he was an old child and would simply have to follow the successful friends who had remained at home. And was it certain that all the trouble to which one would have to put him would bear fruit? Perhaps nobody would even succeed in getting him to come – he himself had said that he could no longer understand conditions at home – and so he would in spite of everything remain in his alien state, embittered by the counsels given him, and separated from his friends still more. But if he really should follow the advice and be crushed here, if he should not be able to adjust himself, with his friends nor without them; would it not be better for him if he stayed abroad, the way he was? For could one under such circumstances assume that actually he would get along?

For these reasons one could not, if one were really willing to keep up any correspondance, let him know of details such as one would explain to the most distant acquaintance. The friend had been absent from home three years, and explained this very unsatisfactorily by the uncertainty of the political conditions in Russia, which would not admit even the briefest absence of a small businessman, while a hundred thousand Russians were riding quietly around the world.

But in the course of these three years a great many things had changed for George. To be sure, his friend had heard of the death of George's mother, which had occured about two years ago, and since which George had lived with his old father; the friend had expressed his condolences in a letter of such coldness that it seemed to be explained only by the fact that such an occurence in the outside world was simply inconceivable. George had plunged into his business since then with much more energy. Perhaps his father had prevented real activity on his part while his mother was alive, by insisting solely upon asserting his views. Perhaps his father had become more reticent since his mother's death, although he was still active in the business; perhaps – and this seemed more probable – a few felicitous accidents had played a much more important role; at any rate, business had been flourishing these two past years most unexpectedly. They had had to double the personnel; the earnings were five times more than formerly and further progress seemed likely.

But his friend had no idea of this change. In the old days, the last time perhaps in that letter of condolence, he had wanted to persuade George to emigrate to Russia and had expatiated on the prospects that existed for George's business in St. Petersburg. His friend's earnings were small compared with the expansion of George's business now. But George was not inclined to write his friend about his commercial successes, and now, after all that had gone before, it would really have looked strange.

Thus George limited himself to writing his friend about unimportant happenings, as they accumulate in the memory, while one muses about them on a quiet Sunday. He had no other desire than to leave undisturbed the impression of his hometown which his friend had developed in this long interval, and which he surely found to his liking. Then it happened that in three letters, following one another at long intervals, George had notified his friend of the engagement of some man to a girl, equally unknown, until the friend, entirely against George's intentions, had begun to get interested in this curiosity.

But George preferred writing him about such things, rather than admitting that he himself had become engaged a month ago to Miss

Frieda Brandenfeld, a girl from a well-to-do family. Often he discussed this friend with her as well as the special relationship they maintained by correspondence. "I suppose he wont come to our wedding then," she had said, "and still I have a right to know all your friends."

"I dont want to disturb him," George had replied, "dont misunderstand me, he probably would come, at least I think so, but he would feel forced to it and would be hurt, perhaps he would even envy me, and then go back alone, certainly dissatisfied and incapable of getting rid of this dissatisfaction. Alone – do you know what that means?" –

"Yes, but may he not hear of our wedding in some other way?"

"That, of course, I can't prevent, but it is improbable, considering his mode of living."

"If you have such friends, George, you should never have become engaged." "Well, we're both responsible for that; but I would not have it otherwise even now."

And since she, then, breathing heavily under his kisses, had objected: "It really hurts me," he thought it unavoidable to write his friend everything.

"That's the way I am, and he will have to take me that way," he said to himself, "I can't carve a human being out of myself that perhaps would be more suitable for friendship than I am."

And, in fact, he had announced his engagement in the long letter to his friend he was writing this Sunday afternoon, in the following words: "The best news I have saved for the last. I have become engaged to Miss Frieda Brandenfeld, a girl from a well-to-do family that settled here long after your departure, and that you probably will not know, for that reason. I hope to have an opportunity to tell you more about my fiancée; I will only say today that I am very happy and that the only change in our relations is that you will have instead of a very ordinary friend, a really happy one. And then you will have in my fiancee, who wishes me to send her regards and who will herself write you soon, a sincere friend, which is not without importance for a bachelor. I know many things prevent you from visiting us. But dont you think that our wedding might offer the right opportunity to throw all the impediments over board? But however that may be, please act without taking us into consideration, just as you see fit."

With this letter in his hand, George sat at his desk a long time, his face turned to the window. Smiling absent-mindedly, he hardly answered an acquaintance who passed by and greeted him from the street.

At last he put the letter in his pocket and crossing the room went through a little hallway into his father's room in which he had not been for months. There was never any real necessity for his going there, for he saw his father during business hours every day. They ate lunch together in a boarding house, although they had dinner separately. Then both sat for a little while, in the common living-room, each with his newspaper, unless George, which happened most frequently, went to see a friend or, as now, visited his fiancee.

George was astonished to see how dark his father's room was this sunny forenoon. Strange, that the high wall rising beyond the small courtyard should throw such a shadow. His father was sitting at the window in a corner which was decorated with diverse souvenirs of his mother, and he was reading the newspaper which he held sidewise in front of his eyes, with which operation he attempted to compensate his feeble eyesight. On the table there were the remains of breakfast, of which he evidently had not eaten much.

"Ah, George," said his father walking towards him at the same time. His heavy bath-robe opened while he was walking, the ends fluttered about him. "My father is still a giant," thought George to himself.

"It's really unbearably dark here," he said aloud.

"Yes, it's really dark," his father replied.

"Did you close the window?"

"I'd rather have it like this."

"It's quite warm outside," said George, as if adding an epilogue. He sat down.

His father took the breakfast dishes away and placed them on a box.

"I simply wanted to tell you," George continued, while observing absent-mindedly the motions of the old man, "that I finally did announce my engagement to St. Petersburg." He took the letter from his pocket, and let it wander back again.

"To St. Petersburg," asked the father.

"Why, to my friend," George said, looking for his father's eyes. – "In business he's entirely different," he thought to himself, "The way he sits here, his arms crossed over his broad chest."

"Yes, to your friend," his father said emphatically.

"You know, father, I first intended not to tell him anything about my engagement. For reasons of consideration simply. He is a difficult man. I said to myself, he may find out about my engagement from other sources, although that is hardly probable, considering his solitary mode of living – I cannot prevent it, anyway – but he should not find it out through me."

"And now you have changed your mind again?" his father asked, putting the large newspaper on the window sill and upon the paper his glasses which he covered with his hand.

"Yes, I thought it over again. If he is a good friend, I said to myself, my happy engagement will be happiness for him. And therefore I no longer hesitated to send him the announcement. But before mailing the letter, I wanted to tell you about it."

"George," his father said, pulling his toothless mouth apart, "now listen! You have come to me with this affair to talk it over. That is doubtless to your credit. But it is nothing, less than nothing, if you now do not tell me the whole truth. I do not want to stir up things that do not belong here. Since the death of our dear mother certain disagreeable things have happened. Many things escape me in business, perhaps no attempt is made to hide it from me – I do not want to assume now that it is being hidden from me – I am no longer strong enough, my memory fails me. I no longer have control over many things. That is first of all the running down of nature, and secondly the death of your mother has affected me much more than you. – But since we happen to be discussing this letter, I must beg you, George, not to deceive me. It is a small matter, not worth a breath, so dont deceive me. Have you really a friend in St. Petersburg?"

George got up, embarrassed. "Let's leave my friends alone. A thousand friends cannot replace my father. You know what I think? You do not take enough care of yourself. But old age demands its rights. You are indispensable for me in business, you know that well enough; but if business should threaten your health, I should prefer closing it tomorrow. This can't go on. We shall have to introduce a new mode of living for you. But something fundamental. You sit here in the darkness, while you could have a nice light in the living-room. At breakfast you simply nibble a bit, instead of nourishing yourself thoroughly. You sit here, with the windows closed, and the air would be so good for you. No, Father! I will get the doctor, and we will follow his advice. We shall exchange rooms – you must take the front room, and I will stay here. It will not be a change for you, everything will be moved over there. But we'll do that in due time, you might lie down now a bit, you need absolute rest. I'll help you undress, you'll see I can do it. Or perhaps you would prefer moving to the front room at once. Then for the time being you might lie down in my bed. That's a good idea."

George was standing beside his father, who let his head with the scraggly white hair sink to his chest.

"George," his father said softly, without emotion.

George knelt down at once beside his father; he saw the pupils in the tired face of his father, over-large in the corners of his eyes, staring at him.

"You have no friend in St. Petersburg. You have always been a practical joker, even with me. Why should you have a friend there, of all places? I cannot believe it."

"Think for a minute, father," said George, lifting his father from the arm-chair and taking off his bathrobe. The old man seemed very weak. "It's almost three years ago that my friend was here for a visit. I can still remember that you did not care much for him. At least on two occasions I denied him before you, although he was sitting with me in my room, for I could easily understand your aversion to him. My friend has certain peculiarities. But then at other times you got along with him very well. I was so proud that time that you were listening to him; you nodded and asked questions. If you think about it, you will surely remember it. He told incredible stories about the Russian Revolution, for instance, how he during a business trip in Kiev he saw a riot and a priest on a balcony who cut into the palm of his hand a wide crucifix of blood, raising his hand in an appeal to the crowd. I remember you yourself repeating this story from time to time."

In the meantime George had succeeded in getting his father to sit down again and he began to take off his drawers and his socks. At the sight of the not particularly clean underwear, he blamed himself for having neglected his father. It certainly should have been his duty to watch over his father's laundry. He had not yet talked with his fiancee about his father's future, but silently they had presupposed that his father would remain in the old home. But now he decided briefly and decisively to take his father along with him into his future household. It might be that such care would come too late.

He carried his father in his arms to the bed. A fearful feeling was in him, as he began to notice how during the few steps to the bed his father was playing with the watch-chain on his chest. He could not at once put him to bed, he clung so firmly to the watch-chain.

But hardly was he in bed, when everything seemed all right. He drew up the covers himself. He did not look up at George with unfriendly eyes.

"Of course you remember him, father don't you?" asked George, nodding encouragingly towards him.

"Am I covered up now?" asked his father, as if he did not know whether or not his feet were sufficiently covered.

"So you're beginning to like it in bed already?" said George, putting the cover closer around him.

"Am I well covered up?," asked his father once more, seeming most attentively to await a reply.

"Just be quiet, you're well covered."

"No!" his father cried, hurling the answer against the question. He threw the cover off so hard that it unfolded and stood for a moment erect in bed. Only one hand he held lightly against the ceiling. "You wanted to cover me up, I know, my chappie, but I'm not yet covered up. And even if it is my last strength, it's enough for you, too much for you. Of course, I know your friend. He would be a son according to my heart. For that reason you deceived him all these years. Why otherwise? Don't you think I wept about him? That's why you lock yourself in your office, nobody must disturb you, the boss is busy – only that you may write your false letters to Russia. But fortunately nobody warned the father to find out about his son. The way you thought just now you had conquered me, so that you could flop down on me without my stirring. And then my Honorable Son decides to get married!"

George looked up at the terrifying picture of his father. The friend in St. Petersburg, whom his father knew suddenly so well, captivated his imagination, as never before. He saw him lost in immense Russia. He saw him at the door of the empty business which had been looted. He saw him standing amid the debris of the shelves, the shreds of the merchandise, the falling gas-fixtures. Why had he gone so far away?

"But look at me!" his father called, and George ran, almost without thinking, to the bed, but stopped on the way.

"Because she raised her skirts," his father began to say in a flute-like voice. "Because she raised her skirts, the trollop," and in order to picture it, he raised his shirt so high that the scar from his war days could be seen on his upper thigh. "Because she raised her skirts like this, like this, like this, therefore you went to her, and in order to satisfy yourself with her without being disturbed, you have dishonored your mother's memory betrayed your friend, and put your father in bed, so that he cannot move. But he still can move, or can't he?"

And he stood clear and threw his legs into the air. He was luminous with cunning.

George was standing in a corner as far as possible away from his father. Some time ago he had decided to observe everything very accurately, so that he might not be surprised in a roundabout way, from behind or from above. Now he remembered again his long forgotten decision and forgot it, as one draws a little thread through the eye of a needle.

"But your friend is nevertheless not betrayed," his father cried, and his index finger bobbing to and fro affirmed it. "I have been his representative here."

"You're joking," George was unable to refrain from saying this but recognized his mistake, and bit his tongue, although too late – his eyes rigid – so that he bent with pain.

"Yes, of course, I am joking! A joke! Excellent word! What other consolation did an old widowed father have? Look – and for the moment of the reply be still my living son. What was there left for me, in my back room, persecuted by unfaithful employees, old to the very bones? And my son raced jubilantly through the world, concluded business affairs which I had prepared, stood on his head with joy, and avoided his father with the enigmatic face of a man of honor. Don't you think I loved you? I, from whom you came?"

"Now he is going to bend forward," thought George "if he should fall and crush his head." These words hissed through his brain.

His father bent forward, but did not fall. Since George, contrary to his expectations, did not come nearer, he rose again.

"Stay where you are, I don't need you! You think you still have the strength to come here and you hold back, merely because you are so minded. But you are mistaken. I am still much the stronger. Alone perhaps I might have had to draw back, but your mother has now given me her strength; I know all about your friend; the list of your customers is in my pocket."

"There are pockets even in his shirt" said George, thinking this would bring his father to his senses. He thought this only for a moment, for always he forgot everything.

"Just stick to your fiancée and be condescending to me. I will sweep her away from you, you will never know how."

George made a grimace, as if he did not believe it. His father merely nodded towards George's corner, affirming the truth of his statement.

"You really amused me when you asked me if you should write your friend about your engagement. Why, he knows everything, you fool, he knows everything, I wrote him, because you forgot to take my writing material away from me. That's why he has not been back for years, he knows every thing a hundred times better than you yourself. Your letters he crushes, unread, in his left hand, while holding my letters in his right hand to read them."

Enthusiastically he swung his arm over his head. "He knows everything a thousand times better," he called.

"Ten thousand times" said George, to sneer at his father, but the words had a deadly serious sound even in his mouth.

"For years I have been waiting for you to come with this question. Do you think that anything else interests me? Do you think that I am reading newspapers? There," and he threw the page of a paper, which somehow had been carried to the bed, in George's direction, an old newspaper with a name with which George was unfamiliar.

"How long you hesitated before becoming mature. Your mother had to die, she could not experience that day of joy, your friend is perishing in his Russia, three years ago he was as yellow as death, and I, just see, how things are with me. Haven't you eyes to see?"

"So you spied on me?" said George.

Pitifully his father: "You probably wanted to say that sooner? Now it's not the thing to say."

And louder: "Now you know what was going on outside yourself. Before you only knew about yourself. You really were an innocent child, but in reality, diabolical! – Listen: I now condemn you to death by drowning."

George felt himself chased out of the room; in his ears rang the blow with which his father had crashed onto the bed. While on the stairs, over the steps of which he raced as over an oblique plane, he stumbled against the cleaning woman who was about to go upstairs to arrange the rooms after the night. "Good Lord," she called, and covered her face with her apron. But he was already gone. He jumped out of the doorway, something drove him across the streetcar tracks to the water. Already he had hold of the parapet, like a hungry man clutching his food. He swung over it, being an excellent athlete. Clutching the railing with weakening hands, he saw an omnibus which would break his fall most easily, cried softly: "Dear parents! Yes, I have always loved you," and let himself go down.

At that moment a very heavy traffic was crossing the bridge.

Translated from the German, and adapted, by EUGENE JOLAS.
[FEBRUARY 1928]

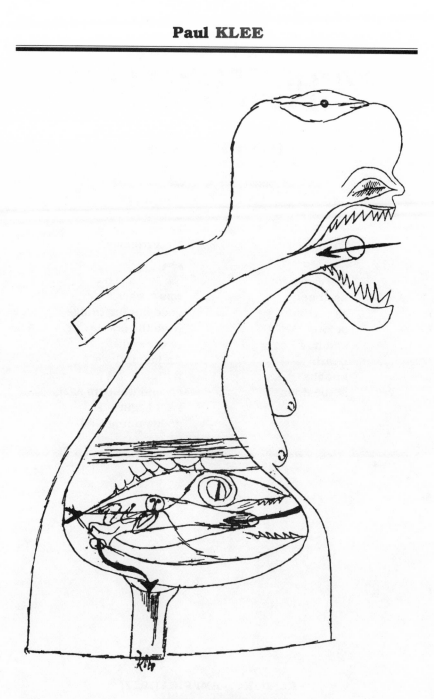

Paul Klee

Fish-Man : Man-Eater

[NOVEMBER 1929]

FROM «MANHATTAN ANTHOLOGY»

by Alfred Kreymborg

WHORE.

EVERYBODY
used her
as earth
before
and now
Death
knocks
at the door.

MISANTHROPE.

THIS FELLOW
was always
goddamning things
from the cradle
to the sod.
And doubtless
if he
should wake up again
he'll begin
goddamning God.

[NOVEMBER 1927]

– READ IN . . . AMERICA [1927]

"Gertrude Stein, living in France, has apparently forgotten English – at least the kind of English this reviewer speaks."

Detroit *News*.

Fernand Léger

Composition

[JUNE 1930]

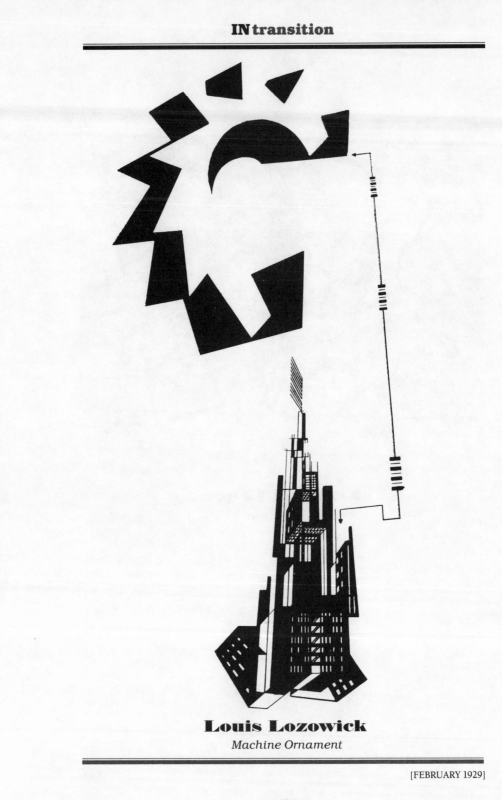

Louis Lozowick
Machine Ornament

[FEBRUARY 1929]

EXTRACT FROM A NOVEL

by Robert McAlmon

SITTING NEAR A TURN IN THE LEVEE OLD MAN WOODS TALKED TO NI. "I TELL you the flood's going to break that dam. Them college engineers won't stop it with rocks, or none of their worked-out-on-paper ideas. Besides they didn't start piling rock soon enough to have a bank sufficiently strong when the waters hit the levee."

Ni believed Woods right, simply because of an instinct of inevitability in him, rather than through belief in the old man's judgment. The flood would be an economic fatality for some in the valley, bringing its loss of cotton crops. Futile, however, as the attempt to forestall the fatality, this was the way to do, to go on working doggedly, expecting the best and accepting what happened.

It was Saturday. Ni was anxious to be in town as he knew that the negroes had thrown a barbecue during the day, and there was to be a negro dance on. He intended to go to it even if Paul or the Lymans did not go. Driving back to the town the sun was still clear; the day was mistless, but oncoming evening brought a brighter brightness as Ni's consciousness became less aware that heat was causing intense brooding in the infinity of sky. The red glow gleaming through the opaque clarity was less viciously hot. Ni found Paul Ellenthorpe and the two Lymans at the shack. Pauls' eyes were bloodshot from weeks of work in mosquito-ridden, oven-hot, swamps.

"Hell, Ni, we haven't had much talk this summer, have we? Clarence says you're on your heels to be East. I'll give you letters to my brother, and friends there, even if nothing much comes through letters of introduction, generally.

"At least I'll know somebody there, that way. But I'll get on somehow."

"When Elihu came back from the army he stayed in New York. I had my brother take him around, but he got afraid and came back without spending two weeks to locate a job in the East. That's no way to get ahead," Paul said.

"I know. Too much mother, and sister, in both Clarence's and Elihu's life. But look at Elihu. His looks won't let him be taken seriously, and nobody goes in for locating diamond-in-the-rough men if they can't blow their own whistle. He'd only end up as an employe. Elihu hasn't executive stuff in him. A good cotton crop might make Clarence and Elihu well off here."

"Damn my health," Ellenthorpe protested. "I was lined up with the Subway company in New York, but just as I was well under way the strain got me. It's the heat here I object to, and the lack of companionship. A man stagnates with no stimulus."

"Hey, if you guys want a shower bath before dinner, you'd better start," Elihu called from the shack, where he was drying himself with a none-too-clean towel. "And that bum, Ni, had better fix us up a high class meal. Grill the steak brown tonight, Ni."

In time the meal was on the sand, and the men chewed at a juicy steak. Clarence ate quickly, to lean back and jabber. "Well Ni, old-timer, you'll be gone in the fall. You know, I could make a job for you at our office when Paul's out of the valley. It's hell here in the winter time; lonely; and you're a talkative beezer."

"Lay off the kid," Elihu brooded. "Ni ain't a hick yet like you and me, but he'd get to be one down here. I'll miss his cooking, but hell, the chink will have us back over his greasy slop-jar."

"Send me books and magazines to Imperial Valley. I'll be busy with the new engineering partnership, but I want to know what's going on," Paul Ellenthorpe said.

"You're a soft bird, Paul," Clarence said. "I'll bet there's a girl back East more than it's books you're missing. Hell, Elihu, you and me'll join the El Dorado club even if the politics they talk there drive a guy blotto. They have a good nigger cook."

Paul chuckled. "Dat boy am some exalted personage, Ah say. It seems he took religion on the astral plane some time back. He ain't just common folk. He serves good food, but if anyone registers a kick, he looks spiritually wounded and retires to the kitchen to take up communion with the loftier souls."

"Have some more beer, Paul," Clarence invited. "What do you think you'll do back East, Ni? Journalism mebbe?"

"Don't ask me," Ni answered. "I hate newspaper work; I detest advertising; but – I'll try anything, and won't stick it long. There are enough in my family leading settled lives. I'd as soon be a hobo as not."

"Bosh, what does all the intellectual life amount to?" Clarence said. "You don't get more kick out of life. You might as well give up. Suppose you get headed for something and a war breaks out, or you get hit by a truck."

"Who's talking about intellectual life?" Ni said irately. "All I want is to move around and keep interested, and I haven't a private income. I'm ready to take it, or leave it, as regards anything in life. But I'd pass out with boredom in this valley. Cotton crops don't inspire me, and to hell with whether the flood breaks the dam, except for Paul's sake."

"Don't begin thinking nothing matters at your age, Ni," Paul advised.

"It isn't the thinking, it's the feeling that nothing matters that is destructive. Besides that sort of thing happens inside one. We don't decide how we think or feel, much. My capacity for keeping discontented is helped with all the temperamental parphernalia necessary. May be that means I think things can, do, matter."

"I know how you feel, Ni. It's hell," Paul answered. "You're still randy. Not that I've lost my sex either, but I used to pace the streets thinking I'd do anything. The fear of infection got me through. I couldn't be promiscuous. And, a man gets emotionally involved with girls of his own class. Where would I be now if I had been caught by marriage? I had a nice time in Italy and France though for a year, before the war."

"Hell," Ni jerked out, "Can't an American find anything in America? It's rot too that the European countries know so well how to live. I know an Italian who writes me crazier letters than I'd ever write, and the French young writers have been knocked in the belly as hard as anyone."

"I'll jog over town," Elihu Lyman broke in. "If you guys settle whatever you're talking about, send me a wire. Anyone going across the cotton fields with me? We might as well join the boneheads in the village and talk irrigation politics."

Soon the four went across the cotton field. On the edge of town they passed camps of people who had already begun to drift into the valley as cotton pickers, or in anticipation of a few days well paid work if the flood broke the levee banks. Ni left the others to investigate the remains of the negro barbecue. No negroes were about but the remnants of food, canteloupe husks, chicken bones, corn fritters, and half empty beer bottles, were strewn about where the central fire had been.

Ni went to the dance hall. Some old mammies and greyheaded males, were sitting around chattering and wheezing with laughter as they joked.

"Wheee-he-he-eough, Mistah Prentice, shuah, didn't you'all know dat whiskey wuz tea. Wheee-he-he-ho-oooh, I near burst. You'all is crazy ef you tink Sol Marston is gibbin'way any ob his liquor. Dat boy got religion all right, but 'e shoah laks his drink to hisself."

Ni stood at the door watching the glistening, beaming, black faces, extra greasy from food gorging at the barbecue.

"Howdy honey," an old negress who did Ni's laundry called to him. "I done save you a chicken lak ah sez ah would, but honey, ah shuah had to do battle foah it".

"Great Lula, but I knew you would. You sure do know what food was meant for," Ni answered, and went to Joe's for a drink, as dancing would not begin among the negroes for a while. When he returned, reckless impulsiveness was on him. The sound of music excited him. The dance hall was alive with gay young bucks, and maidens dressed grandly for the occasion. The older people at first sat around, smiling wistfully out of their shining black faces. As they tapped their feet and shrugged their shoulders, however, they lost their wistfulness, and forgot their years, and soon were dancing vehemently. Ni stood in the doorway. No other white men were about, and but one or two Mexicans who had come only to look on. An Indian girl, with a flabby, early matronized body, watched the proceedings with curious apathy. Ni discovered she lived with one of the negro men.

In the orchestra a violinist swayed and rocked and shouted like a dog howling at the moon. A pianist bounced on the piano stool, doing jig steps with his feet as he played. A drummer banged madly at his bass and snare drums. Now and then he grabbed a potato whistle to make shriek-ing, yodeling, calliope noises. Negro laughter and chatter flowed, volup-tuous timbred, through the evening air. After watching a time Ni found the flesh odour in the room, as of bee-hives, oppressive to him. He didn't want to stand watching when he could not be a part of the proceedings. As he started back to Joe's, to join Harry Gallego for a last drink, he heard a voice say, "Evening honey, is youah lonely? Ah's right down good com-pany mahself."

Ni looked at the speaker, a young half-breed negress he had seen about town. She was not of the community negroes. He thought she was a girl imported by the one white restaurant keeper in town, and if so, she served as prostitute a good portion of the un-mated male population. He laughed, looking at her dubiously. She was slender, full bosomed, and hot with animal magnetism.

"Doan youah want company. Ah's lonely mahself, and ah doan want to go in with them no-count niggers. Ah's creole, from New Orleans." Her voice was persuading. Ni wanted to talk to her, to hear her soothingly mellow voice talk on, to hear her laughter.

"No, I have to go on," he told her, thinking, however, it would have been different were the town not so small and gossipy, and the prejudice against negroes so intense in the town.

The water had risen twelve inches during the night, and already during the last four days every rancher in the valley who could get away was working on the levee. Gunnysacks were filled with sand and piled along the banks to restrain the flood waters. During rest periods Ni heard ranchers complaining because this or that rancher was not doing his share of work. "He won't have any crop to work on if the flood breaks. This is a community matter, but you can trust him to let somebody else do his civic work."

Other men boasted that they hadn't slept for 24 or 36 hours. Every-where was great disregard for ordinary routines. Everywhere were men pumped full of excited consciousness of their own necessity in this crisis. When one rested, he was taking his first rest, and had to rush back at once to direct Indians, or Mexicans, or other ranchers. There was not a man on the job who did not know that if the flood was controlled, it would be because of his advice, and that if the flood broke, it was because some-one had failed to follow his directions.

Back from the levee banks stood a huge thatch-roofed shack which had been speedily erected to serve as kitchen. The grounds about the place had begun to be soggy with water coming up from underneath because of flood water pressure. Not fifty feet from the kitchen the horses were hitched and fed, and the odor of ammoniacal manure permeated the air. The cooks were a horribly dirty, one-armed Mexican; an old Scotchman with a cross dog disposition, the sort of man vicious-tempered from isolated living and hardships; and assistants; waiters, kitchen boys, and volunteer helpers. All cursed and reviled each other, cursed the men at work for their appetites, the location for its uncleanness, the management of the Water company for lack of preparation for such emergencies, and such equipment as there was as inadequate. Flies were about every pot, pan, and dish of food; flies congregated in millions from stink pools and manure piles. Neither the Mexican or Scotch cook bothered to wash their hands after excretion. Some men would not eat the food, at first; others ate on indifferently, saying, "This ain't no time to be delicate."

Through day and night, autos, trucks, wagons, came and went with loads of men, of cement lime, of gunny sacks. The heat sweltered. The flood waters put steaming humidity into the air so that it was stifling to breathe. Heat and humidity writhed and coiled about men and horses; horses dropped in their harness. Men felt sick at stomach, and rested in what shade there was. But the water was still rising.

Ni had not had more than four hours sleep out of twenty-four for three days. He had to rush from gang to gang, seeing that gunnysacks and men were working where conditions looked most dangerous.

At noon next day the crisis seemed bye. Ranchers departed, and all gangs worked in a desultory manner. Ni sat munching a sandwich at an intersection of the levee channel. Down the levee some twenty Mexicans worked without energy. Suddenly a shouting arose. It increased to excitement. Ni jumped up. A moment later he heard the rush of water. The levee had burst. At first the water seeped through, but once the small break occurred the rush of water swept away masses of the bank. There was no stopping it now, and cotton fields, stockfarms, ranch houses, and roadways would be knee deep in water. Only the passing of flood season would permit the repair of the levee banks. Ni got into a boat and rowed into the backwater to circle around where the twenty Mexican men were trapped on the levee. After hot rowing under cottonwood brush, he reached the men. They were calm now, and smoked indifferently, seemingly at ease because the flood waters had made a decision for them. The work of piling rock and sandbags was over for the summer, which put them out of a job, but that was for tomorrow's thinking.

The next day men were standing about town discussing the flood, boasting of work they'd done, each one giving his reason why the thing and happened, and would not have happened IF.

[AUGUST 1927]

SIGNATURE ANONYME

by Archibald MacLeish

As FOR MYSELF
My name is helved to this iron

I was a stranger in all the lands of the earth
I had no home in the lands where the rain falls

Nor a town where the street dogs knew me
The sound of my feet in the road or the smell of my shoes

I was of doubtful blood
I was born of the race of the Gaels in the outland

(It is a troubling thing
To remember the singing of rivers you have not heard)

My brother's grave is over the north water
In the sand where they fought

The grave of my son is made over the water
There in the green knoll is he laid

I do not know the land where my grave will be
This craft is a hard craft I follow

I have no skill in the new tongue I was born to
Neverthless I can not be still

You that pity
Labor done in pain at night and in bitterness

Think if you read these words in a better time
Of the shape of my mouth forming the difficult letters

[APRIL 1927]

Archibald MacLEISH

POEM DEDICATED TO THE ADVANCEMENT OF AVIATION...

by Archibald MacLeish

BUT THAT'S ALL DIFFERENT NOW. THEY'VE GOT IT FIXED.
They give the prizes to Authentic Artists.
They put no Colley Cibbers in their lists.
They know the Homers and the Hacks apart.
(You tell the works of Homer by the blurbs)
They know the bum ones from the Edna Ferbers
And Miss Millay's Own work from what's not hers.
They never get the salt and sugar mixed —

They know too much. And when all's done and said,
When all the lady novelists and neat
She-poets are (if worms still be) worm's meat
And names in magazines, i.e., are dead.
No unknown kid will get their laurel stem.
By Yee! They'll have no Keatses crowding them!

[SEPTEMBER 1927]

SOME OPINIONS [1929]

the revolution of the word according to transition
weary parisians and expatriots turn sour on the king's english and set
out to reform it to their needs and who cares.
— from a page-review by Georges Currie in the *Brooklyn Eagle*

TOURIST DEATH
(for Sylvia Beach)
by Archibald MacLeish

I PROMISED YOU THESE DAYS AND AN UNDERSTANDING
Of light in the twigs after sunfall

                              Do you ask to descend
At dawn in a new world with wet on the pavements
And a yawning cat and the fresh odor of dew
And red geraniums under the station windows
And doors wide and brooms and the sheets on the railing
And a whistling boy and the sun like shellac on the street

Do you ask to embark at night at the third hour
Sliding away in the dark and the sails of the fishermen
Slack in the light of the lanterns and black seas
And the tide going down and the splash and drip of the hawser

Do you ask something to happen as spring does
In a night in a small time and nothing the same again

Life is neither a prize box nor a terminus
Life is a haft that has fitted the palms of many
Dark as the helved oak
                         with sweat bitter
Browned by numerous hands
                         Death is the rest of it
Death is the same bones and the trees nearer
Death is a serious thing like the loam smell
Of the plowed earth in the fall
                               Death is here
Not in another place not among strangers
Death is under the moon here and the rain

I promise you old signs and a recognition
Of sun in the seething grass and the wind's rising

Do you ask more
               Do you ask to travel forever

[FEBRUARY 1929]

Man Ray

Photographic Study

*Man Ray is an American who has lived in Paris
several years, doing painting, sculpture and
photography. Within the past year, he has
evolved an abstract moving picture which may
be an important development in
cinematographic art.* [JUNE 1927]

[FEBRUARY 1929]

André Masson

La Rencontre

[JUNE 1930]

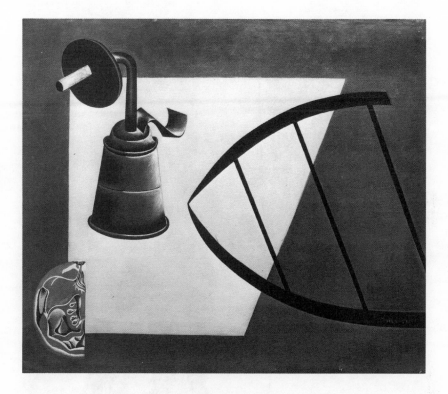

Joan Miró

Painting

[DECEMBER 1927]

L. Moholy-Nagy

Jealousy

*L. Moholy-Nagy lives in Berlin. He is also a
member of the Bauhaus of Dessau.*

[FEBRUARY 1929]

Francis Picabia
Painting

[MARCH 1928]

THE WORK OF PABLO PICASSO

by Elliot Paul

THE RELUCTANCE OF SENSITIVE OBSERVERS TO PASS JUDGEMENTS UPON their contemporaries, and especially to state rather obvious truths which are tacitly accepted among themselves, makes it appear in after years as if each epoch had misunderstood itself more completely than was actually the case. During the past twenty years, the just reverence which French domination of painting had inspired for decades has made critics all the more timid about giving Picasso his full due.

No artist, even before the days of the camera, had for his object the mere representation of objects. The problem of space and the inter-relations of its divisions was dimly in the minds of Giotto and his contemporaries. How long the early Italian painters felt the integrity and continuity of lines before it was definitely stated that they were not primarily the outlines of tangible articles it is now impossible to say. It is enough that principles of composition have developed, that ideas of perspective have expanded as science has progressed, that color and light have come to be understood as one and the same thing.

The twentieth century opened with such a wealth of tradition and information that progress in painting was difficult to expect. As soon as Picasso began working in his Montmartre studio, an eager young Spaniard with infinite good-nature and enthusiasm, his natural gifts were recognized. It was acknowledged that he could draw marvellously well, that he had profound human insight into character and that his outlook was fresh and significant.

He began by improving upon Toulouse-Lautrec, since he was surrounded by the types the latter had caricatured. But Picasso's early paintings were diabolical, where Toulouse-Lautrec's were merely grotesque. The instinct for growth, for continual renewal of his inspiration was so strong in Picasso that his first supporters deserted him at once. Relieved of the burden of their endorsement, Picasso has never faltered. He seems to have turned from the masters nearest him in point of time and travelled right back to the primitive sources, failing at no point to learn the vital lesson.

From Gauguin, Picasso derived support for his love of the exotic. In the early "Cubist" landscapes the influence of Cezanne is best discerned. The linear perfection of Ingres, Daumier's integrity of form, El Greco's distortion for emphasis, Botticelli's radiance were in turn examined, revered and appropriated by Picasso.

It is only those who fear for their individuality and doubt their originality who shun influences. Picasso treated the work of all his masters as if it had been left unfinished, or perhaps he chose the masters whose principles were capable of further application.

His impatience with the then existing conventions of painting is evidenced in the first reproduction in this number, which dates about 1905. He had not relinquished Daumier's method of building forward from the background, but in the hands and the vessel he burst all previous restraint. Three years later, in the second painting, it will be seen that he has modified the scale of the head and the body in order to harmonize their lines and that the implied continuation of the principal lines influence the background.

Having reached that point of departure, it is not strange nor illogical that, in studying a given set of objects, Picasso's vigorous imagination should see the continuations of their planes and curved surfaces. As the space he created became thus animated, it was natural that the outlines should diminish in importance and that he should chose his own color scale instead of feeling bound by the haphazard tints of nature. The third reproduction is from the most pronounced Cubistic period. The figure of the model almost disappears and the intersecting planes suggested by its surfaces become visible and balanced three-dimensionally.

There is nothing unreal about the parts of the figures in geometry books which are indicated by dotted lines. Poussin felt the same aversion for dead space on a canvas, however plausibly excused by its supposed representation of the sky, the earth, the sea, or the floor of a room, or even the bosom of a lady. The French master introduced objects arbitrarily into the vacant spaces, and his array of articles is certainly, from a rational point of view, more incongruous than Picasso's array of planes.

Having liberated himself from representation or comment, Picasso's adventurous spirit was free to organize the entities he had created. No device the primitives or classicists had used to beautify or amplify their paintings was lost upon him, but he has been able to put their discoveries to a purer use than they did, since he felt

Pablo Picasso
1906

Pablo Picasso

1921

*A friend once sait to Pablo Picasso, "Since you
can draw so beautifully, who do you spend your
time making these queer things?"
"That's the reason," replied Picasso.*

[SUMMER 1928]

no obligation to identify the shapes he used, nor to apologize for his enthusiasm under the cloak of mysticism.

For a time, Picasso was carried away by his own discoveries but he soon decided that mere complication of detail was as bad for Cubism as it was for illustrative drawing. From that time on, he has striven for simplicity until in 1927, as illustrated by the cover design, his austerity is almost equal to that of Euclid. But a comparison of the cover design with the painting of the boy and the jug discloses subtle and unmistakable qualities in common.

The drawing of the two nude figures, the fourth of the reproductions, was preliminary to the period in which he painted the famous "Rose Nude" and if placed beside one of his Toulouse-Lautrec caricatures shows an indefinable mastery of relationships which later has become one of the most baffling and significant factors of his art. The next painting, finished in 1921, combines this quality with the selected Cubistic technique, warmth without sentimentality, simplicity without obviousness. The last sketch is an amazing display of virtuosity, in which the essential lines and rhythms of two boxers are captured in one instant of lightning draftsmanship.

To underestimate Picasso's scope is to misunderstand his art, which is the life-blood of the art of our epoch. His work has gained as its elements of suprise have ceased to bewilder us. What seemed at first most strange, appears in two short decades to be most inevitable. He has, as Gertrude Stein has remarked, organized the esthetic world as Napoleon organized the political world of his day, and with an effect quite as permanent.

Katherine Anne PORTER

MAGIC

by Katherine Anne Porter

AND MADAME BLANCHARD, BELIEVE THAT I AM HAPPY TO BE HERE WITH YOU and your family because it is so serene, everything, and before this I worked for a long time in a fancy house – maybe you don't know what is a fancy house? Naturally. . . everyone must have heard sometime or another. Well Madame I work always where there is work to be had, and so in this place I worked very hard and saw a lot of things, things you wouldn't believe, and I wouldn't think of telling you, only maybe it will rest you while I brush your hair. . . You'll excuse me too but I couldn't help hearing you say to the laundress maybe someone had bewitched your linens, they fall away so fast in the wash: Well, there was a girl there in that house, a poor thing, thin, but popular with all the men who called, and you understand she could not get along with the woman who ran the house. They quarrelled, the madam cheated her on her checks: you know, the girl got a check, a brass one, every time, and at the week's end she gave these back to the madam, yes, I think that was the way, and got her percentage, a very small little of her earnings: it is a business you see like any other – and the madam used to pretend the girl had given back only so many checks, you see, and really she had given many more: but after they were out of her hands, what could she do? So she would say, I will get out of this place, and curse and cry then. The madam would hit her over the head. She always hit people over the head with bottles, it was the way she fought, my good heavens Madame Blanchard, what noise there would be sometimes with a girl running raving downstairs, and the madam pulling her back by the hair and smashing a bottle on her forehead.

It was nearly always about the money, the girls got in debt so, and if they wished to go they could not without paying every sou marqué. The madam had full understanding with the police, the girl must come back with them or go to the jails. Well, they always came back with the police-men or another kind of man friend of the madam: she could make men work for her too, but she paid them very well for all, let me tell you: and so the girls stayed unless they were sick: If so, if they got too sick, she sent them away again.

Madame Blanchard said, You are pulling a little here, and eased a strand of hair: and then what?

Pardon — but this girl, there was a true hatred between her and the madam, she would say, I make more money than any body else in the house, and every week were scenes. So at last she said one morning, I will leave this place, and she took out forty dollars from under her pillow and said, Here's your money! The madam began then to shout Where did you get all that, you — ? And accused her of robbing the men who came to visit her. The girl said keep your hands off or I'll brain you: and at that the madam took hold of her shoulders, and began to lift her knee and kick this girl most terribly in the stomach, and even in her most secret place, Madame Blanchard, and then she beat her in the face with a bottle, and the girl fell into her room where I was making clean: I helped her to the bed, and she sat there holding her sides with her head hanging down, and when she got up again there was blood everywhere she had sat. So then the madam came in again and scream-ed, Now you can get out, you are no good for me any more: I don't repeat all, you understand it is too much. But she took all the money she could find, and at the door she gave the girl a great push in the back with her knee, so that she fell again in the street, and then got up and went away with the dress barely on her.

After this the men who knew this girl kept saying, where is Ninette? And they kept asking this, so that the madam could not say any longer, I put her out because she is a thief. No she began to see she was wrong to send this Ninette away, and then she said, She will be back in a few days.

And now Madame Blanchard, if you wish to hear, I come to the strange part, the thing recalled to me when you said your linens were bewitched. For the cook in that place was a woman, colored like myself, like myself with much French blood just the same, like myself living always among people who worked spells. But she had a very hard heart, she helped the madam in everything, she liked to watch all that happened, and she gave away tales on the girls. The madam trusted her above everything, and she said, Well, where can I find that slut? because she had gone altogether out of Basin street before the madam began to ask of the police to bring her again. Well the cook said, I know a charm that works here in New Orleans, colored women do it to bring back their men: in seven days they come again very happy to stay and they cannot say why. It is a New Orleans charm for sure, for certain, they say it does not work even across the river. . . And then they did it just as the cook said. They took the chamber pot of this girls from under her bed, and in it they mixed with water and milk all the relics of her they found there: the hair from her brush, and the face powder from the box, and even little bits of her nails they found about the edges of the carpet where she sat by habit to cut her finger and toe nails: and they dipped the sheets with her blood into the water, and all the time the cook said something over it in a low voice: I could not hear all, but at last she said to the madam, Now spit in it: and the madam spat: and the cook said, When she comes back she will be the dirt under your feet.

Madame Blanchard closed her perfume bottle with a thin click: Yes, and then?

Then in seven nights the girl came back and she looked very sick, but happy to be there. One of the men said, Welcome home, Ninette! and when she started to speak to the madam, the madam said, Shut up and get upstairs and dress yourself. So Ninette, this girl, she said, I'll be down in just a minute. And after that she lived there quietly.

[SUMMER 1928]

NOTICE

To READERS :

To insure prompt receipt of copies sub-scribe through our Paris office. Single copies may be secured from bookstores listed in this issue.

In subscribing please send drafts in French francs when possible.

To CONTRIBUTORS : Read *transition* before submitting manus-cripts. We welcome new work but not the kind that might be accepted else-where. Imitations of James Joyce and Gertrude Stein are automatically re-jected.

We cannot carry on correspondence concerning manuscripts nor guarantee to return them.

In no case will manuscripts be returned unless accompanied by an *international postal coupon* and a self-addressed envelope. Americain and British stamps are useless to us.

The rate of payment for contributions is 30 francs the printed page.

To BOOKSELLERS :

For new orders, additional copies and re-turns of unsold copies, in America write Gotham Book Mart 51 West 47th Street New York.

In England apply to Wm. Jackson Ltd. 16 Took's Court, Cursitor St. London E. C. 4.

[NOVEMBER 1927]

TROPICS

by Alfonso Reyes

THE VICINITY OF THE SEA HAS BEEN ABOLISHED:
It is enough to know that our shoulders protect us;
that there is a huge green window
through which we may plunge for a swim.

It is not Cuba, where the sea dissolves the soul.
It is not Cuba – that never saw Gauguin,
*   that never saw Picasso –*
where negroes clothed in yellow and green
roam about the dyke, between two lights,
and where the vanquished eyes
dissemble their thoughts no longer.

It is not Cuba – that never heard Stravinski
orchestrate the sounds of marimbas and guiros
at the burial of Papa Montero,
that pompous rascal with his swinging cane.

It is not Cuba – where the colonial yankee
fights the heat by sipping cracked ice
on the terraces of the houses;
*   – where police disinfect*
the sting of the last mosquitoes
that hum in spanish still.
*   It is not Cuba – where the sea is so clear*
that one may still see the wreck of the Maine,
and where a rebel leader
dyes white the afternoon air,
fanning in his rocker,
wearily smiling, the fragrance
of cocoa nuts and mangoes from the customs house.

No: here the earth triumphs and commands
— it calms the sharks at its feet;
and between the cliffs, last vestiges of Atlantis,
the sponges of poisonous algae
taint the distance, where the sea hangs in the air
with a green gall like violet.
    It is enough to know that our shoulders protect us:
the city opens to the coast
only its service doors.

    In the weariness of the wharves
the stevedores are no sailors:
they carry under the brim of their hats
a sun of the fields:
men color of man,
sweat makes you kin to the donkey
— and you balance your torsoes
with the weight of civilian pistols.

    Heron Proal, hands joined and eyes lowered,
carries the holy word to the people;
and the sashes of the shirt-sleeved officers
hold the overflowing of their bellies
with a sparkling row of bullets.

        The shadow of birds
dances upon the ill-swept squares.
There is a noise of wings on the high towers.

        The best murderer in the country,
old and hungry, tells of his prowess.
A man from Juchitlan, slave enchained
to the burden upon which he rests,
seeks and catches, with his bare foot,
the cigar which the siesta dream
had let fall from his mouth.

        The captains who have seen so much,
enjoy, in silence,

the mint drinks in the doorways;
and all the storms of the Canary Islands;
and Cap Vert with its motley lighthouses;
and the China ink of the Yellow Sea;
and the Red Sea glimpsed afar
                   — once cleft by the Jewish prophet's rod;
and the Rio Negro where float
the caravels of skulls of those elephants
that helped along the Deluge with their trunks;
and the Sulphur Sea
   — where the horsemen perished, men and goods;
and that of Azogue that gives teeth of gold
to the Malayan pirate crews,
— all this is revived in the smell of sugar alcohol,
and, wearing the thin blue, three-striped caps,
they leave the captured butterflies,
while whirling clouds of smoke float up
from pipes with cherry stems.

           The vicinity of the sea is abolished.
The errant yelp of brass and wood-winds
rides around in a street-car.
It is enough to know that our shoulders protect us.

           (A huge green window behind us . . .)
the alcohol of the sun paints with sugar
the crumbling walls of the houses.
(. . . through which we plunge for a swim.)

           Honey of sweat akin to the donkey;
and men color of men
contrive new laws,
in the midst of the squares
where bird-shadows roam.

   And I herald the attack on the volcanoes
by those who have their shoulders to the sea:
when the eaters of insects
will drive the locusts away with their feet,

Alfonso REYES

– and within the silence of the capitals,
we will hear the coming of sandalled foot-falls,
and the thunder of Mexican flutes.

Vera Cruz, 1925.

Translated from the Mexican by the MARQUISE D'ELBÉE.

[FALL 1928]

CUT-OUTS FOR THE KIDDIES [1927]

"Feeling it our duty to read both (Miss Stein's *Elucidation* as originally printed and corrected version), we did so, then we cut up the supplement and the magazine into little pieces, and pasted them in another order. This failed to make any sense either, so we next cut up the two versions again, pasted them on typewriter paper, and, standing at the foot of a tall stairway, threw them with all our might. We then collected them in the order in which they landed, but still the words, while they were all very nice words, didn't make sense, so we gave it up."

Boston *Transcript.*

SEA-GHOST

by Laura Riding

A GHOST ROSE WHEN THE WAVES ROSE,
When the waves sank stood columnwise
And broken: archaic is
The spirituality of sea,
Water haunted by an imagination
Like water previously.

More ghost when no ghost,
When the waves explain
Eye to the eye . . .

Three dolphins made the day legendary,
And the ventriloquist gulls,
Their three-element voice and angularity.
But one natural ghost at sea
Outranks the legends,
Ages the memory with restlessness,
The volcanic mind long cool in water and man
Except at night, when the sea is feverish
And a warm drizzle assails the eye
With the inhabitants of the shoreless
Premonition of earth and water,
Day and night, man and ghost.

[JUNE 1927]

AND THIS IS LOVELINESS
by Laura Riding

BECAUSE THE ARMS, EYES, STANDING GRACE
And other praiseworthies
Please other arms and eyes and graces,
This is not beauty in them,
It is a stupidness.
   Beauty is a kind word.

Each part knows what it is,
And this is truthfulness.
Each part knows what it does,
And this is goodness.
Each part alone is stupid,
And this is loveliness.

But beauty flatters like a germ,
Turns to a richness,
Swells up the limbs,
Puffs out the faces,
Infects the mouths with majesty
And looking-glass grimaces,
Spreads like dropsy
Among praise worthies,
Betraying stupidness
To its stupidities,
Beauty to kindness,
Words, beauties.

[DECEMBER 1927]

IN A CAFE

by Laura Riding

THIS IS THE SECOND TIME I HAVE SEEN THAT GIRL HERE. WHAT MAKES ME SUSPI-cious is that her manner has not changed. From her ears I should say she is Polish. If this is so, is it not dangerous to drink coffee here? Does anyone else think of this I wonder? Yet why should I be suspicious? And why should her manner not remain unchanged? She has probably been cold, unhappy, unsuccessful or simply not alive ever since I saw her last. Quite sentimentally I wish her success. The man who is making sketches from pictures in the Art Magazine may find her little Polish ears not re-pulsive. For good luck I turn away and do not look at her again. I, who am neither primitive nor genteel, like this place because it has brown curtains of a shade I do not like. Everything, even my position, which is not against the wall, is unsatisfactory and pleasing: the men coming too hurriedly, the women too comfortably from the lavatories, which are in an unnecessarily prominent position – all this is disgusting; it puts me in a sordid good-humour. This attitude I find to be the only way in which I can defy my own intelligence. Otherwise I should become barbaric and be a modern artist and intelligently mind everything, or I should become civilized and be a Christian Scientist and intelligently mind nothing. Plainly the only prob-lem is to avoid that love of lost identity which drives so many clever people to hold difficult points of view – by *difficult* I mean big and obviously re-ligious points of view which absorb their personality. I for one am resolved to mind or not mind only to the degree where my point of view is no larger than myself. I thus have a great number of points of view no larger than the fingers of my hand and which I can treat as I treat the fingers of my hand, to hold my cup, to tap the table for me and fold themselves away when I do not wish to think. If I fold them away now, then I am sitting here all this time (without ordering a second cup) because other people go on sitting here, not because I am thinking. It is all indeed, I admit rather horrible. But if I remain a person instead of becoming a point of view, I have no contact with horror. If I become a point of view, I become a force and am brought into direct contact with horror, another force. As well set one plague of cats loose upon another and expect peace of it. As a force I have power, as a per-son virtue. All forces eventually commit suicide with their power, while vir-tue in a person merely gives him a small though constant pain from being continuously touched, looked at, mentally handled; a pain by which he learns to recognize himself. Poems, being more like persons, probably only squirm every time they are read and wrap themselves round more tightly. Pictures and pieces of music, being more like forces, are soon worn out by the power that holds them together. To me pictures and music are always like stories told backwards; or like this I read in the newspaper: "Up to the last she retained all her faculties and was able to sign checks."

It is certainly time for me to go and yet I do not in the least feel like going. I have been through certain intimacies and small talk with everything here, when I go out I shall have to begin all over again in the street, in addition to wondering how many people are being run over behind me; when I get home I shall turn on the light and say to myself how glad I am it is winter, with no moths to kill. And I shall look behind the curtain where my clothes hang and think that I have done this ever since the homocidal red-haired boy confided his fear to me and I was sorry for him and went to his room and did it for him. And my first look round will be a Wuthering-Heights look; after that I shall settle down to work and forget about myself.

I am well aware that we form, all together, one monster. But I refuse to giggle and I refuse to be frightened and I refuse to be fierce. Nor will I feed or be fed on. I will simply think of other things. I will go now. Let them stare. I am well though eccentricly dressed.

[OCTOBER 1927]

GOOD VALUE [1927]

"Contains 182 pages."

Samuel Dashiell, New York *Evening Post.*

AUTUMN DAY

by Rainer Maria Rilke

LORD: IT IS TIME. SUMMER WAS VERY GREAT.
Lay thy shadow on the sunny hours
and on the fields let loose thy winds.

Command the last fruits to ripen,
give them still two southerly days,
press them to fulfilment and hunt
the last sweetness to the heavy wine.

Who still has no house, builds no more,
who still alone, will long remain so,
will wake, read, write long letters,
and in the lanes will here and there
unsettled wander, as the leaves are driven.

Translated from the German by
ZORA PUTNAM WILKINS.

Rainer Maria RILKE

REMEMBRANCE

by Rainer Maria Rilke

AND YOU AWAIT, AWAIT THE ONE THING
your life without end to augment;
the mighty, the marvelous,
the awakening of stones,
depths turned back to you.

Dusk falls on the bookcases,
the volumes in gold and brown;
and you think of lands traveled over,
of pictures, of the garments,
of women lost once more

And all at once you know: That was it.
You raise yourself, and before you stand
from a long departed year
anguish and dread and prayer.

Translated from the German by
ZORA PUTNAM WILKINS.

[SEPTEMBER 1927]

PRESENTIMENT

by Rainer Maria Rilke

I AM LIKE A PENNANT FROM AFAR ENCIRCLED.
I forebode the destined winds; I must live them
while nothing down below has yet begun to stir;
the doors are still closing softly: in the chimneys there is quiet;
not yet do windows quiver and still the dust lies heavy.
Already I know the storm: I am stirred like the sea.
I stretch and strain, fall back again,
and hurl myself up, and am all alone
in the great storm.

Translated from the German by ZORA PUTNAM WILKINS.

[SEPTEMBER 1927]

Diego Rivera

Mural

*[From the following issue:] The name of the
Mexican painter Rivera was given in the last
number of* transition *as Piedro Rivera. His name
is Diego Rivera.*

[FEBRUARY 1929]

FAULA AND FLONA

by Theo Rutra

THE LILYGUSHES RING AND TING THE BILBELS IN THE IVILLEY. LILOOLS sart slingslongdang into the clish of sun. The pool dries must. The morrowlei loors in the meaves. The sardinewungs flir flar and meere. A flishflashfling hoohoos and haas. Long shill the mellohooloolooos. The rangomane clanks jungling flight. The elegoat mickmecks and crools. A rabotick ringrangs the stam. A plutocrass with throat of steel. Then woor of meadowcalif's rout. The hedgeking gloos. And matemaids click for dartalays.

[JUNE 1929]

ANDRE MASSON

by Theo Rutra

THE LOORABALBOLI GLIDES THROUGH THE ALGROVES SUDDENLY TURNING upon itself. There is a spiral spatter of silver. A thunderbelt lies in white. The rolls drum down the hidden malvines, where the gullinghales flap finwings casually. The feathers of the salibri glint in the marlite. Then the loorabalboli sings: "O puppets of the eremites, the weedmaids fever love. Send Octobus to shores of clay; thieve younglings out of sheaves of ice." And troutroots dance. There is a blish. A wonderlope whirs through the floom.

[FEBRUARY 1929]

Philippe SOUPAULT

POEM

by Philippe Soupault

my thirst is too big
I stop and wait
for the light
Paradise paradise paradise

(Authorized translation from the French by EUGENE JOLAS.*)*

[APRIL 1927]

SOME OPINIONS [1929]

– Transition is the most representative magazine of modern tendencies
in the English language today . . . – Bernard Fay in *La Revue Hebdomadaire*

Kurt Schwitters

Workman's Picture

*Kurt Schwitters is a German living in Hannover, who conceived independently
the idea of using materials other than pigments for flat compositions in color.
During the past several weeks he has been engaged solely in answering
messages of congratulation he received on his fortieth birthday.*

[JUNE 1927]

DESCRIPTIONS OF LITERATURE
by Gertrude Stein

A BOOK WHICH SHOWS THAT THE NEXT AND BEST IS TO BE FOUND OUT when there is pleasure in the reason.

For this reason.

A book in which by nearly all of it finally and an obstruction it is planned as unified and nearly a distinction. To be distinguished is what is desired.

A book where in part there is a description of their attitude and their wishes and their ways.

A book which settles more nearly than has ever been yet done the advantages of following later where they have found that they must go.

A book where nearly everything is prepared.

A book which shows that as it is nearly equally best to say so, as they say and say so.

A book which makes a mention of all the times that even they recognize as important.

A book which following the story the story shows that persons incurring blame and praise make no return for hospitality.

A book which admits that all that has been found to be looked for is of importance to places.

A book which manages to impress it upon the young that those who oppose them follow them and follow them.

A book naturally explains what has been the result of investigation.

A book that marks the manner in which longer and shorter proportionately show measure.

A book which makes no mistake in describing the life of those who can be happy.

The next book to appear is the one in which more emphasis will be given to numbers of them.

A book which when you open it attracts attention by the undoubted denial of photography as an art.

A book which reminds itself that having had a custom it only needs more of it and more.

A book which can not imbue any one with any desire except the one which makes changes come later.

A book explaining why more of them feel as they do.

A book which attracts attention.

A book which is the first book in which some one has been telling why on one side rather than on the other there is a tendency to shorten shorten what. Shorten more.

A book which plans homes for any of them.

A book a book telling why when at once and at once.

A book telling why when said that, she answered it as if it were the same.

A book which tells why colonies have nearly as many uses as they are to have now.

A book which makes no difference between one jeweler and another.

A book which mentions all the people who have had individual chances to come again.

A book in translation about eggs and butter.

A book which has great pleasure in describing whether any further attention is to be given to homes where homes have to be homes.

A book has been carefully prepared altogether.

A book and deposited as well.

A book describing fishing exactly.

A book describing six and six and six.

A book describing six and six and six seventy-two.

A book describing Edith and Mary and flavouring fire.

A book describing as a man all of the same ages all of the same ages and nearly the same.

A book describing hesitation as exemplified in plenty of ways.

A book which chances to be the one universally described as energetic.

A book which makes no mistakes either in description or in departure or in further arrangements.

A book which has made all who read it think of the hope they have that sometime they will have fairly nearly all of it at once.

A book in which there is no complaint made of forest fires and water.

A book more than ever needed.

A book made to order and the only thing that was forgotten in ordering was what no one objects to. Can it easily be understood. It can and will.

A book which places the interest in those situations which have something to do with recollections and with returns.

A book with more respect for all who have to hear and have heard a

Gertrude STEIN

book with more respect for all who have heard it.

A book more than ever read.

A book by and by.

A book not nearly so much better than ever.

A book and fourteen. The influence of this book is such that no one has had more than this opportunity.

A book of dates and fears.

A book more than ever a description of happiness and as you were.

A book which makes the end come just as soon as it is intended.

A book which asks questions of every one.

A book fairly certain of having admirers when at once there are admirers of it.

A book which shows that agreeableness can be a feature of it all.

A book which makes a play of daughter and daughters.

A book which has character and shows that no one need deceive themselves as to the sending of gifts.

A book which has a description of the selection and placing of chairs as an element in Viennese and American life.

A book which standardizes requests and announcements.

A book which urges and reasonably so the attraction of some for others.

A book in which there is no mention of advantages.

A book attaching importance to english and french names.

A book which has to be carefully read in order to be understood and so that the illusion of summer and summer and summer and summer does not remain deceiving. So much so.

A book narrowly placed on the shelf and often added. Added to that.

A book of addresses invented for the sake of themselves.

A book and a bookstore. A book for them. Will they be in it.

[SUMMER 1928]

SOME OPINIONS [1929]

... that irritating hodgepodge of genius and nonsense ... transition ...
Lewis Gannett in the New York Herald-Tribune.

THE LIFE OF JUAN GRIS
THE LIFE AND DEATH OF JUAN GRIS

by Gertrude Stein

JUAN GRIS WAS ONE OF THE YOUNGER CHILDREN OF A WELL TO DO merchant of Madrid. The earliest picture he has of himself is at about five years of age dressed in a little lace dress standing beside his mother who was very sweet and pleasantly maternal looking. When he was about seven years old his father failed in business honourably and the family fell upon very hard times but in one way and another two sons and a daughter lived to grow up well educated and on the whole prosperous. Juan went to the school of engineering at Madrid and when about seventeen came to Paris to study. He tells delightful stories of his father and Spanish ways which strangely enough he never liked. He had very early a very great attraction and love for french culture. French culture has always seduced me he was fond of saying. It seduces me and then I am seduced over again. He used to tell how Spaniards love not to resist temptation. In order to please them the better class merchants such as his father would always have to leave many little things about everything else being packages carefully tied up and in the back on shelves. He used to dwell upon the lack of trust and comradeship in Spanish life. Each one is a general or does not fight and if he does not fight each one is a general. No one that is no Spaniard can help any one because no one no Spaniard can help any one. And this being so and it is so Juan Gris was a brother and comrade to every one being one as no one ever had been one. That is the proportion. One to any one number of millions. That is any proportion. Juan Gris was that one. French culture was always a seduction. Bracque who was such a one was always a seduction seducing french culture seducing again and again. Josette equable intelligent faithful spontaneous delicate courageous delightful forethoughtful, the school of Faintainebleau delicate deliberate measured and free all these things seduced. I am seduced and then I am seduced over again he was fond of saying. He had his own Spanish gift of intimacy. We were intimate. Juan knew what he did. In the beginning he did all sorts of things he used to draw for humourous illustrated papers he had a child a boy named George he lived about he was not young and enthusiastic. The first serious exhibition of his pictures was at the Galerie Kahnweiler rue Vignon in 1914. As a Spaniard he knew cubism and had stepped through into it. He had stepped through it. There was beside this perfection. To have it shown you. Then came the war and desertion. There was little aid. Four years partly illness much perfection and rejoining beauty and perfection and then at the end there came a definite creation of something. This is what is to be measured. He made something that is to be measured. And that is that something.

Therein Juan Gris is not anything but more than anything. He made that thing. He made the thing. He made a thing to be measured.

Later having done it he could be sorry it was not why they liked it. And so he made it very well loving and he made it with plainly playing. And he liked a knife and all but reasonably. This is what is made to be and he then did some stage setting. We liked it but nobody else could see that something is everything. It is everything if it is what is it. Nobody can ask about measuring. Unfortunately. Juan could go on living. No one can say that Henry Kahnweiler can be left out of him. I remember he said "Kahnweiler goes on but no one buys anything and I said it to him and he smiled so gently and said I was everything." This is the history of Juan Gris.

[JULY 1927]

POPULAR APPEAL [1927]

"Hopelessly muddled and unintelligible."

New York *Times.*

THE BROOKLYN BRIDGE
(A Page of My Life)

by Joseph Stella

DURING THE LAST YEARS OF THE WAR I WENT TO LIVE IN BROOKLYN, IN the most forlorn region of the oceanic tragic city, in Williamsburg, near the bridge.

Brooklyn gave me a sense of liberation. The vast view of her sky, in opposition to the narrow one of NEW YORK, was a relief — and at night, in her solitude, I used to find, intact, the green freedom of my own self.

It was the time when I was awakening in my work an echo of the oceanic polyphony (never heard before) expressed by the steely orchestra of modern constructions: the time when, in rivalry to the new elevation in superior spheres as embodied by the skyscrapers and the new fearless audacity in soaring above the abyss of the bridges, I was planning to use all my fire to forge with a gigantic art illimited and far removed from the insignificant frivolities of easel pictures, proceeding severely upon a mathematic precision of intent, animated only by essential elements.

War was raging with no end to it — so it seemed. There was a sense of awe, of terror weighing on everything — obscuring people and objects alike.

Opposite my studio a huge factory — its black walls scarred with red stigmas of mysterious battles — was towering with the gloom of a prison. At night fires gave to innumerable windows menacing blazing looks of demons — while at other times vivid blue-green lights rang sharply in harmony with the radiant yellow-green alertness of cats enjewelling the obscurity around.

Smoke, perpetually arising, perpetually reminded of war. One moved, breathed in an atmosphere of DRAMA — the impending drama of POE'S tales.

My artistic faculties were lashed to exasperation of production. I felt urged by a *force* to mould a compact plasticity, lucid as crystal, that would reflect — with impassibility — the massive density, luridly accentuated by lightning, of the raging storm, in rivalry of POE'S granitic, fiery transparency revealing the swirling horrors of the Maelstrom.

With anxiety I began to unfold all the poignant deep resonant colors, in quest of the chromatic language that would be the exact eloquence of steely architectures — in quest of phrases that would have the

Joseph Stella

Brooklyn Bridge

[JUNE 1929]

greatest vitriolic penetration to bite with lasting unmercifulness of engravings.

Meanwhile the verse of Walt Whitman — soaring above as a white aeroplane of Help — was leading the sails of my Art through the blue vastity of Phantasy, while the fluid telegraph wires, trembling around, as if expecting to propagate a new musical message, like aerial guides — leading to Immensity, were keeping me awake with an insatiable thirst for new adventures.

I seized the object into which I could unburden all the knowledge springing from my present experience — "THE BROOKLYN BRIDGE."

For years I had been waiting for the joy of being capable to leap up to this subject — for BROOKLYN BRIDGE had become an ever growing obsession ever since I had come to America.

Seen for the first time, as a weird metallic Apparition under a metallic sky, out of proportion with the winged lightness of its arch, traced for the conjunction of WORLDS, supported by the massive dark towers dominating the surrounding tumult of the surging skyscrapers with their gothic majesty sealed in the purity of their arches, the cables, like divine messages from above, transmitted to the vibrating coils, cutting and dividing into innumerable musical spaces the nude immensity of the sky, it impressed me as the shrine containing all the efforts of the new civilization of AMERICA — the eloquent meeting point of all forces arising in a superb assertion of their powers, in APOTHEOSIS.

To render limitless the space on which to enact my emotions, I chose the mysterious depth of night — and to strengthen the effective acidity of the various prisms composing my Drama, I employed the silvery alarm rung by the electric light.

Many nights I stood on the bridge — and in the middle alone — lost — a defenceless prey to the surrounding swarming darkness — crushed by the mountainous black impenetrability of the skyscrapers — here and there lights resembling suspended falls of astral bodies or fantastic splendors of remote rites — shaken by the underground tumult of the trains in perpetual motion, like the blood in the arteries — at times, ringing as alarm in a tempest, the shrill sulphurous voice of the trolley wires — now and then strange moanings of appeal from tug boats, guessed more than seen, through the infernal recesses below — I felt deeply moved, as if on the threshold of a new religion or in the presence of a new DIVINITY.

The work proceeded rapid and intense with no effort.

At the end, brusquely, a new light broke over me, metamorphosing aspects and visions of things. Unexpectedly, from the sudden unfolding of the blue distances of my youth in Italy, a great clarity announced PEACE — proclaimed the luminous dawn of A NEW ERA.

Upon the recomposed calm of my soul a radiant promise quivered and a vision — indistinct but familiar — began to appear. The clarity became more and more intense, turning into rose. The vision spread all the largeness of Her wings, and with the velocity of the first rays of the arising Sun, rushed toward me as a rainbow of trembling smiles of re-surrected friendship.

And one clear morning of April I found myself in the midst of joyous singing and delicious scent — the singing and the scent of birds and flowers ready to celebrate the baptism of my new art, the birds and the flowers already enjewelling the tender foliage of the new-born tree of my hopes — "The Tree of My Life."

[JUNE 1929]

[APRIL 1927]

A QUARTER OF AN HOUR BETWEEN GOD AND THE OFFICE

by Lorincz Szabó

BLESSED BE THOU, LOVELY
morning that pour
your warm wave into my face;
when I step over
my sad threshold: oh!
the peace of God
lies behind me already,
be blessed still,
lovely quarter of an hour,
when the rumbling street-cars
hurl me to the city,
the mills, the boring offices,
the fetid prisons
of the cowardly day,
when through the souls and through the windows
shines the oblique light!
                    Now
I belong to myself, furtively I receive
into my rejuvenated eyes
the warmth of gentle life,
the bright stockings of hastening girls,
the gipsy desires of misery
chained to money,
and I embrace my brothers running with me
in the street-cars that are hurled
to the city of money,
accursed prisons
of the inquisitor-day,
and dreaming with me of all the beauty
and weeping with every joy,
for this is the last farewell to life
this moment before the office,
in the sun-sprinkled street, this moment,

Lorincz SZABÓ

revolt of my rested senses,
daily hope for liberty,
unique and holy quarter of an hour
between God and the office.

Blessed be thou, lovely
trip in the street-car,
golden morning,
for having really stayed by me,
and joyously
accept the salute of those about to die.

Translated from the Hungarian by L. GARA and M. LARGEAUD.

[SEPTEMBER 1927]

FEARLESS IN ITS ATTACKS [1927]

"Onslought and ravage upon the English language."
Saturday Review of Literature.

LETTER FROM GREENWICH VILLAGE

by Genevieve Taggard

EIGHTH STREET, FROM THE 6TH AVENUE EL., TO THE SLICK REMODELLED Brevoort always seems to be especially New York. Sometimes when passing the newspaper stand under the El stairs near the cigar store, I experience the vague inclination to gather up the whole display of current stuff – to, see, perhaps, if by doing so I can really get at what is happening in the world. Most of us come to New York because of an obsession to find out, I suppose, – after trying all the transcendental recipes . . . (all the world's in your own back-yard, etc.) Well, I walk from 6th to 5th, and that's an end to it.

6th is more chaos than ever – add to trucks, trolleys and the smashing, El pipes and timbers and construction huts, and then add steam-shovels. Beneath the wooden planking is a raw cavern, a Grand Canyon, – a net work of more scaffolds, a few electric light bulbs. Out of the enormous dark, negroes climb in clay-covered rubber boots.

There's a nice new sky-scraper hotel at the other end of the block – 1 Fifth Ave. Seen from Macdougal, the effect of the proud thing is nice and theatrical. Macdougal looks like the centre street in a little French town . . . the life of the best skyscraper is only twenty years. Just now this our tower still has Xs on all the windows, Xs like tick-tack-toe marks. Nice custom. To keep a workman from plunging himself or something else, through a supposed emptiness. Some contractors make circles, but Xs are much nicer.

Aside from this, a few other things are happening in New York. There is a fine movie called *Sunrise*, directed by Murnow, using all the movie conventions with delicious seriousness. Then there is an O'Keefe show . . .

Stieglitz says something about cremating the pictures when he and O'Keefe die . . . Mr. Gorham Munson is giving a course on Prose Style at the New School For Social Research, and his class is publishing a magazine called *The Figure in the Carpet*. Mr. Orage has also been giving a course in writing . . . all literature brilliantly laid out with measuring rods, like the Eternal City in the Book of Revelations. As if it had been finished long ago. As if the fertility of America might not joggle or transform the values a little. Max Rheinhardt plays to papered houses; the Irish players fall flat. The Guild does the lesser O'Neil sumptuously. Robert Frost tells us that he is writing plays. Now that is news and good news. The New Playwright's Theatre has produced four plays, in an experimental fashion that deserves praise. But their plays undo all the excellence of the production. Dos Passos has made the sets, and they have been the strongest element in the theatre. The Playwrights excite my interest until I see with each production their conventionalities and their limitations reiterated. Mr Bertrand Russell has been lecturing here on things like, Why Russia has Failed and the Companionate Marriage. But if you want platform artists, Darrow is more amusing. He knows human nature, whereas Mr Russell has just been discovering it since the war, having devoted himself before that time to mathematics and philosophy. People keep coming to tea shaking a copy of *The Enemy*, but after they go you read your own copy again and discover all over again that the hard hitting Mr. Tory Lewis boils down shortly to a very small substance. His anti-arty attempts are to be applauded. But the man is scatter-brained in the extreme, and ill informed (which won't do for anyone who makes such a point of intelligence). A good Communist could make a monkey of him very easily. The strange thing is that he hungers for Communist doctrine. Only being that static thing, an Englishman, he can't bear the labels. And he offers us – think of it – after all the onslaughts on the shallow minded, the emotional minded – sympathy with the Catholic revival, and this recipe for international relations: the white races and the black races should be polite to one another. Like Sandino we say. Say it with bullets.

There's a fine Russian Industrial show just opening, and a marvelous Mexican show at the Art Center. Which brings us to Latin America. Diego Rivera went through New York on his way to Russia, and for one day was rushed from Wey's Gallery to the Metropolitan Museum, to Mr Pach's to the Daily Worker... and eventually, to a dinner for Theodore Dreiser, also enroute. With this difference, Diego was going third, of course, and Dreiser was going first. Also, of course, Dreiser didn't know who this big guy in the flannel shirt with the great laughing face like a luscious mural was. But he felt somebody in the room. The blue Dreiserian eyes kept going down the table to size up the new comer. Well, the two of them went off on the same boat, first and third – very nice, that was, – and if you will, perfectly fitting.

The Rivera drawings have been hard to see. Now at last the famous murals that stand on the walls of the Ministery of Education in Mexico City will be reproduced in a book that will be published next fall by Harcourt Brace, with, I am told, a very acute preface by Ernestine Evans. There is talk of a production of a ballet, entitled H.P. by Carlos Chavez for which Rivera has done some delicious sketches ... tropical fruits, American Marines and Germanic mermaids, all intermingled. Chavez is the musical sensation of the year. His music has the perfect energy and the perfect clarity of a composer of the first importance. His playing of his recently written Piano Sonata at the first Copland = Sessions Concert of Contemporary Music, was wonderful and bewildering. The last movement in a mighty jazz tempo is astonishing. Besides H.P., Chavez has written two ballets on Astec themes, and shorter pieces which are being speedily included in concert programs here and in Paris. Aaron Copland, writing in the New Republic says:

"It (his music) exemplifies the complete overthrow of nineteenth century Germanic ideals which tyranized over music for more than a hundred years. It propounds no problems, no metaphysics. Chavez' music is extraordinarily healthy, it is clear and clean sounding, without shadows or softness. Here is absolute music if ever there was any."

Put it this way: 1927 was the year in which HIM by E.E. Cummings was published, and 1928 will be the year in which it is produced. People have not quite yet discovered this way of putting it, but let us get it straight, in an extravagant manner of speaking. I would rather see Him produced than any play I have ever read. The only actors I know who have enough finesse to do it are the Chinese in a stock company on Houston street. As luck will have it, Cummings inhabits another language; it is being produced by the Provincetown in March.

That's about all the intellectual currents ... Oh, I beg your pardon, Witter Bynner has written a parody on the President's Daughter, in the manner of Frankie and Johnny, beginning;

Nannie and Warren were lovers ...

P.S. Time passes. The X's have been washed off 1 Fifth Ave. Dreiser came home from Russia, and wrote an excellent series of articles about his trip. (Please Wyndam Lewis, don't say that because I mention Dreiser and Russia, and Transition prints this letter that the plot you super-discovered is super-thickening.) And what is even more interesting, *Him* has been produced, and Mr Wolcott has made a ninny of himself, along with a few other gentlemen. The Provincetown has gotten out a little pamphlet, printed by that printer-angel, Mr Sam Jacobs, which I enclose to the editors of *Transition*. Did you ever run across the press notices on the first Ibsen plays which Shaw reprinted in his Quintessence? How like, how like. The production was excellent, I thought. The girl who played Me had the simple gravity, the slow childish feeling of the lines. Johnstone, who played the title-role was very bad at it, and since the pace and tone of the Cummings lines create the mood of the play, I think his lacks had more to do with the critical coldness than anyone has suspected. As a whole *Him* plays superbly; the author was quite right in thinking it could play on Broadway. It could – given a few changes in Broadway, perhaps. *Strange Interlude*, (some one has called it Interlewd), and *Him* are the only recent plays which have the fascination of writing about the modern heart and mind. O'Neil after everything is said and done, has written stupidly and ambitiously. Cummings, in every segment of his play has the tone, the structure, the angles and emphasis that make our time.

[SUMMER 1928]

Yves Tanguy
Landscape

Among the Surrealiste group, Yves Tanguy has achieved distinction within the past few months. He is 27 years old, and French. A year and a half ago he began to paint, without instruction. . . . [MAY 1927]

ROSARY SONGS

by Georg Trakl

1. To the nurse

WHEREVER YOU GO THERE IS AUTUMN AND EVENING,
Blue deer that steps beneath the trees,
Lonely pool at eventide.

Softly sounds the flight of the birds,
The sadness of your brows,
And your little smile.

God has curved your eyelids.
Stars seek at night, o Child of Holy Friday,
The arch of your brow.

2. Nearness of death

O THE EVENING WALKING INTO THE DARK VILLAGES OF CHILDHOOD,
The pool under the willow trees
Fills with pestilential sighs of sadness.

O the forest that softly lowers its brown eyes,
While out of the bony hands of the lonely man
Sinks the purple of his ecstatic days.

O the nearness of death. Let us pray.
In this night there will be unloosed on languid cushions
Yellow with incense the slender limbs of lovers.

3. Amen

DECOMPOSITION GLIDES THROUGH THE WORM-EATEN ROOM;
Shadows on yellow wall-paper; in dark mirrors there vaults
The ivory sadness of our hands.
Brown pearls trickle through the dead fingers.
in the silence
An angel's blue poppy-eyes are opened.

Blue is also the evening;
The hour of our dying, Azrael's shadow,
That darkens a little brown garden.

(*Translated from the German by* EUGENE JOLAS.)

[APRIL 1927]

TOTO VAGA

by Tristan Tzara

I

ka tangi te kivi
kivi

ka tangi te moho
moho

ka tangi te tike
ka tangi te tike

tike

he poko anahe
to tikoko tikoko

heare i te hara
tikoko

ko te taoura te rangi
kaouaea

me kave kivhea
kaouaea

a-ko te take
take no tou

e haou
to ia

to ia ake te take
take no tou

II.

ko ia rimou ha ere
kaouaea
totara ha ere
kaouaea

poukatea ha ere
kaouaea
homa it te tou
kaouaea
khia vhitikia
kaouaea
takou takapou
kaouea
hihi e
haha e
pipi e
tata e
apitia
ha
ko te here
ha
ko te here
ha ko te timata
e-ko te tiko pohue
e-ko te aitanga a mata
e-te aitanga ate hoe-manuko

III.

ko aou ko aou
h i t a ou e
make to te hanga
h i t a ou e
tourouki tourouki
paneke paneke
oioi te toki
kaouaea
takitakina
ia
he tikaokao
he taraho
he pararera
ke ke ke ke
he parera
ke ke ke ke

[JUNE 1930]

MAZEL-TOF

by I.M. Veissenberg

THE SMALL TOWN IS ROARING, FOR THE RABBI IS SINKING RAPIDLY. AND FROM THE first it is evident that the doors of heaven are closing.

Heartrending cries, mingled, are carried by the air. In the doorways of stores, saleswomen with pale faces stand weeping, and turn quiet and intense glances to the end of the street, over there. Chave Gittel, who sells pots and pans, runs excitedly along, her face flushed. She meets another woman, says something avidly, waves her hands.

And Hirshl, the teacher, hurries, with his thin stringy neck pulled out, hands in his back pocket, sharp elbows sticking out like the wings of a goose about to fly. A small schoolboy, with tiny feet and red flaming cheeks, runs after him.

"To the bes-hamidrach! To the bes-hamidrach!"

The bes-hamidrach is overcrowded. Teachers and pupils from all the schools have been poured together into one mass.

A Jew with a red sash tied around him stands before the shrine with outstretched hands, praying. In a whining voice he says the Tfila Lemosha, line after line, and the crowd repeats it so heartily and with such sorrow and disturbance that the children stand with open mouths and staring eyes ... There near the wall, a man hides his face in the psalm book with a bitter sigh, raises his eyes to the ceiling, closes them again, and remains so, motionless and with his neck outstretched, like Isaac before the offering. They all are praying, repeating prayers, and the rabbi's name has been applied in prayers over and over again, his initials beginning the sentences. The crowd prays, on and on.

*
* *

In the rabbi's yard they trample one another. Plain people, cobblers, tailors, – stand with fixed gaze. Young chasidim walk around in circles, their dangling sashes tripping their feet, scarcely speaking to one another. The teachers and pupils return from the bes-hamidrach. The teachers stand in a separate group, looking at each other, chatting quietly among themselves. School children, playful, simple youngsters, climb the fence around the rabbi's garden. They crawl over the ice-house roof and stretch out lengthwise and crosswise upon it. All their faces are turned toward the rabbi's windows. The sexton and members of the household run in and out, confused. Young men get under their feet. When one of them is asked what is new, he extends his hands, sighs and hurries away. Under the piazza roof, a large crowd of women stand, pushed into the corner, making faces and holding their aprons ready to cry.

Suddenly from the house comes a hustle and bustle. The crowd moves. The doctor tells them to pray to the Lord! Someone shouts from the window. The crowd remains stupified, and the women get loose, cutting through the men who give way for them. The women run with a yell into the street. There more women join them. On the way to the market place, the women are divided into two groups, one running to the synagogue, the other to the cemetery.

In the marketplace the men turn around like lost silent sheep until a worse bulletin is brought. The crowd remains frozen and trembling lips whisper:

Blessed Be Thy judgement!
Blessed Be Thy judgement!

*
* *

Now the crowd is left with nothing, without hope, without consolation. Just one, – to express sorrow for the rabbi's wife and orphans, and to count them. The gathering moved to one side, abandoned itself to God's leading and to his judgement they took for love.

The sexton is already running to the post office with long written telegrams. The windows of the room in which the rabbi was lying flame up reddishly and a thin cold rain drops from the leaden sky, drops upon the body as the parts of the body curl up and shrink. Women put up their collars and huddle their heads into their shoulders. Teachers huddle into the large red shawls around their necks, and their faces grow darker, bluer and more sunken. Lips and eyes tremble.

Then at night chasidim begin to drive in from the surrounding small towns and toward morning there is a commotion, the streets get no rest from cabs and carriages. At dinner time all the stores are closed and the whole crowd gathers in the rabbi's yard.

A cry is heard at the door. Open! Open! The coffin appears and the whole crowd moves.

They go into the bes-hamidrach to pray for the dead. It becomes crowded. No room for a pin. They stand, heads over heads. Men and women together, and over the tables and altar, everywhere, it is full and black. The burning light of the hanging chandeliers throws out heat. All the faces grow red, are covered with sweat, and the air is suffocating, hot and muggy. The coffin is put before the shrine, and the chasidim catch one another by the shoulders, their eyes reaching out of their heads. They hang in the air, one on top of the other, scrambled together. Then it is quiet, and everybody's eyes are concentrated on the center. Soon a thin small voice is heard, "Too great a penance you take, Lord, for our sins! You tore away our king of the torah and, more than that, you took away the tongs without which we can do nothing . . ."

And again it becomes quiet amid the women and girls, with kerchiefs on their heads covering half their eyes.

The coffin is moved, and the crowd begins to pack through the doors and the windows pushed open.

The street is already blocked. A chain of chasidim occupies one side and the crowd accompanying the coffin stretches like a long belt with thousands of faces. All the way, prayers are said, and the son and heir follows at the head, resting his forehead on the coffin, his face hidden.

In the cemetery, among the trees, the grave is already prepared and the final coffin is ready. During the burial they put the rabbi into the open grave and salute him with a mazel-tof and the whole crowd turns toward the son. "Mazel-tof, rabbi! Mazel-tof!"

*
* *

The grave is covered. The new rabbi says a prayer for the dead.

And a consolation, a new hope begins to blossom. Faces lighten again and in the eyes a new light begins to dawn. Everyone gathers around the rabbi, to see how godliness has reposed upon his pale face.

In the cemetery it is quiet. The trees shake softly, as if in prayer.

Translated from the Yiddish, and adapted, by SOFIA HIMMEL.

[JANUARY 1928]

HAS A PUNCH [1927]

"I must admit that this sample leaves me wobbling."
Brentano's *Book Chat.*

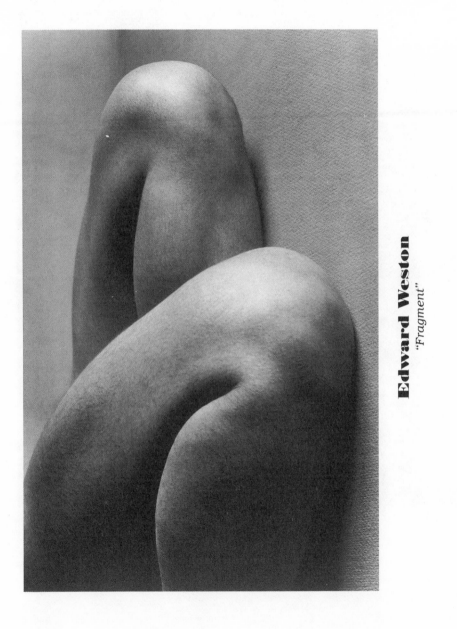

Edward Weston
"Fragment"

[JUNE 1930]

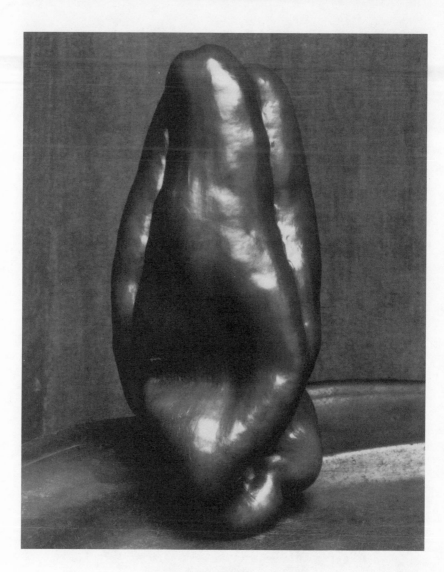

Edward Weston

"Pepper"

*Edward Weston is an American photographer
living in Carmel, Cal.*

William Carlos WILLIAMS

IMPROVISATIONS

by William Carlos Williams

THAT POEM JAYJAY

THAT DAY THAT THE JAYS PASSED US IN A TAXI AT THE ETOILE AND THEY waved their hands and smiled and he blushed crimson we took dinner at Seevées or when first E. appeared after fifteen years absence and I wished for a civilized world it was like the day Bill Bans sulked, twice he sulked, once at Chateau Thierry not when the smart young American rushed up to us at the table in the hotel and wanted to take us for a tour of the battlefield for ten dollars but because Susie was like she gets when she wants to sing but she wasn't that way that time but it was because of the brandy Bill had he isn't a bit French he is an American so he didn't roar or anything like when we were bringing the mustard back from Dijon way up on the seventh floor rue Vichy her mother was on the fire escape at seven a. m. when the taxi pulled up and all the neighbors stuck their heads out of the windows and she had on a bright red evening wrap the old driver, he was old, and he insisted on talking and she was American so she stopped and listened he said *ah c'est beau l'amour*, when I was young he said I too came home with the sun but if he had known he would not have been so fatherly because simple kindness is lost on Americans who – all over Paris differently from the Parisians but she was able to listen because she knows what a laboratory Paris is for dissociations one is split and the particles fly to Iceland and Buenos Ayres if you only KNEW what that does to me feverishly at a turn of his head low is high – is to lean from a crystal stem at chess slap jesus on the back and PROVE why Man Ray can never take off photo, NEVER, therefore photography is an art but could YOU stand on a table drunk and one by one take off your stockings at balance and let your tanned legs flame by the champagne darkly soft and low by pneumatique all the surface of the cathedral angels split off by the flames of war so that devils and angels are indistinguishable but slap him rudely on the back and his delicacy is at once apparent after all, Jake, aren't we all a little bit that way soft and low, Mengelberg holding the orchestra in his arms like Lincoln did the baby and rocking them while they puke and scream, soft and low, a great mother she said but we have to carry our men and fool them, nurse them take them take them between our breasts and sleep away the day on a newspaper on the grass and that is why Gertrudes Picassos, the blue and grey period look so well because they have such narrow frames and they are so close together in a row that it looks like the bottom of a great decoration that would be pretty if the top did not extend through the ceiling and is so lost in the clouds Van der Bile trembling-simply-together the new places touch and make it what she is, and do you mean to say these are all lost women, in a row naked before him at so much a piece Paris is not like that now but the scalp is yellow just the way she rubbed the lotion on it.

WELLROUNDEDTHIGHS

It is the pad that protects the adolescence, insulating it against the injury of knowledge and so permitting the strength for knowledge to grow, rather than the quite bare wire on which the colored swallows sat, the very small egg buried in the thick roaring womb that rides the elephant and turns three somersaults as if Jockey Joe Sloan did a snappy jig act between what's his name, the fellow that took Nijinsky's place, did that elbow trick *SALADE* and the scraped off evening in the Bois piece. Poor Nijinsky with a wife and Diaglieff, one driving him to rehearsals and the other dragging him home and both in love and noendtoit with the drill drill drill. He tried to manage himself but the English ass didn't get him his boots on time so he had to go insane diametrically opposite as if the Edinborough Review should say something uncertain it's the thunder that holds the lightning as much as to say: when the machine scrapes and screams carrying the advertisements of ladies hose around the curve, there is a machine implied that accidently carries the train and its occupants along. Without the roar to insulate the petty pimple of their comprehension there would not be a ground in which the MASS could accumulate, THUS conversely the Essentiality of the blatant and perfectly stupid excrescence like the New York Journal is mechanically sound and morally effective – and the whole mass is knit, generating the game of football – with its organized cheers. Baseball is something else the ball being harder, smaller, different in color and you hit it with a stick, that is although Babe Ruth may shine for a season there will always be a strong party opposed to him as a factor detrimental to the spirit of the game which is silent, saturnine, close to the principles of physics and lyric poetry.

William Carlos WILLIAMS

THE DEAD GROW

The most striking anachronism in N.Y. is of course the Metropolitan Museum of art with a slab by clever Paul to able John at the right of the entrance, badly worded, where Stonebridge of Hartford put a weight in the balance when he was sick of the ton of stuff he had lifted and the worst is that it spills over on the tall-buildings but it doesn't do it enough, like the rotten Stock Exchange like a dirty face without Pallas Athenas in it and the Telephone building and that crappy stuff – but the bronze tablets by Manny aren't so bad but nobody ever sees them thank goodness it would clip one ball if they did and that's what I mean, there isn't a more potent anachronism in the city than the museum – it is right because it's deadly, the detail of the ornaments and plates and vases even one or two pictures, the Burmese jewelry, they're the essence of the quietness, it's that that forks the noise out of its hole but if it weren't for the roar there wouldn't be any museum because the price of exchange depends not so much on the spiritual values but on the fat which has just this to do with art that it collects everything that is cast off by the dead and puts it on like the *peschecani*, you know, Thenewrich, the fellow who just has written a novel, without knowing that Leonardo invented the toilet-seat – you see the poet's daughter all nice and ripe, as Ken says, is noisy around the knees, that's what gives her the pull, Kiki in spite of her noise is made of quietness but the roar is full of pulp into which nerves and sinews grow a this and that anti-roar, is, valuable as it is to something or other like the history of Ireland or Ulysses, a compendium, very dangerous to growth. It is quite stark in its gentleness, it wants to – needs to have a kind of starvation on which to thrive and so make the kind of flabby shank devotees and condoms that John enjoyed when he was tired – it is a monument to John's fatigue when he felt the lead loose in his pencil, as Pop used to say, So it's dangerous and that's why we have prohibition, we don't need alcohol, WE DON'T NEED ALCOHOL, we have all the noise we want but even poverty can make noise enough to be heard in those places I'd like to see anyone he heard because he was poor here – here we are NOT ALONE, we're enclosed TOGETHER.

We don't know there is nothing because the essential noise won't let us hear it whispered so we don't need to play chess but there where the oil is burnt out the emptiness is being felt by the muscle – so we grow and they atrophy: they tried to make a noise with the war but it was a very silly deception, all we had to do was to know they couldn't make a noise and there it was.

[SUMMER 1928]

POEM

by Louis Zukofsky

COCKTAILS
and signs of
"ads"

flashing,
light's waterfalls,

Bacchae
among electric lights

will swarm the crowds
streamers of the lighted

skyscrapers

nor tripping
over underbrush

but upon pavement

and not with thyrsus
shall they prick

the body of their loves
but waist to waist

laugh out in gyre —
announced then upon stairs,

not upon hills,
will be their flight

when passed turnstiles,
having dropped

coins
they've sprinted up

where on the air (elevated)
waves flash — and out —

leap
signaling — lights below

[FEBRUARY 1929]

WHY DO AMERICANS LIVE IN EUROPE?

[Fall 1928]

Transition has asked a number of Americans living in Europe to write brief stories of themselves – their autobiographies of the mind, self-examinations, confessions, conceived from the standpoint of deracination.

The following questions were asked:

1. – Why do you prefer to live outside America?

2. – How do you envisage the spiritual future of America in the face of a dying Europe and in the face of a Russia that is adopting the American economic vision?

3. – What is your feeling about the revolutionary spirit of your age, as expressed, for instance, in such movements as communism, surrealism, anarchism?

4. – What particular vision do you have of yourself in relation to twentieth century reality?

Gertrude STEIN

THE UNITED STATES IS JUST NOW THE OLDEST COUNTRY IN THE WORLD, THERE always is an oldest country and she is it, it is she who is the mother of the twentieth century civilisation. She began to feel herself as it just after the Civil War. And so it is a country the right age to have been born in and the wrong age to live in.

She is the mother of modern civilisation and one wants to have been born in the country that has attained and live in the countries that are attaining or going to be attaining. This is perfectly natural if you only look at facts as they are. America is now early Victorian very early Victorian, she is a rich and well nourished home but not a place to work. Your parent's home is never a place to work it is a nice place to be brought up in. Later on there will be place enough to get away from home in the United States, it is beginning, then there will be creators who live at home. A country this the oldest and therefore the most important country in the world quite naturally produces the creators, and so naturally it is I an American who was and is thinking in writing was born in America and lives in Paris. This has been and probably will be the history of the world. That it is always going to be like that makes the monotony and variety of life that and that we are after all all of us ourselves.

Hilaire HILER

WHEN ALBRECHT DÜRER WAS ASKED BY LETTER WHY HE REMAINED SO LONG IN Venice he replied "Because here I am considered a gentleman; at home a loafer". The accumulation of the combined thought waves of millions apathetic or hostile towards any form of creative graphic or plastic expression showing the slightest originality, naturally affects the mental life of a creative artist living in such an atmosphere.

In America there are no facilities for the enjoyment of leisure or apparatuses for reflection.

Considerable time must be wasted in self justification both verbally and introspectively and many questions settled which are otherwheres taken for granted.

The spiritual future of America appears too remote to allow of predictions of any value at the present moment.

My feeling about the revolutionary spirit of my age is pessimistic in the extreme.

I feel that a painter occupies a place of real unimportance in an age such as ours. So unimportant is the whole field of visual aesthetics that it is left as unworthy of the attention of any first rate minds as a refuge for morons, unbalanced neurotics, and dull nonentities.

WHY DO AMERICANS LIVE IN EUROPE?

Robert McALMON

IN RESPONSE TO YOUR QUESTIONNAIRE: IN GENERAL YOU ASSUME MUCH TO BE true that is yet in the controversial stage; yet to be proved by history. We, deracinated ones, if we are deracinated, may not all have come to Europe impelled by some motive of the heart and mind. I came, intending to return, or to travel much. I felt in America that Europe was finished, decayed, war- and time-worn out. There it seemed that in Europe the sense of futility would be too enveloping. However there is the rot of ripe fruit, and there is the blight and decay of green fruit.

1. I prefer Europe, if you mean France, to America because there is less interference with private life here. There is interference, but to a foreigner, there is a fanciful freedom and grace of life not obtainable elsewhere. From various Frenchmen I gather that these statements do not apply to French citizens in a strong sense. It may be well to live in foreign countries; and to be definitely "deracinated." In that case the deficiencies of the land which accidentally gave us birth need disturb us no more than the legal, social, and human, infringments on our 'rights' bother us elsewhere. If by Europe you mean England, Italy, or Germany, I think America an exciting, stimulating, imaginative, country with the fresh imagination of youth and ignorance.

2. Is Europe dying, and is Russia adopting the American economic vision? Russia is a big and raw and primitive country with a mixture of many races. Before the war was the world accepting the German state-controlled standard of life? It's a quick judgment to make on Russia. And if Europe is dying, her various countries seem obstinately to cling to their convictions and rights. There seems not to be the breath of fatalism, shattered morale, or acquiescence, that goes with approaching death. By the few hundred years time that Europe is dead what may not have happened in America?

As to America's spiritual future, that is too involved a question to discuss, as religion, sentimentality, idealism, are so generally confused with an understanding of the word spiritual. Sensually Americans appear sentimental rather than aware, and childishly incapable of facing facts that France has faced for generations. England in this aspect may be decayed, as English people are aware, but 'decorous' to an extent that is unhealthy, publicly, whatever they are privately. As far as America's or Europe's future then, I visualize it as for the individual who does not look to a mass movement which lets him flow in its current on to victory. Possibly writers and artists in America will stop scolding about the state of society in their own country, once enough have become deracinated so that it is realized that all countries have their defects. Then art may ensue.

3. I don't feel that my age has a revolutionary spirit, artistically, or politically. The Declaration of Independence, a real revolution, took place sometime back. Impressionism, futurism, cubism, and abstract art-isms, were all pre-war concepts, and there does not appear on the horizon any new

originative forces. Beneath the coerced acceptance of the machine age I sense fear and caution, reaction, and sentimentality which is worse than decay. Communism is the natural, temporary outcome of the democratic concept, and reaction against it may at any time force an aristocrat-political theory, and that won't be new or revolutionary. Surrealism may be like Dada, nothing. At least the works of various sur-realists are unlike enough to furnish no clue, and Isadore Ducasse and Rimbaud, preceded sur-realism, utilized metaphysics, abstractions, darkness and madness and death, with perhaps greater force intellectually and emotionally, leaving aside the hysteria and commotion. Anarchism is temperamental and our generation did not invent the temperament. On the other hand our generation seems cowed and ready to conform, to submit or to run away. What it is they are conforming none of them, that is, us, know; not even the sixty year old peace conference gatherers.

4. My vision of myself in relation to 20th century reality is one of remaining myself, or hoping to. If that is impossible, what bad luck. By the time Menckens, Pounds, Enemies, and Sur-realists give their messages on what is wrong and what should be done, Transition comes along with a questionnaire. In any case, answers are contradictory, chaotic, and ineffectual with the wall of lost souls seeking a platform or expressing personal bias and frustration. I wouldn't dare mount one of the platforms in a rocky sea. Bad as it may be I'll do my own swimming. As to cosmic relationship, is there no God and isn't war hell, and there is the peace pact. May you, however, have answers from beings with more interpretive zeal.

George ANTHEIL

WHEN I RECEIVED YOUR LETTER ADDRESSED TO EXILES, I WAS ASTONISHED TO think that I was probably an exile, but it is undoubtedly true. The time flies to advantage in Europe, whereas much of it is wasted in America explaining battles that have been won years ago. My Polish origin means that I love the ground upon which I was born, New Jersey, with a love that it is difficult to explain, or understand.

Nevertheless musically it is absolutely impossible to live in America. I am a musician, a composer, and this type of artist needs vast organizations such as opera companies and symphony orchestras to write for to produce his works. It is not as simple or as inexpensive as printing a book, for example.

A young composer has absolutely no future in America, because, even if he attains the very peak of eminence, he cannot hope to make a livelihood, whereas in Europe he stands a chance of making anywhere from a decent three livelihood (after the early years of struggle) to even the accumulation of a fortune. This is because of the hundred first class operas in Europe which give performances every night in the season, a liberal amount of them being fairly modern. But America has only two first class operas, and it is seldom indeed that they give a really modern opera.

Moreover a young man casts his lot with that which is ascending, not decending. Europe is upon the ascent. Since the war forty new operas have appeared in Germany alone, while in the United States no new first class opera companies have appeared. Moreover instead of the three symphony orchestras that New York City had seven years ago, it now only has one. Contrast this with the four symphony orchestras that Paris boasts. Consider also the lavishness with which vast sums of money are thrown to old virtuosi; the absolute refusal to spend a penny upon any composer who can be called a composer, or who is even remotely recognized in other countries.

I have every hope that this condition in America will change, but I do not see how they can build two hundred operas overnight, or train the public to hear them, and as this will take some little time, I prefer to stay in Europe in the meantime, and learn how to write operas by actually hearing my own symphonies and operas for existing organizations. I trust that this will be no spot on my so far stainless Americanism for the *New-York*: 1928 group, but simply a very practical economic standpoint.

I think that answers your first, second, and fourth question. As to number three ... I am emphatically for what I have seen of the surrealistic painters and writers. Eternal revolution, and eternal change ... some day I may even turn traitor to these ... but that day has not yet come, and those who again turn to say that youthful Paris is wrong, will again live to see the day when they will rue their words. The old fools never learn.

Kay BOYLE

WRITING FOR AN AUDIENCE IT IS NECESSARY TO DECIDE WHETHER OR NOT explanations are necessary. They are not necessary. Neither human, intellectual, metaphysical or scientific. Explanations murder like a knife the perception. Explanations are the lie making it possible to accept the truth. If I, let us say, am seeking to live an absolute revolt against superiorities which even the most restless abuse but do not question, a dissection of my peculiar honor is beside the point. Explanations are invented as the apology for the action; invariably a collection of words as important as a lace handkerchief in a slaughter-house.

Any froth that blew around the Winged Victory, Greek contemporaneous froth explaining, cannot put a head on the woman today. It was an act and not an explanation which removed the head, and to that the blood responds, permitting no outraging of it, while the explanation says no more than this: my own senses, experiences, appetites, my contemporaries have confused me *let me explain myself*.

For this I have turned Indian, in an attempt to catch the sound of my own kind. But the hoofs galloped in another direction. For this I turned American to understand, but there were no Americans speaking for themselves. As a class they speak for a situation. Beginning with the composite figure of the American intellectual expressed for the moment in Mr. Matthew Josephson, and ending with the Unknown Soldier, each citizen functions with pride in the American conspiracy against the individual.

Do you object to a white bath every morning before breakfast? No, I like a white bath every morning before breakfast. But I say that it is a white bath every morning before breakfast and it is nothing more than one way of getting clean water into a receptacle without spilling a drop. Thanks to the efficacy of plumbing. But get into it with a literature in your head and get out of it clean to write the literature. To me there is in America no conviction which questions the value of inventions that protect the flesh from everything except the importance of being cared for.

The mechanics of America have afforded its intellectuals the opportunity to find words for what somebody else did. They preach, but they do not predict, for it has already historically taken place. They invent a lyrical explanation for form, and form has none whatsoever mystic-outline following necessarily the structure of action and not of evasion.

(I do not speak here of those artists who have subjected invention and hence given it another value. Steiglitz, Antheil, Sheeler, Man Ray, would, as individuals, have brought importance to any matter.)

In France this identical leeching upon a situation exists in the Surrealistes. They, too, depend upon bewilderment and ignorance in the minds of their audience for their success. They are livelier than the American Composites and they have an honor for they leech upon a situation created by other artists – possibly the Académie Française – but at least by men who make use of the same medium. The Americans, with a bastardly recognition for a thing stronger and better-equipped for life than themselves, are explaining a situation which has forgotten them. The American artist is no product of America's zeal, but he is one of those who has chosen to get outside it. Some of them leave the background and accept simpler conditions: Ezra Pound of the first. And the question is still to be answered: to what can one return?

Americans I would permit to serve me, to conduct me rapidly and competently wherever I was going, but not for one moment to impose their achievements upon what is going on in my heart and in my soul. I am too proud and too young to need the grandeur of physical America which one accepts only at the price of one's own dignity. I am making a voyage into poverty because I am too proud to find nourishment in a situation that is more successful than myself.

Cling, gentlemen, to the skyscraper by toe-finger-eyelash, but do not come to Europe. Here nothing is done for you. You must write your own literature, you must walk up and down stairs, and you must drink like gentlemen.

WHY DO AMERICANS LIVE IN EUROPE?

Berenice ABBOTT

To TRY TO ANSWER THESE QUESTIONS SEEMS ONLY TO SINK ONE MORE AND MORE into a maze of complexities, impossible to answer. However, I do not prefer to live outside America indefinitely. To live in Europe – in flight – as a solution can not satisfy. All this talk of deracination in this particular post-war exodus seems greatly overestimated. The very complex nature of America is, if possible, better understood from a distance than at close range. The extent of one's Americanism is put to a severe test, and that extent denotes the depth of the artist's capacity. What is more Irish than Joyce, more Spanish than Cervantes? To learn from Europe by affiliation-imitation and not by contrast is negation. America's artists must evolve from a civilization new-revolutionary in short, vastly different. The material at hand for artists should be limitless if they have the strength and vision to adjust themselves to a rapidly changing civilization, with or without the individuals, consciously or not, its very youthful energy will carry it on. In time, that dynamic momentum is bound to produce artistically and otherwise and when it has quieted down, become refined, it is in danger of becoming aesthetic. A spiritual future built on a material basis may be very great even if it is not the custom.

But why worry about the future? What about the engineers, the architects, Antheil, the comic movies, "Gentlemen prefer Blondes"? What about our Scientists, in fact? Why Surrealism, for instance? Microbes! (question number three) the biggest movements are not named . . .

Harry CROSBY

I

WHY DO YOU PREFER TO LIVE OUTSIDE AMERICA?
I prefer to live outside America

(1) because in America the *stars* were all suffocated inside
(2) because I do not wish to devote myself to perpetual hypocrisy
(3) because outside America there is nothing to remind me of my childhood
(4) because I prefer perihelion to aphelion
(5) because I love flagons of wine
(6) because I am an enemy of society and here I can hunt with other enemies of society
(7) because I want to be in at the death (of Europe)
(8) because I like tumults and chances better than security
(9) because I prefer transitional orgasms to atlantic monthlies
(10) because I am not coprophagous
(11) because I would rather be an eagle gathering sun than a spider gathering poison.

(12) because by living outside of America New York can still remain for me the City of a Thousand and One Nights

(13) because the Rivers of Suicide are more inviting than the Prairies of Prosperity

(14) because I prefer explosions to whimperings

II

How do you envisage the spiritual future of America in the face of a dying Europe and in the face of a Russia that is adopting the American economic vision?

> In the pagan unafraidness of a Girl
> and because she is unafraid
> > Chaste
> and because she is constant to her
> desires
> > Chaste

> > but the men are afraid and
self-righteous
> and disordered in their minds
> and weak
> and sunless
> and dry as eunuchs

III

What is your feeling about the revolutionary spirit of your age, as expressed, for instance, in such movements as communism, surrealism, anarchism?

The revolutionary spirit of our age (as expressed by communism, surrealism, anarchism, madness) is a hot firebrand thrust into the dark lantern of the world.

> In Nine Decades
> a SUN shall be born.

IV

What particular vision do you have of yourself in relation to twentieth century reality?

In relation to twentieth century reality and by reality I mean the *real* under-the-surface reality of our age I have the vision of myself as a spoke in the wheel of this reality moving

away from Weakness
toward Strength
away from Civilized Sordidness
toward Barbaric Splendor
away from Whimperings
toward Explosions
away from Ashes
toward Fire
away from Malted Milk
toward Straight Gin
away from Shame
toward Nakedness
away from Furnished Souls
toward Forged Souls
away from Canaries
toward Lions
away from Mesquinerie
toward Madness
away from Plural
toward Singular
away from Moon
toward Sun.

Kathleen CANNELL

I DO NOT PREFER TO LIVE OUTSIDE AMERICA. I WOULD PREFER TO LIVE IN AMERICA if I could make enough money to do so. It happens that I have lived more than half of my life in Europe. During the war I spent a number of years in New York, where I had not been since the age of seven. In spite of the fact that I never made enough money to be even reasonably comfortable there, I have never been so much alive as at that period. I find the American life and climate stimulating. Americans in Europe are apt to go soft.

I am too self-centered to answer your second question. The only spiritual future which preoccupies me is my own and it leaves me no time for prophecy.

I was at one time an ardent and rather active Communist. I have since become convinced of the vanity of *movements*, preferring to turn my good old American instinct for reform upon the only person over whom I have any control — myself.

I love living in the twentieth century. It is full of everything that has ever been in the world and of some new things. People who pine for other ages would have pined wherever they lived. To wail against your age is a confession of weakness.

H. Wolf KAUFMAN

I PREFER TO LIVE OUTSIDE OF AMERICA CHIEFLY BECAUSE I ONCE HAD MONEY enough to leave America with and the desire to leave America at the same time. It was a coincidence and I took advantage of it. There has never been a coincidence since. I have never had both the desire to go back and the money to go back with at the same time.

I first conceived the notion of leaving America because I was disatisfied with existing conditions. I didn't like the grade of books the bookshops were selling. I bought a copy of Frank Harris, after saving my money for six weeks, and the bookdealer who sold me the book was arrested by a big-eared nitwit who stood around and watched the transaction. But what made me more angry than ever was that the janitress of my apartment house, or to put it more exactly the janitress of the apartment house in which I rented a two room back apartment, objected to my sitting on the front door steps and waiting for my wife to come home when I had lost the key to the door. It wasn't dignified, she said, it didn't look nice and the other people in the building complained.

Since I have come to know Paris I have become less irritable. I don't like the sound of the French language, I don't like the Russian taxi-drivers, I would like to have some good American coffee at the same time that I eat my meat, and I would like the newspaper for which I work to pay me enough to enable me to go to concerts when the notion strikes me. But I have come to the conclusion that there would be just as many irritable things in Berlin, or Vienna, or Moscow, or Hong Kong. Which doesn't mean that I don't intend to go to some of those places. I do. If, of course, I ever want to go and have the money to go with at the same time.

I am not particularly enthusiastic about America in any manner, shape or form. But I do have the feeling – Lord knows why – that the "spiritual future of America" is worth watching as it evolves. And I think Russia is worth watching. A little later than America, though. England is stagnant. The best that England seems to be capable of is the inane cleverism of Alduous Huxley and the not-so-clever stupidities of Wyndham Lewis. France has all the leeway in the world. Therefore the French are inclined to lean back and take things easy. France is a country of French. England is a country of English. Spain is a country of Spaniards. Therein lies their greatest weaknesses.

I hate to use the word "melting-pot". But the American is a combination of half a dozen nationalities. After the ingredients get well mixed up I think some sort of result must burst forth. The first definite American result thus far has been a sort of dynamo-like powder blast. That is only a first re-sult. It isn't enough. Something else is coming. A couple of years ago, way down on Hudson street, I saw a little circulating library in a confectionery shop. The best sellers there were Dreisers's *An American Tragedy* and Hemingway's *The Sun Also Rises*. The owner told me that most of his customers wanted to read the books but later inevitably told him they were "rotten". Nevertheless, they read them. I may be a hopeless optimist. I cannot help feeling that if they read good books long enough, whether they understand them or not, whether they like them or not, sooner or later a bit of understanding will burst through. I cannot help feeling that if they buy good pictures long enough because they have the money and think it's the proper thing to do, sooner or later they will learn to distinguish between red and purple.

The critics brayed in their usual nearsighted fashion after listening to George Antheil in Carnegie Hall. But they ranted all over the front pages of the newspapers. The goddam fools didn't realise that what they were saying, in effect, was, "Here is important stuff that we don't like." Otherwise, why pay so much attention to it?

No, I think America will some day sprout forth. If you mix blue and yellow you get neither color for some time. Then, after mixing long enough, you may get a beautiful green. Give 'em time. Here's how. But – here's how from across the ocean.

IN MEMORIAM:
HARRY CROSBY

[June 1930]

HOMAGE TO HARRY CROSBY

by Kay Boyle

... While deep within our hearts shall smoulder
Strange fire growing young not older.
(Harry Crosby)

TO BE LIVING NOW, TO BE LIVING, ALIVE AND FULL OF THE THING, TO BELIEVE in the sun, the moon, or the stars, or in whatever is your belief, and to write of these things with an alertness sharp as a blade and as relentless, is a challenge that is a solemn privilege of the young. In any generation there are but few grave enough to acknowledge this responsibility. In ours, Harry Crosby stands singularly alone.

Maybe it would be a good thing if history were never set down. It imposes a tradition of standards that has to do with the experiences of other people and it makes criticism a literary right instead of a lonely deliberation of the heart. It puts a judgment upon man before he is conceived even, and judgment on the life he has not begun to live. And if a man write down his poetry and his life, they are doomed before they are written by the poetry and the lives that have been done before.

But there should be no confusion, no question, in judging the work of a young man who took his time and his contemporaries to heart. With all the nobility of his belief in them, and all the courage of his determination to make his life a testament of stern and uncompromising beauty, he wrote his poems and wrote his diary in words that never faltered in their pursuit of his own amenable soul.

The results are: one of the few important diaries ever printed; some of the finest and most moving descriptions of foreign places, of weather, of times of day; the speech of a young man who was so absorbed in the display of life that he had no time nor inclination for cynicism or for slander. Add to this some of the most delightful love poems of our time, and a lively sense of humour.

A page of his diary, written one April first goes as follows:

'The ramparts, and the sun is strong and lizards are basking in the crannies of the wall and I look down from the battlements over the new city and upon the steep grassy slope a girl is digging up dandelions while a dirty-faced tot ("a totty in her courses") clings tenaciously to her skirts hampering her labors. Red slippers and black stockings and the glint of a knife in the Sun and a herd of goats and a brushwood fire and the watching of her shadow and the mediaevalness of the ramparts and the strong interior feeling and Carcassone perhaps the outward symbol of the soul.'

And in one of his books of poems there is a poem:

'I have invited our little seamstress to take her thread and needle and sew our two mouths together. I have asked the village blacksmith to forge golden chains to tie our ankles together . . . I have arranged with the coiffeur for your hair to grow into mine and my hair to be made to grow into yours . . . but though we hunt for him all night and though we hear various reports of his existence we can never find the young wizard who is able so they say to graft the soul of a young girl to the soul of her lover so that not even the sharp scissors of the Fates can ever sever them apart.'

There was no one who ever lived more consistently in the thing that was happening then. And with that the courage to meet whatever he had chosen, with no consistency except the consistency of his own choice, and always the courage to match it, His heart was open like a door, so open that there was a crowd getting into it. And with his mind it was the same way. His protection was not in closing himself up when he found he was invaded, but in retreat. Retreat from knowing too much, from too many books, from too much of life. If he crossed the sea, it was never a stretch he looked upon as wide rolling water, but every drop of it stung in him because he did not know how to keep things outside himself; every rotting bit of wreck in it was heaped on his own soul, and every whale was his own sporting, spouting young adventure. If he went into retreat, into his own soul he would go, trailing this clattering, jangling universe with him, this ermine-trimmed, this moth-eaten, this wine velvet, the crown jewels on his forehead, the crown of thorns in his hand, into retreat, but never into escape. Either they would get out and leave him, the young boy making his own choice, or they would stay inside. But other than this there was no middle way.

> '. . . then if ever come (he wrote)
> Days which weigh upon the heart,
> Lead me quietly away
> Lead me quietly apart.'

TO THE CLOUD JUGGLER

by Hart Crane

In Memoriam: Harry Crosby

WHAT YOU MAY CLUSTER 'ROUND THE KNEES OF SPACE
We hold in vision only, asking trace
Of districts where cliff, sea and palm advance
The falling wonder of a rainbow's trance.

Your light lifts whiteness into virgin azure . . .
Disclose your lips, O Sun, nor long demure
With snore of thunder, crowding us to bleed
The green preemption of the deep seaweed.

You, the rum-giver to that slide-by-night, —
The moon's best lover, — guide us by a sleight
Of quarts to faithfuls — surely smuggled home —
As you raise temples fresh from basking foam.

Expose vaunted validities that yawn
Past pleasantries . . . Assert the ripened dawn
As you have yielded balcony and room,
Or tempests — in a silver, floating plume.

Wrap us and lift us; drop us then, returned
Like water, undestroyed, — like mist, unburned . . .
But do not claim a friend like him again,
Whose arrow must have pierced you beyond pain.

HARRY CROSBY
A Personal Note
by Stuart Gilbert

"LET US SUPPOSE," MONTAIGNE HAS WRITTEN, "THAT A PLANK IS FIXED BETWEEN the twin towers of Notre Dame Cathedral, quite wide enough for a man to walk along it; however great may be our philosophical wisdom, however staunch our courage, they will not embolden us to walk that plank as securely as we should, were it resting on the ground." The mere thought of that dizzy walk in air between the skyey towers, above Our Lady's pinnacles, was enough, a later writer tells us, to make some of Montaigne's readers blanch and sweat with fear. And yet how jauntily you and I parade that selfsame plank when it is laid out on the pavement of normal experience, little plainmen who rarely lift eyes above the shop windows and studiously avert our gaze from the insistence of the sun!

Harry Crosby could stroll that dizzy, aerial plank as easily, as carefree, as though he were walking down a garden alley of his country home; not that, through defect of imagination, he ignored the danger, but because he knew and welcomed it. If he ever felt a qualm of vertigo, it was, I imagine, when he tried to walk the plank laid out on *terra firma*, that safe and sensible promenade of whimpering "hollow men". He feared the *terre à terre*, the normal, as most of us fear celestial heights.

Seeing Harry Crosby for the first time, one was at once impressed by the lithe, faunal elegance of his poise, but most of all, perhaps, by the curious remoteness of his gaze. In the Parisian *salon* where we first met he seemed out of place, unseeing, as though his eyes, by some trick of long-sightedness or a queer Rœntgen quality of their own, were watching some aerial pageant across the walls, out in the blue beyond. Such aloofness was almost disconcerting at first; "a difficult man," one thought, "and perhaps an arrogant man," and turned for solace to the Marie Laurencin flowers, pink and blue petals of artificial light glimmering from the wall. But, when one spoke to him, there was nothing aloof, nothing of arrogance, in Harry Crosby. An expert in the conversational *vol plané*, he could descend without the least gesture of condescension from his eyrie and talk lightheartedly of the latest recipe for cocktails and the dilative influence of limp Parisian ice on their gay Gordon hearts, or of his latest *trouvaille* in New York 'slanguage'.

I never heard him speak ill, or harshly, of any individual – and that is to say much; his only enemies were Mrs Grundy and Mr Bowdler, legendary types. He never refused a service to a friend or even an acquaintance, and his generosity was unbounded, whether it was a case of paying the fine of some reveller whom the local police had sequestrated or of salving a poet on the rocks.

Clearest, perhaps, of my memories of Harry Crosby is an interminable automobile drive from a country village where I was staying, to Saint-Dizier, where *transition* is printed. Summer was ending and from vineyards stripped of a record grape-harvest (the wine of 1929 will yet be talked of when you and I are dead) wraiths of night mist were creeping to blur the pale French roads. Crosby's chauffeur, a dreamer and an incurable collector of *contraventions*, seemed unable to find his way; we were lost time and time again and Saint-Dizier seemed a mirage on a moonlit horizon. Yet there, we knew, *transition's* galley-pages were impatiently awaiting correction, and we were all rather cold and very hungry. Villages on the way seemed as dead as if the war had traversed them. Benighted peasants grunted misleading counsel. Crosby, seated beside the chauffeur, was content. To have lost the way – that was, I think, to him the best *hors d'œuvre* for the belated dinner, still far away, the spice of the adventure. Any fool can find his way, a poet alone knows how to lose it. Our hostess had pressed on us a road-map when we were leaving. The writer of these lines – more shame to him! – insisted on stopping to examine the map (like "any fool") by the light of the headlamps. *We had brought the wrong map!* Harry Crosby laughed, like a mischievous child who has taken (as they say in France) the key of the fields and is playing truant. Presently a rabbit flashed grey across the road, right under our wheels. Despite demurs from ravenous materialists, Crosby stopped the car and we had to spend a quarter of an hungry hour or more examining the road, and the edges of the forest which it ribboned, to discover the wounded animal. The cruelty of leaving it to a lingering death was, to Crosby, inconceivable.

Journey's end at last, and, after a hurried meal, we installed ourselves in a neighbouring café where, with the aid of "little glasses" of *fine champagne*, we set about the inky rite of proof-correction. Harry Crosby in his aviator's overalls (he had intended to take a flying lesson that morning near Paris but fog had, to his great disappointement, prevented it) created something of a sensation in the sleepy little town. Under the drastic invigilation of *transition's* Editor, Mr Jolas, a posse of proof-readers hunted down the inverted m, the bisected w, furtive misalliances of the lower case and neologies twisted into solecisms. Crosby and I, to whom our Editor allotted the same pages, had a little contest as to who would 'spot' the greater number of misprints; *amour propre* was saved, for we ended in a dead heat – a flattering result (for me), for Crosby had the airman's eye for typographical misfires. (I believe that my detection, at a first reading, of the unique printer's error in his book of poems, *Transit of Venus*, promptly ensured me a welcome place in his esteem!) Despite the superficial chaos of his writing he was an extremely careful artist; he brought to his work the vigilance and attention to detail which won for him his pilot's certificate after an exceptionally brief series of flights under 'dual control'.

Another memory of Harry Crosby, my last. He has just returned from the aviation field and is snugly ensconced in an enormous bed with a bulky

Shakespearian concordance propped on his knees. He has just looked up the references to "bed" in the works of his favourite poet, and is chuckling over them.

"To bed, to bed: sleep kill those pretty eyes!"

"My bosom as a bed shall lodge thee."

"Madam, undress you now and come to bed."

"You were best to go to bed and dream again."

"A banished woman from my Harry's bed."

"To bed, to bed! There's knocking at the gate: come, come, come come!"

Shakespeare, the Elizabethans, had an inevitable appeal for Crosby. Those were spacious times before the world had been straitwaistcoated with cables, iron roads and airlines. "Life ran very high in those days." Sonnets, *Sea-Ventures*, the "art of surfeit" ... "Hot herringpies," as we read in *Ulysses*, "green mugs of sack honeysauces, sugar of roses, marchpane, gooseberried pigeons, ringocandies. Sir Walter Raleigh, when they arrested him had half a million francs on his back including a pair of fancy stays." That was a world of gentlemen-poet-adventurers, made for Harry Crosby and his company, followers of the westward sun.

But now the earth has no mystery left, no undiscovered country to explore, no perilous seas of fairyland. We have, no doubt, the air – but, for all his airmanship, the pilot must make his goal of some known spot of charted earth. A bare three hundred years ago and Crosby would have been in his element,

> *A gallant knight*
> *Singing a song,*
> *In quest of Eldorado.*

All that is ended. In a mere decade the rich, energetic man of to-day can enjoy, or anyhow sample, all that this little old world of ours has to offer of diverting and exotic. "And behold all is vanity and vexation of spirit." There remain, of course, vast unexplored territories of the mind, dream-cities to visit, cloud-capped palaces to explore; but the high-priests of madness and modernity have blocked the way with their dopes and denials – *No Thoroughfare: Sens (le bon sens) Interdit* – till only one virgin adventure (if 'adventure' that can be called which is inevitable in life: an end) seems left, the final, futile plunge "down the Valley of the Shadow" to

> *the undiscover'd country from whose bourn*
> *no traveller returns ...*

HARRY CROSBY AND TRANSITION

by Eugene Jolas

I FEEL THERE IS NOTHING I CAN ADD TO STUART GILBERT'S MOVING ARTICLE: *Harry Crosby, a personal note.* The qualities he describes there of a comrade in life and letters were generously revealed to all those to whom Harry Crosby gave his friendship. I want rather to speak of him in his capacity as a friend of *transition*, which, while involving necessarily our personal friendship, nevertheless goes far beyond that.

In the spring of 1928 I received the following letter from Harry Crosby: "I have inherited a little money, and if you approve, I would like to send you $100 (strictly anonymous) for you to send to the poet who in your judgment has writen the best poem in the first twelve numbers of *transition*. But for God's sake, don't make a prize out of it. Instead of going to some fathead organisation, I should like this small amount to go to someone who will spend it on cocktails and books rather than on church sociables and lemonade. It you accept this, please forget it as quick as possible."

This charming and quixotic offer came at a time, when the coffers of *transition* – thanks to censors and other such cretins – were somewhat depleted, and it enabled us to pay promptly a few writers who needed the money.

A year passed by during which time Harry Crosby sent me some manuscripts – always with the modest suggestion to destroy them if I did not like them, and invariably accompanied by some Heinesque aphorisms and encouraging notes with regard to the offensive *transition* was then carrying on.

In the spring of 1929 I was faced with the problem of getting a certain amount of outside financial help. Harry Crosby's response was immediate, and in view of the unavoidable depletion of my editoral ranks at that time, he seemed the obvious person, by virtue of his keen understanding and fervor for *transition's* aims, to join us. His collaboration was, up till the end, generous, comprehending and unstinted, and full of that human charm that all those felt who came near him.

He was a mystic of the sun-mythos. This was not a literary caprice on his part, his very being was involved in it, he felt the planetary concussions, the fire-god was primordial in his soul. This chthonian faith colored his creative writings. His spirit was still fermenting at the time of his death. He was still groping, and we who watched his evolution noted with satisfaction that he was rapidly gaining more discipline and mastery over his instrument. Fate cruelly wrenched the lyre from his hand at a moment, when the creative spirit was burning brightest in him.

With his death I feel that not only *transition*, but the entire American revolutionary minority has lost one of its staunchest and most promising members.

A Requiem for Harry Crosby!

CINEMA OF A MAN

by Archibald MacLeish

In Memoriam: Harry Crosby

THE EARTH IS BRIGHT THROUGH THE BOUGHS OF THE MOON
    like a dead planet
It is silent it has no sound the sun is on it
It shines in the dark like a white stone in a
    deep meadow
It is round above it is flattened under with shadow

          *
       * *

He sits in the rue St. Jacques at the iron table
It is dusk it is growing cold the roof stone glitters
    on the gable
The taxies turn in the rue du Pot de Fer
The gas jets brighten one by one behind the windows
    of the stair

          *
       * *

This is his face the chin long the eyes looking

          *
       * *

Now he sits on the porch of the Villa Serbelloni
He is eating white bread and brown honey
The sun is hot on the lake there are boats rowing
It is spring the rhododendrons are out the wind
    is blowing

          *
       * *

Above Bordeaux by the canal
His shadow passes on the evening wall
His legs are crooked at the knee he has one shoulder
His arms are long he vanishes among the shadows
    of the alder

*
* *

He wakes in the Grand Hotel Vierjahreszeiten
It is dawn the carts go by the curtains whiten
He sees her yellow hair she has neither father nor mother
Her name is Ann she has had him now and before
      another

*
* *

This is his face in the light of the full moon
His skin is white and grey like the skin of a quadroon
His head is raised to the sky he stands staring
His mouth is still his face is still his eyes are staring

*
* *

He walks with Ernest in the streets in Saragossa
They are drunk their mouths are hard they say *qué cosa*
They say the cruel words they hurt each other
Their elbows touch their shoulders touch their feet
      go on and on together

*
* *

Now he is by the sea at St-Tropez
The pines roar in the wind it is hot it is noonday
He is naked he swims in the blue under the sea water
His limbs are drowned in the dapple of sun like
      the limbs of the sea's daughter

*
* *

Now he is in Chicago he is sleeping
The footstep passes on the stone the roofs are dripping
The door is closed the walls are dark the shadows deepen
His head is motionless upon his arm his hand is open

*
* *

Those are the cranes above the Karun River
They fly across the night their wings go over
They cross Orion and the south star of the Wain
A wave has broken in the sea beyond the coast of Spain

HARRY CROSBY

by Philippe Soupault

I SAW HARRY CROSBY ONCE IN MY LIFE. HE WAS RUNNING AROUND IN A circle and proposing a thousand solutions which he abandoned with a promptitude he did not want to hide. His great mistake, in my estimation, was that he accepted being a victim without protest.

The world in his hands was nothing but a ball he set revolving. But he, too, revolved around that ball.

The years passed and his circle narrowed. Friendship, love, poetry became words. Death remained the only reality.

SLEEPING TOGETHER

by Harry Crosby

these dreams for Caresse
"fermons les yeux pour voir"

FOR A PROTECTION

I SEE PART OF YOUR FACE PART OF YOUR MOUTH MOVING IN SALUTATION MAKING amends for the light wind that unravels your hair. I realize that the snowball I am bringing to you for a plaything is inadequate. There is for background a white colonnade a mere incident in the measure of the dream which is brought to a close by your turning into a heavy silk fabric which I wind around me as a protection against the cold wind which no doubt made itself felt in my dream because all our bedclothes had fallen off during the night.

WHITE SLIPPER

A WHITE AEROPLANE WHITER THAN THE WORD YES FALLS LIKE A SLIPPER FROM the sky. You come dancing over the silver thorns of the lawn and by holding up the corners of your rose-and-white skirt you catch the white slipper which I kick down to you from the sun.

WHITE CLOVER

THERE IS A CLAIRVOYANCE OF WHITE CLOVER, A COMING TOWARDS ME OF THE white star-fish of your feet, an aeolus of drapery. Your hand on the knob of the door is the timidity of the new moon, your hair over your shoulders a cataract of unloosened stars, your slender arms the white sails you lift to the mast of my neck. Not even the silkiness of newdrawn milk can compare to your skin, not even the cool curves of amphora can compare to the cool curves of your breasts, not even the epithalamiumic gestures of an Iseult can compare to your queenliness. Your ears are the littlest birds for the arrows of my voice, your lap the innocent resting place for the hands of my desire. And as you sit nude and shy on the edge of our bed I wonder at the miracle of the opening of your eyes.

In Memoriam: **HARRY CROSBY**

SAFETY-PIN

AUDACIOUSLY YOU PUT ON THE HAT BELONGING TO THE LADY AND WALK WITH ME down the abrupt declivity to the sea. A large body of water confronts us whereon is no ship wherein is no fish (so we are told by the skeleton of the fisherman) so that we are spared the anxiety of sharks. You are preparing to undress and are taking off your rings preparatory to putting them in the conch-shell which I hold up to you. You are having difficulties with a safety-pin while I remain an appreciative spectator. We are interrupted by the four winds whistling together over the burial of the dead but though we searched up and down the beach we found no corpse and we were forced or rather you were forced to return to the problem of the safety-pin which refused to open for the simple reason that your fingers were inadequate to the occasion.

HUMAN FLESH AND GOLDEN APPLES

LIKE THE HORSES OF DIOMEDES I AM BEING NOURISHED WITH HUMAN FLESH while you are eating the golden apples of the Hesperides. I suppose they are the apples of the Hesperides for they are so very big and gold. There is a clean sound of gravel being raked. The shadows under your eyes are blue as incense. Your voice is the distant crying of night-birds, your body is the long white neck of the peacock as she comes down the gravel path. Your mouth is an acre of desire so much as may be kissed in a day, our love the putting together of parts of an equation, so that when they knocked on the door at nine o'clock I could not believe that you were in the country and I alone in a hotel in New York forced to take consolation in the bottle of white rum that I bought last night from the elevator boy.

I BREAK WITH THE PAST

IN A HOT OFFICE BUILDING A MAN IS DICTATING A LETTER TO A BRIGHT-EYED stenographer who has just graduated from the College of Progress. Dear Madam I regret to inform you that your swans have sleeping sickness, but I am far away in the country wandering across the golf links your bright-colored scarf around my neck. I cannot seem to find you. I look into every bunker. I ask the caddy with the gluttonous face. I call out loud to the birds. I keep remembering how good-looking you are with your bedroom eyes and your new-moon ears. I begin to run. It is growing late for the red wolf of the sun has almost disappeared into his cavern of night. I run over the wooden bridge. I break with the past and race into the future over the far end of the links feeling myself fly through the air towards two sensations of light which turn out to be your eyes. When I wake up I am as tired as a marathon runner.

GOLDEN SPOON

Your BODY IS THE GOLDEN SPOON BY MEANS OF WHICH I EAT YOUR SOUL. I DO NOT seek to find the explanation for this curious sensation which is more visual than tactile. But I am afraid of the army of silver spoons marshaled in array under their commander-in-chief Silver Fork who is about to give the command to march against the golden spoon which I hold desperately in my mouth.

AUNT AGATHA

A LEG SHOULD BE MORE THAN A LEG YOU SAID AND I AGREED. THERE ARE caterpillars underfoot you said and I agreed for I could feel my bare feet squashing a liquid something. The secret of love is to be animalistic you said and I agreed for I like panthers. But when you said let us go to call on Aunt Agatha I tied you face downward across a chair, turned up your clothes with the utmost precision and was just on the point of lashing you with a silver switch when there was a shriek of laughter as the Gay Duchess and Elsa de Brabent burst into the room to tell us that their niece Little Lady Lightfoot had been expelled from school for having been caught in the act of kissing the Yellow Dwarf. Here the dream ended for I felt you pressing knowingly into my arms and I realized that it must be long after seven to judge by the position of the sun as reflected in the twin mirrors of your eyes.

IT IS SNOWING

We ARE PREPARING OURSELVES FOR THE HORRORS OF WAR BY VIEWING AN autopsy. A trained nurse depressingly capable sits by a stove reading aloud from the Madonna of the Sleeping Cars while you insist on telling me that for three years the chorus girls have not come to Touggourt. There is a turmoil of passionate red except for my hands which are two drifts of white snow lying upon the cool shells of your breasts. It is snowing and there are people in galoshes and when we wake up it is snowing and there is the sound of the men shovelling the snow off the sidewalks. It is one of those cold grey days when the wise thing for us do is to go to sleep again like bears in the wintertime.

WHITE AEROPLANES IN FLIGHT

We ARE FLYING. BELOW US THE LAND IS A SHEET OF NOTEPAPER SCRAWLED OVER by the words of roads and rivers. A cemetery is a game of chess. A ploughed field is an accordeon. Black hayricks are crows. We are one of an

In Memoriam: HARRY CROSBY

astonishing pack of white aeroplanes a million million in number filling the sky with a myriad white points of light hunting after the red fox of the sun. We lose him among the clouds. We find him again. But he eludes us and burrows out of sight into the blue tunnel of the sea and you and I are confronted by the unpleasant problem of having to alight in the Place Vendôme because we must cash a cheque at the bank before we can take a room at the Ritz. We awake to a bang. It is the femme de chambre closing the windows of our room while Narcisse is barking to be let out.

MIRACULOUS MESSAGE

I AM IN A PARLOR CAR. I AM IN A DINING CAR. I AM IN A SLEEPING CAR. I HAVE THE upper berth so that I cannot look out the window but I have the apprehensive feeling of things happening in the dark outside. A bearded creature carrying a telegram in his mouth as a dog often carries a newspaper is trying to get on the train. I know in advance it is for me believing what I cannot prove. I feel that I am indivisible with the telegram but I am not able to put my hand through the steel side of the car. I have already decided to hide it under the roof of my tongue when I am sleepily aware of a body stirring in my arms and of the utter uselessness of the telegram which could not possibly contain such a miraculous message as your "Are you awake Dear."

EMBRACE ME YOU SAID

EMBRACE ME YOU SAID BUT MY ARMS WERE RIVETED TO THE MOST EXACTING OF walls, embrace me you said but my mouth was sealed with the huge hot fruit of red wax, embrace me you said but my eyes were seared by the severities of two thousand winters – embrace me you said in such a low and feline voice that my eyes began to open like frightened shutters, in such a low and feline voice that my mouth became unsealed like red ice in a bowl of fire, in such a low and feline voice that my chains dropped like silver needles to the floor and my arms were free to encircle the white satin nudity of your voice which I tore into thin strips of music to store away in my heart whose desert had been threatened with vast armies of female laborers marching down dusty roads strewn with the prickly leaves of the cactus plant.

A PROGRESS UPWARD

OCCURING AT RARE INTERVALS IS A DREAM OF FAIRY-TALE LIGHTNESS MORE swift than the flight of tennis-balls. This dream consists of a progress upward towards a light metallic fire (sweet-smelling as a sun-ray) which pours like honey into a minute orifice rigidly exact whose organ of hearing is adjusted to the harmony of your hands.

WHITE FIRE

YOUR THROAT IN MY DREAM IS A SENSATION OF LIGHT SO BRIGHT SO SUDDEN THAT I am dominated by the image of white fire far beyond the moment of ordinary awakening.

REVIRGINATE

A SWIFT METALLIC MONSTER WITH EYES MORE PRECIOUS THAN DIAMONDS RICH IN the secrets of sun and wind whirs with the whizzing sound of an arrow into the direct centre of my dream from which you turn sleepily with what *is* the matter what *is* the matter until we both fall asleep again under you grey squirrel coat which I pull over our heads for it is bitter cold.

ANIMAL MAGNETISM

ALL THE SAILORS ARE LAUGHING. IT IS CONTAGIOUS. ALL THE WHORES ARE yawning. It is contagious. And all night long we wear ourselves out trying to laugh and yawn at one and the same time.

FAREWELL TO TRANSITION

[June 1930]

ANNOUNCEMENT

WITH THIS NUMBER I BRING TO A CLOSE THE DIRECTION OF *TRANSITION* over a period of three years. I am now suspending the magazine indefinitely, as I can no longer afford the expenditure of time and labor necessary to its preparation.

The transitional period of literature appears to be drawing to a close. But our experimental action, I feel sure, will constitute an impulsion, and a basis on which to construct for some time to come.

I take this opportunity of expressing my gratitude to those who, at one time or another, have been friends and collaborators of *transition*, especially: the late Harry Crosby, Stuart Gilbert, Matthew Josephson, Elliot Paul, Robert Sage, Sylvia Beach, Sonia Himmel, Maria Jolas, and Maive Sage.

EUGENE JOLAS.

FAREWELL TO
transition
A Letter to Eugene Jolas from
Robert Sage

London, 20 March 1930.

DEAR GENE:—

The knowledge that *transition* has come to the end leaves me with a feeling of sadness. My unavoidable activities outside of Paris these past months have deprived me of the closer association with you and the magazine that I once enjoyed: they have kept me too, I realize with regret, from materializing the various compositions which in optimistic moments I had hoped to write and send to you. But throughout my other occupations *transition* and its battles have been frequently in my thoughts, and it was always pleasant to know that the magazine existed and that a new number would be appearing sooner or later.

Now that *transition* is to be discontinued there will be a decided void. It is true that numerous other periodicals of a literary or radical nature are appearing both in Europe and the United States, but none of them seem (I am naturally somewhat partisan) to have the scope, freedom or unified aim which made *transition* unique. That the concentrated tangible expression of *transition*'s fight has ceased and that there will be no Number 21 and Number 22 and Number 23 to anticipate means that another appreciable dose of spice will be lacking from an ideologico-literary menu which at present is not over-laden with courses for exacting palates.

Yet a superb collection of souvenirs, both personal and literary, remains. 40, rue Fabert is an historic address for me, as it must be for you and several others. I shall always remember that little fourth floor room with its single window looking out on the Esplanade des Invalides and the dim vision of Sacré-Cœur on the hill across the city. And I shall remember the just-visible clock on the Gare des Invalides – sometimes a diabolic reminder of luncheon dates being missed, sometimes a convenient alibi for an apéritif at the corner bistrot, the Métro, Chez Francis or Ferarri's. The walls of Room 16 should be saturated with arguments, jokes, discussions, worries, mockeries and those pleasant meandering conversations which at college we called pea-talks. I always preferred the talks en famille, but how many people managed to break through the inefficient consigne downstairs to tap hesitantly at the door of 'the business and editorial offices' of *transition*! Delightful people and impossible people, who always stayed on and on (totally disorganizing the unpleasant but necessary task of completing the business details) until they were rallied by the irresistible suggestion of, 'How about a little drink down on the corner?'

FAREWELL TO transition

I recall, especially during the summer of 1928, the ritual of opening the morning mail, invariably rich with amusements and doubly so when a mail boat had arrived from New York the previous day. There were the unbelievably bad manuscripts from americans who interpreted modernism as an unsystematic garbling of words and from englishmen who apparently thought emancipation meant the spilling of the nastiest thoughts left over from puberty. There were threatening unpoetic letters demanding whether *transition* were going to publish that poem sent a year ago – *yes or no*!! There were those precious newspaper clippings which, with few exceptions, ran true to form – preliminary sneers at the Joyce-Stein contributions (the names, for some reason, were always linked together), the inevitable wisecrack about the small 't' in *transition* and the naive speculations about the magazine being composed on the terraces of Montparnasse cafés. And then, in magnificent contrast, the occasional appearance of an excellent manuscript from some person completely unknown.

It amuses me, too, to remember the freak results of publishing some of the manuscripts submitted. There was a certain short story which was so victoriacrossish in its servantgirl philosophy, so pompously sentimental in its style, such a complete burlesque of what a good short story should be that you could not resist publishing it. The author was overjoyed at its acceptance and, as far as we ever knew, no reader of *transition* ever found any objections to it. Then there were a number of stories which were on the border, which were finally accepted with misgivings – and which were immediately selected by the reviewers as the only worthwhile things in their respective numbers.

No one, apparently, discovered the ultra-assininity of an essay published in the first number as a test of the reader's discrimination, and I fear that few noticed the quite remarkable merits of the finest things which *transition* published during its three years of existence.

It sometimes seems, curious that even people of some intelligence cannot get beyond the lazy habit of accepting readymade classifications for all phenomena which come to their attention. To the end *transition* remained for the columnists of the United States and for many others a manifestation of Montparnasse. The more I have lived in Paris the less certain I have been as to the exact definition of that mysterious and derogatory word Montparnasse. It may mean the cafés in the vicinity of the Carrefour Raspail, or it may mean the Montparnasse quarter (which comprises probably a thousand times as many humble french working people as it does artists, near-artists or pseudo-artists), or it may mean a more or less definite social atmosphere of affectation, drunkenness, freakishness, unmorality, perversity (or perversion, if you prefer) and degeneration. In any case, however the word be interpreted, there is little actual application to *transition*. No one directly concerned with the publication of the magazine has ever been an habitué of the Montparnasse cafés, a resident of the district or a contributor to the atmosphere. But, because american reviewers like to think of Montparnasse as the 'artists' colony' and because they never took the trouble to understand *transition*'s rather simple aims, they persisted in putting *transition* and Montparnasse together, just as they persisted in finding an inexistent relationship between

Gertrude Stein's everlasting strumming on a single key and James Joyce's rich cosmic symphony.

But I am going astray. I am, as you know, sentimental, and I should like to evoke just one or two more of the many souvenirs before dropping the subject. Our promenades together through Paris, those stimulating impromptu strolls about the Boulevards, the Champs-de-Mars quarter, the Place de l'Alma and the alley-streets between the Place Saint-German-des-Prés and the Place Saint-Michel will always be happy memories, but I do not wish to speak of them now for I hope that the day will soon come when I may return to Paris and we shall be able to resume these walks – not forgetting an occasional Pernod or bière allemande en route. Unfortunately, however, I suppose, I am destined never to go with you again to that charming little town in the Haute-Marne, Saint-Dizier, where *transition* passed through the mysteries of a french printing plant. My memories of Saint-Dizier nevertheless are vivid ones – the station restaurant with its superb old dry Vouvray which we speedily exhausted, the amiable waitress who served the cobwebby bottles while they lasted, the abominable monument to the morts de la guerre, the thin canal and its locks where the barges descended in a seasick manner before continuing toward Paris, and the cheerful holly tree in the postoffice park. And that cold room where we corrected proof throughout the day except for the intervals of consultation with the suspecting Father Christmas. And then those evenings in the Café du Commerce whose buxom patronne was proud of the english she had picked up during the war but regretfully confessed that she could not keep pace with *transition*, and whose patron, fresh back from 'la chasse', was afraid to talk to you in german when there were customers about but became generous to a quite unfrenchlike degree with a bottle of Courvoisier (to his wife's dismay) as the evening wore on. And those eerie walks through the deserted and shadow-haunted town when even the cafés had closed their doors . . .

Inextricably associated with the recollections of my first days with *transition* and my first visits to Saint-Dizier is the shadow of Elliot Paul, rotund and bewhiskered and as mischievous as a Katzenjammer Kid. It is pleasant to remember those ridiculous games of croquet at Colombey-les-Deux-Eglises and the expert cheating that took place as we thumped the balls over the knobby ground in back of your home. But above all I shall always remember that peculiarly perfect summer evening when we all went out into the field beside the 'croquet grounds' and Paul's accordeon pumped out everything from *Nearer My God to Thee* and *The Trail of the Lonesome Pine* to russian folk dances and George Antheil, while we sat on the grass and watched the sun spurt deep colors into the sky beyond the rambling Haute-Marne hills . . .

But these things are only an atom of the experiences that have rolled out of the *transition* cornucopia. The magazine brought many people together, for better or for worse. More than one fine friendship developed, numerous valuable acquaintships were made. That sensibilities were occasionally trampled and a few vivid enmities produced was, I suppose, an inevitable by-product. People who are interested in writing have, or are supposed to have, ideas: frequently, however, they are not devoid of stubborn instincts. And individuals thus dually equipped are apt to clash in the manner of strange bulldogs. There were the lady geniuses (should it be geniæ?) who shrieked their loves and hates in print and a few males who tried for vengeance through dubious methods. Personalities sometimes intruded where objective ideology was more appropriate. But most of the sparks cooled with a few months of perspective and there was little permanent damage done.

The only betrayal sufficiently shameless to remain unforgiven seems to me to be that of Harold Salemson, the industrious young literary man about town. The lurid and distorted series of articles which he sold to an american newspaper syndicate should certainly blackball him forever in Paris. Taking Harry Crosby's suicide as a starting point, he wrote, as you know, a garbled 'cross-section of life in the american art colony of Paris' which resembled the 'findings' of a cub reporter from Kalamazoo who had come to Paris to 'investigate conditions'. In this series, which is doubly ghastly in its capitalization of the Crosby tragedy, the reader is presented a confused picture in which Crosby and a vague sensation-seeking 'cult,' James Joyce, transition, Montparnasse (inevitably), the Quat'z'Arts ball, Gertrude Stein, drugs, drink, Link Gillespie, etc., etc. all appear to be somehow involved in a wild and degenerate communal orgy. Hot stuff for the folks back home to marvel over with their Sunday morning pancakes, but utterly false in its correlations and malicious in its implications. The other quarrels and misunderstanding are lost in the multitudinous pleasant tangents of transition, but such a traitorous peddling of gossip and inaccuracy must remain a dirty blotch on the records.

Three of transition's contributors have died, – Howard Weeks, a Detroit newspaper man who might have become a fine writer had it not been for prohibition; Baronness Elsa Freitag von Loringhoven, whose eccentrically vicious talent was far from negligible, and Harry Crosby. Although I had always just-missed meeting Crosby I experienced a sharp shock when I bought a two-day-old Paris newspaper in Budapest one morning and read of his suicide. It was the sort of thing that puts ice in one's blood. To me it seemed a terrible mistake, for life promised more to him than to most of us and his true core of poetic talent would surely have crystalized had he persevered. Yet I know but little of his life and none of us can judge the solutions others adopt for their own problems. The affair was, of course, sensationalized and provided ample material for such obscene articles as those which Salemson readily sold; it gave ground for much smug moralizing and indignant ranting about the life which is supposed to be lived by the 'american art colony in Paris.' From what little I have heard I believe it was true that Crosby was eager to taste all the sensations life could offer him; and, having the means, he did so. Well, why not? Such an ambition may not appeal to you or to me, but what is there against someone else trying to achieve it? The attainment requires the courage and fixity of purpose which, bent in other directions, produce great poets, great scientists, great businessmen. It seems to me that Crosby's course was more admirable than a sanely mediocre avoidance of all sensation and danger.

It would be futile to make these comments and reminiscences of the past three years more than a skeleton, and of transition itself I shall speak even more briefly, for I know that you, who are so vastly closer to its life, are well aware of its successes and failures. Yet, in summarizing its achievements, your last letter omits many of the factors which reinforced the magazine's central aims. *transition* created a tremendous advance focus on the new work of James Joyce and inspired the illuminating series of essays written about that work before its completion, it pioneered in presenting english translations of Fargue, Benn, Perse, Kafka, Ribemont-Dessaignes, Soupault, Breton, several of the Soviet authors and other important european writers, it introduced into english the more valuable elements of surréalisme, it started the process of destroying the humdrum realism and stylistic banality which have so long characterized american fiction, and as you emphasize, it fired the first shots in the revolution of the word, related the primitive mentality to the reality of the presentday and brought forward the dream magic of man's mind. It accomplished these things and many others. It was for a long time the only possible outlet for writers whose conception or form was unorthodox. I am sure that you would be the first to admit that, in welcoming experimentation, *transition* sometimes printed manuscripts of small value. But better to have encouraged the man who tried to break away from the wornout conventional and failed than to have admitted only the man who succeeded in fabricating stories according to pattern. I cannot help but believe that *transition* was a tremendous inspiration to all those interested in the progress of modern literature and in its being moulded into a vehicle more in touch with the times. And this was a service which formed a splendid raison d'être. Through it *transition* must be given its place as an influence on american literature in a period which may accurately be called transitional.

I had intended to outline at some length my reasons for believing that *transition* should go just a bit farther, but at the last moment I have decided to refrain. Perhaps after all it is better for *transition* to become silent while the ideas proposed are still fresh than to continue, and risk becoming repetitious and monotonous. In any case it is useless to regret: better to be thankful that *transition* has existed, with its discoveries, its battles, its controversies, its ideas and its superb work in revivifying literature. Although my name trailing along on the reverse of the title page has not meant much in the past few issues I have been content to see it there for sentimental reasons. Life for me has been pleasanter since 1927 because of *transition's* existence, and I feel certain that many others can honestly say the same thing. Possibly I am unjustifiably prejudiced, but I suspect that after the twenty numbers of *transition* american literature will be a little different just as all literature has been a little different since the publication of *Ulysses.*

I wish you the best of luck for the final number, which, because I know nothing of the contents, I await with even more eagerness than usual. There is so much more that I should like to say, but I am counting on your coming to London as soon as you have corrected the last page of proof. And I know an excellent pub where we can talk over the rest.

Always your friend,
BOB.

TRANSITION AND FRANCE

by Philippe Soupault

At THE MOMENT WHEN EUGENE JOLAS HAS DECIDED TO SUSPEND THE publication of *transition*, it does not seem to me unimportant to look back and examine the role played by this review.

At a time when we stood in France before the collapse of all poetic values, when those most qualified to consider poetry had become discouraged, and when, for reasons that seem to me superfluous to enumerate here, those same persons turned their attention in other directions, *transition* represented the only living force, the only review which did not despair of poetry, and thus authorized the poets to continue their work.

Let me cite only one example of the consequences of *transition*'s existence, to wit, the *Revolution of the Word,* which Jolas proposed not only to our activity, but still more to our spirit. The question at stake here was not — as it always was in the case of the ignominious Marinetti's futurism — a game in which only the form was considered, but rather a project for an entente between action and poetry. In 1927, 1928, and 1929 we could not accept more or less witty speculations, attempts at a play on words, or simple attempts of a more or less moralising nature. *transition*, therefore, at that period, was a geometric link.

It was the only "direction" one could have taken without risking defeat from the very beginning.

At the present time we should, therefore, feel less regret at the disappearance of a review which has reached its goal. It can die in peace, the direction has been suggested, the impulse has been given.

THE PURSUIT OF HAPPINESS

AS WAS TO BE EXPECTED, *TRANSITION* HAS AFFORDED UNITED STATES officials, and their understudies in the various commonwealths, continuous opportunities to display their maudlin instincts.

No. 3 was found by Mr. Fuller, manager of the Old Corner Book Store of Boston, arsewiper to the late J. Frank Chase, and patron saint of the book review pages of the Boston *Herald* and the Boston *Transcript* "to contain material in violation of the Massachusetts law."

No. 4 was turned back by the Philadelphia customs officials on the ground that it was copyrighted material.

No. 5 was held up needlessly and without justification for weeks by the port authorities of New York.

No. 6 has been confiscated by the same gentlemen and refused admission on the ground that it contained obscene matter.

Needless to say, the editors of *transition*, being more than sixteen years of age and of sound mind, have no respect whatever for the law, and certainly none for the underpaid and scant-witted crew the citizens of the United States hire to annoy them. Occasionally it may be necessary to print a few extra copies in order to circumvent them, but our subscribers will be served and the bookstores will be supplied.

Yet the spectacle is ludicrous. The general laws of the United States are framed by crooks, if money is involved, and by bigots, if it is a case of morals. They are voted into effect by nincompoops in exchange for local bridges, post offices, or even Fourth of July seats upon reviewing stands. They are enforced by the delinquent relatives and friends of the men who passed them, except in cases where they might inconvenience the men who drafted them.

There would be little objection to this queer game if its participants were courteous enough not to interfere with those who prefer simpler amusements. *transition* is compiled and printed each month because the editors like to spend their time that way, and it is sent to a group of people who are as much entitled to special consideration in the way of reading matter as are doctors or engineers.

Since the newspaper writers from coast to coast have declared *transition* to be utterly unintelligible, and have proved conclusively from their comments that it was, in fact, quite meaningless to them, any claim that the magazine is likely to corrupt the morals of American youth seems far fetched.

Naturally, we shall continue to print whatever we think best, but inasmuch as the authorities and censors have taken to reading our product, we wish to inform them that we have had special buttonholes sewed into our coat-tails with red, white and blue threads and that we shall henceforth wear therein, for the benefit of any and all who hold office, be it high or low, within the gift of the American people, a small sprig of mistletoe.

THE EDITORS.

[NOVEMBER 1927]

EPILOGUE

THE END OF EUROPE

by Harry Crosby

THE SHATTERED HULL OF A ROWBOAT STUCK IN THE SAND, A FIRE OF driftwood, a bottle of black wine, black beetles, the weird cry of seagulls lost in the fog, the sound of the tide creeping in over the wet sands, the tombstone in the eel-grass behind the dunes.

[JUNE 1929]

Acknowledgments

The publishers, and Phillips & Company Books, would like to thank the following people who helped in the making of this *transition* anthology:

William C. Agee
Gordon Baldwin
Edoardo Bensi
Janet Bowcott
Kay Boyle
Stephen F. Breimer
Roger Bull
John Calder
Diana Collecott
Amy Conger
Virginia A. Creeden
Merry A. Foresta
Elizabeth Friedmann
Jerome Gold
Margaret Harman
Naomi Hoffman
Patricia, Countess Jellicoe
Betsy and Tina Jolas

Constance Keene
Elinor Langer
B. Lerman *(Galerie Louise Leiris)*
Nina Lobanov-Rostovsky
Lynn MacRitchie
Michael Mulcay
Adam Phillips
David Phillips
Terence Pitts
Roy Rubinstein
Sheila Ryan
David Stang
John Stewart
Marcia Tiede
Pamela Todd
Lucien Treillard
Kelley Jeane Younger

Proofreaders: Simone Mauger
Anna Powell
Mary Scott

Exhaustive efforts have been made to contact all contributors whose work has been included in this book, their agents or heirs. Phillips & Company Books would be extremely grateful for information leading to those whom we have not been able to find. To those who have given permission for their work to appear in this anthology, our renewed appreciation:

Poetry and Photograph by BERENICE ABBOTT: © Berenice Abbott/Commerce Graphics Ltd, Inc.
Poetry by RICHARD ALDINGTON: © Madame Catherine Guillaume
Comment by GEORGE ANTHEIL: By permission of the Antheil Estate
Poetry by HANS ARP: © 1963 by Verlags AG Die Arche, Zürich;
Arping by HANS ARP: Copyright 1990 ARS N.Y. / ADAGP
Poetry by SAMUEL BECKETT: Reprinted by permission of Grove Weidenfeld. © 1977 by Samuel Beckett

Acknowledgments

Fiction and poetry by PAUL BOWLES: Copyright © 1928, 1930 by Paul Bowles. By permission of William Morris Agency, Inc.

Fiction, poetry and comments by KAY BOYLE: Copyright © 1990 by Kay Boyle. By permission of Watkins/Loomis Agency, Inc.

Photograph by CONSTANTIN BRANCUSI: Copyright 1990 ARS N.Y. / ADAGP. Courtesy Musée National d'Art Moderne, Paris

Paintings by GEORGES BRAQUE: Copyright 1990 ARS N.Y. / ADAGP. Courtesy Galerie Louise Leiris, Paris

Poetry by BRYHER: By permission of Perdita Schaffner

Wire Sculpture by ALEXANDER CALDER: Copyright 1990 ARS N.Y. / ADAGP. Courtesy Peter A. Juley & Son Collection, National Museum of American Art, Smithsonian Institution

Fiction by ERSKINE CALDWELL: By permission of the Estate of Erskine Caldwell

Poetry and fiction by MALCOLM COWLEY: By permission of Robert Cowley

Poetry by HART CRANE: From *The Collected Poems of Hart Crane*. Copyright © 1933, 1958, 1966 by Liveright Publishing Corporation. Reprinted by permission of W.W. Norton & Company, Inc.

Photograph by HARRY CROSBY: Courtesy Special Collections, Morris Library, Southern Illinois University, Carbondale.

Painting by STUART DAVIS: Collection of Betty and Milton Green, Birmingham, Michigan. © DACS 1990. Photo by © Geoffrey Clements, Courtesy Stuart Davis Catalogue Raisonné, New York

Painting by GIORGIO DE CHIRICO: © DACS 1990

Writing by ROBERT DESNOS: Poem from *Domaine Public* (1953), © Editions Gallimard; Scenario by permission of Dr. Michel Fraenkel

Lines from "The Sons of Our Sons" by ILYA EHRENBURG [Epigraph]: Translated by Babette Deutsch, included in *A Treasury of Russian Verse*, edited by Avrahm Yarmolinsky

Writing by PAUL ELUARD: "A Dream" and "In Company," from *Bibliothèque de la Pléiade*, Vol. 1; "Georges Braque," from *Capitale de la Douleur*. © Editions Gallimard

Frottage by MAX ERNST: Copyright 1990 ARS N.Y. / SPADEM

Poetry and fiction by ANDRE GIDE: © Editions Gallimard

Poetry by ROBERT GRAVES: By permission of A.P. Watt Limited on behalf of The Executors of the Estate of Robert Graves

Paintings by JUAN GRIS: Copyright 1990 ARS N.Y. / SPADEM. Courtesy Galerie Louise Leiris, Paris

Painting by GEORG GROSS: *The Demagogue* by Georg Grosz, © DACS 1990. Courtesy Stedelijk Museum, Amsterdam

Poetry by H.D.: From H.D.: *Collected Poems 1912-1944*. Copyright © by the Estate of Hilda Doolittle. Reprinted by permission of New Directions Publishing Corporation. U.S. and Canadian Rights

Fiction by ERNEST HEMINGWAY: Reprinted with permission of Charles Scribner's Sons, an imprint of Macmillan Publishing Company from *Men Without Women* by Ernest Hemingway. Copyright 1927 by Charles Scribner's Sons, renewal copyright © 1955 by Ernest Hemingway. Photograph of ERNEST HEMINGWAY: Courtesy Sylvia Beach Papers. Princeton University Library.

Poetry and other writings by EUGENE JOLAS and THEO RUTRA: By permission of Betsy and Tina Jolas

Text by JAMES JOYCE: From FINNIGANS WAKE by James Joyce. Copyright 1939 by James Joyce, renewed © 1967 by George Joyce and Lucia Joyce. Reprinted by permission of Viking Penguin, a division of Penguin Books USA Inc.

Acknowledgments

Fiction by FRANZ KAFKA: From THE COMPLETE STORIES by Franz Kafka. Copyright © 1971 by Schocken Books, Inc. Reprinted by permission of Schocken Books, published by Pantheon Books, a Division of Random House, Inc.

Line drawing by PAUL KLEE: Copyright 1989 ARS N.Y. / COSMOPRESS

Painting by FERNAND LEGER: Copyright 1990 ARS N.Y. / SPADEM. Courtesy Musée National d'Art Moderne, Paris

Fiction by ROBERT MCALMON: Copyright © 1990. By permission of Watkins/Loomis Agency, Inc.

Poetry by ARCHIBALD MACLEISH: Copyright © 1927, 1928, 1930, 1962 by Archibald MacLeish. From *New & Collected Poems, 1917-1976*. Copyright © 1976 by Houghton Mifflin Company, Boston

Photographs by MAN RAY: Copyright 1990 ARS N.Y. / ADAGP. Courtesy Jerome Gold (Man Ray Trust) and Lucien Treillard, Paris

Pastel by ANDRE MASSON: Copyright 1990 ARS N.Y. / SPADEM. Courtesy Galerie Louise Leiris, Paris

Painting by JOAN MIRÓ: *The Carbide Lamp*, 1922-23. Oil on canvas, 15×18" (38.1×45.7 cm). Collection, The Museum of Modern Art, New York. Purchase. Copyright 1990 ARS N.Y. / ADAGP

Essay by ELLIOT PAUL: By permission of the Estate of Elliot Paul

Painting by FRANCIS PICABIA: Copyright 1990 ARS N.Y. / ADAGP / SPADEM

Charcoal and pastel by PABLO PICASSO: Copyright 1990 ARS N.Y. / SPADEM. Courtesy Galerie Louise Leiris, Paris

Fiction by KATHERINE ANNE PORTER: "Magic" from *Flowering Judas and Other Stories* [and containing the author's corrections made subsequent to publication in *transition*] copyright 1930 and renewed 1958 by Katherine Anne Porter, reprinted by permission of Harcourt Brace Jovanovich, Inc. and Isabel Bayley, Literary Trustee for the Estate of Katherine Anne Porter

Poetry and fiction by LAURA RIDING: Reprinted by permission of the author, Laura Riding Jackson: "I give full permission and approval to the selection chosen for the appearance of writings of mine in a *transition* collection, with justification felt despite the difference between the date of this publication and the date of my authorship of the selections. I have found in the passing of years a to-me notable consistency between successive stages of my modes of thought and composition."

Poetry by RAINER MARIA RILKE: By permission of Insel Verlag, Frankfurt am Main

Painting by KURT SCHWITTERS: Copyright 1989 ARS N.Y. / COSMOPRESS. Courtesy Statens Konstmuseer, Sweden

Poem and comments by PHILIPPE SOUPAULT: By permission of the author

Writing by GERTRUDE STEIN: By permission of the Estate of Gertrude Stein

Painting by JOSEPH STELLA: *The Voice of the City of New York Interpreted*, 1920-22: *The Bridge*. Collection of The Newark Museum, Newark, New Jersey. Purchase 1937, Felix Fuld Bequest Fund

Painting by YVES TANGUY: Copyright 1990 ARS N.Y. / SPADEM

Poetry by TRISTAN TZARA: Copyright © Editions Flammarion

Photographs by EDWARD WESTON: © 1981 The Arizona Board of Regents, Center for Creative Photography. "Fragment," Courtesy San Francisco Museum of Modern Art, Albert M. Bender Collection, Bequest of Albert M. Bender, 41.2993. "Pepper," Courtesy Center for Creative Photography

Fiction by WILLIAM CARLOS WILLIAMS: *transition*, 1928. Reprinted by permission of New Directions Publishing Corporation., Agents.

Poetry by LOUIS ZUKOFSKY: Reprinted by permission of Paul Zukofsky

ON THE ENDPAPERS: Original advertisements from the pages of *transition*, 1927-1930

DESIGNER: DAVID FORDHAM